ROBERT E. LEE
THE SOLDIER

ROBERT E. LEE IN 1862

ROBERT E. LEE
THE SOLDIER

BY

MAJOR–GENERAL SIR FREDERICK MAURICE

With Portrait, Maps, and Plans

Bonanza Books • **New York**

PREFACE

THIS is neither a life of Lee nor a history of the Civil War of 1861–65. It is an appreciation of Lee's generalship. There are two reasons which justify an addition to the library of books, already extensive, dealing with the great Southern General. In 1915, at a time when the activities and attention of most of us were occupied with another and greater conflict, there were published 'Lee's Confidential Despatches to Davis,' and these throw a new light upon many disputed points which concern both the Civil War in general and Lee's part in it in particular. The second reason is that the Great War has set before us new standards by which to judge generalship. The similarity between many of the problems of the Civil War and of the Great War is striking, and our experiences of the difficulties of solving the problems of the latter should tend to make us more sober in our judgment of those who were confronted with the problems of the former. I believe that Lee's reputation as a general, high as it was before 1914, will be found to be enhanced both by the information which has appeared comparatively recently and by a review of his achievements in the light of our recent knowledge of war.

Lee, himself, said that his practice in battle was to bring his troops to the field in the best possible way and in the best possible condition and then to commit them to God and his subordinates. This has enabled me to deal very lightly with the stories of the battles and to avoid confusing the main lines of my portrait with details and military technicalities. It has also had the advantage that I have been able to escape almost entirely from those many controversies, which have raged round the performances of particular generals on various battlefields.

I have endeavoured, whenever it has been possible, — and Lee's voluminous correspondence has made it often possible, — to give his plans, intentions, and opinions in his own words, and have sought throughout to look at the events of the Civil War through his eyes. The fields of Virginia upon which he fought were but a small, if the most important, part of the whole vast theatre of war, and to enable my readers to refresh their memory of those events in the war with which Lee was not concerned, I have included a chronological table showing in parallel columns those actions in which Lee took a direct or indirect part and those which took place elsewhere.

I must express my indebtedness to Mr. Gamaliel Bradford's 'Lee the American' both for much inspiration and for the assistance given me by his admirable compilation of authorities, which has saved me much labour in research; like most other English soldiers who have studied the history of the Civil War, I owe a debt of gratitude to the late Colonel G. F. R. Henderson; and I am indebted for much courtesy and kind assistance to the Trustees and the Librarian of the Athenæum of Boston and to the authorities of the Library of Harvard University. The Military Historical Society of Massachusetts has kindly placed at my disposal a map from which that at the end of this volume has been prepared.

F. MAURICE

March, 1925

CONTENTS

ILLUSTRATIONS AND MAPS

ROBERT E. LEE
THE SOLDIER

ROBERT E. LEE
THE SOLDIER

• ∴ •

CHAPTER I

THE LEES OF VIRGINIA

THE Lees of Westmoreland County, Virginia, are a family with a long tradition of public service. Genealogists dispute whether they derive from the Shropshire Lees or from some other branch of the English stock, and are prepared to trace their descent from one of William's Norman adventurers who fought on the field of Hastings. Robert Lee took no interest in these researches. It was sufficient for him that he had inherited an honoured name which he was determined to hand on untarnished to his children. When he had done more than his distinguished forbears to make his name illustrious, there were not wanting those who, from affection or from less worthy motives, were ready to nourish in him those little vanities to which even the greatest amongst us are usually susceptible. One of these gentlemen had prepared a tree of the Lee family and had communicated the result of his labours to Mrs. Lee with a proposal for publication. From the trenches of Petersburg came answer in February, 1865: 'I have received your note. I am very much obliged to Mr. —— for the trouble he has taken in relation to the Lee genealogy, and have no desire to have it published and do not think it would afford sufficient interest beyond the immediate family to compensate for the expense. I think the money had better be applied to relieving the poor.' [1]

Such being the opinion of the man most concerned, we need not be anxious to match the exact shade of blue in his blood, but my purpose being to portray the nature and quality of Robert E. Lee's generalship, it is of interest to trace to their origin certain of the characteristics which appear in the soldier. Amongst those which he owed to his forefathers were a sturdy spirit of independence, a readiness to sacrifice all for a cause, and a high sense of duty to the State.

The immediate ancestor of the Lees of Virginia, Colonel Richard Lee, migrated in the reign of Charles I. In a first expedition of investigation he was so charmed with the country and convinced of its possibilities that in 1641 he determined to make his home there. He gave himself to the service of the Colony and became Secretary of State and member of the Privy Council in Virginia. A convinced royalist, he, when the Revolution came in England, assisted Governor Berkeley to hold Virginia for the Crown, so that, after the execution of Charles I, Cromwell had, in order to reduce the Colony

---

[1] Fitzhugh Lee: *General Lee*, p. 21.

to subjection, to send a military expedition across the Atlantic. Berkeley was removed from his post, while Richard Lee, unable to resist, but unwilling to surrender, chartered a Dutch vessel, sailed for Holland, and there gave up to him, whom he at once recognized as Charles II and his lawful sovereign, the Governor's commission, receiving from the exile a new warrant in its place. On Cromwell's death and two years before the restoration took place, he helped Berkeley to proclaim Charles II 'King of England, Scotland, France, Ireland, and Virginia.'

Colonel Richard Lee's second son Richard inherited the Virginia property. He became like his father before him a member of the Council of the State, and had six sons and one daughter, of whom the fifth son, Thomas, succeeded by his energy and ability in establishing the fortunes of the family. Successful in affairs, he rebuilt the home of the Virginia Lees, making Stratford an imposing house and a scene of typical Southern hospitality. The Hanoverians, eager to conciliate the descendant of a staunch adherent of the House of Stuart, treated him with special favour, and he became President and Commander-in-Chief of the Colony, and was eventually nominated its Governor, though he died before the Royal Commission reached him.

President Thomas Lee had eight sons, almost all remarkable men. It was of them their neighbour and friend, George Washington, wrote, 'I know of no county can produce a family all distinguished as clever men as our Lees.' Two of these brothers, Richard and Francis, were signers of the Declaration of Independence, while Richard was the mover of the famous resolution of June 10, 1776, 'That these Colonies are, and of right ought to be, free and independent States.' An uncle of these two distinguished men and the youngest of President Thomas Lee's brothers, Henry by name, was grandfather of a more famous Henry, the 'Light Horse Harry' of the Revolutionary War. Harry was not only a gallant and able leader of cavalry; he was an eager and judicious politician, a man of taste and judgment, and a keen student both of classical and contemporary literature. After the war, Harry Lee was elected to Congress and was chosen to deliver the commemorative address on the death of Washington, in which occurs the well-known description of the Father of his Country as 'first in war, first in peace, and first in the hearts of his countrymen.'

In 1778, 'Light Horse Harry' took a leading part in urging his State to adopt the Articles of Confederation, but twenty years later he showed himself to be a zealous advocate of State rights, declaring certain Federal laws then under consideration to be unconstitutional, adding that if his opinion was correct Virginia had the right to reject them. 'Virginia is my country. Her I will obey, however lamentable the fate to which it may subject me.' He had previously held for three years the office of Governor of Virginia, and his words had the authority of a doctrine to be handed on with consequences of which he had not dreamed to his then unborn son Robert.

Harry Lee married twice. His first wife was a cousin of the daughter of President Lee's eldest son, the owner of Stratford. His second wife and Robert's mother was Anne Hill Carter, the daughter of Charles Carter of Shirley on the James River, the head of a well-known Virginian family. One of her great-grandfathers, Alexander Spottiswood, had fought with Marlborough at Blenheim and had been sent to Virginia to be its Governor.

Robert, the fourth son of the second family, was born at Stratford on January 19, 1807, when his father was forty-nine. The father's health took him to the West Indies away from his family when the boy was barely out of his infancy, and Harry Lee died when Robert was eleven. The child, therefore, owed little to the personal counsels of his father, but it is not unusual to find that the influence of a distinguished and dead parent, especially when transmitted through a devoted woman, is greater than that of a living father, and Robert seems to have absorbed his father's political opinions as naturally as he did his mother's moral teaching. That mother, brought up in the free and generous life of a hospitable Virginian house, was a woman with a sincere and simple faith in God's providence, with which she inspired her son, who made it the guiding principle of his life. It happened that the elder brothers left the house to make their way in the world, and Robert devoted himself to the care of his mother whose health was indifferent. The two became inseparable companions, and much in the man's character may be traced to this association of his youth. The mother's health and widowhood made the home a quiet one, and, as the greater part of the boy's spare time while he was at school was spent with her, he became serious-minded and reserved, and for a man of high principle and strong character unusually gentle. He seems, indeed, to have absorbed so much of his mother's spirit as to have mingled with the manly qualities derived from his forefathers much of womanly modesty and sympathy.

To the circumstances of this quiet upbringing is due the fact that there are few stories of his early life. As is usual in the case of a great man, resort has been had to his schoolmasters for information, but he does not seem to have impressed them particularly. A reserved lad whose chief interest is his home rarely does so. Such details of Robert's youth as have been unearthed by industrious biographers have not been chosen very happily, for when we read of a blameless youth, a faultless career at West Point, and of the young man rebuking by his sober presence the dissipation of an elderly Virginian neighbour, we are left with an unpleasant flavour of priggery. That Robert Lee was not a prig is evident from the fact that all who knew him as boy, young man, or as famous general are agreed that he possessed an extraordinary charm of manner, and the charming prig has yet to be discovered. He seems to have been one of those fortunate men for whom frivolity has few or even no attractions, and to have added to a manly handsome person, to inherited courtesy, to a traditional sense of duty, a naturally serious and somewhat introspective mind.

The father had been not only a student of literature in general, but a perceptive reader of the history of war. He was the author of 'Memoirs of the War of '76,' the best contemporary account of the War of Independence in the South,[1] and was the possessor of a considerable military library. On June 18, 1817, he wrote from the West Indies to his son: 'This is the day of the month when your dear mother became my wife and it is not so hot in this tropical region as it was then at Shirley. Since that happy day, marked only by the union of two humble lovers, it has become conspicuous as the day our war with Great Britain was declared in Washington[2] and the one that sealed the doom of Bonaparte on the

[1] Robert E. Lee issued in 1869 a third edition of this book.
[2] 18th June, 1812.

field of Waterloo.[1] The British General, rising *grada-tim* from his first blow struck in Portugal, climbed on that day to the summit of fame and became distinguished by the first of titles, "Deliverer of the Civilized World." Alexander, Hannibal, and Cæsar amongst the ancients, Marlborough, Eugene, Turenne, and Frederick amongst the moderns, opened their arms to receive him as a brother in glory.'

It may well be that this eulogy of a great soldier written by the father a few months before his death,[2] and therefore amongst the last letters the boy can have received from him, influenced his mind greatly in the choice of a career. We know at least that it was carefully preserved, and it is remarkable that it was written to one who was to be received into that band which the writer pictured as welcoming the great British general.

The educational facilities in Virginia in the early part of the nineteenth century were not great. Great Britain had given the Colonies little help or encouragement in the establishment of schools, and none of the Governors of Virginia before the Revolution had troubled themselves to make provision for systematic teaching. From this neglect Virginia had not recovered during Robert Lee's youth. Jefferson, indeed, wrote of her in 1820: 'What is her education now? Where is it? The little we

---

[1] 18th June, 1815.   [2] General Henry Lee died March 18, 1818.

have to import, like beggars from other states, or import these beggars to bestow on us their miserable crumbs.' Therefore, though Lee in after life wrote gratefully of his first teacher, a Mr. Leary, it is probable that he owed more to his father's library than to his school.

As a younger son he could not look to the inheritance of estates and had to earn a living, but, while his family had few if any connections with the business world and its traditions pointed to the public service as the career for its sons, Robert Lee had none of the facility of expression which distinguished his father and his great-uncles, and this lack, together with the reserve, which may have been its cause, put the law out of court when Robert's choice of a career was in question. It was natural, therefore, that the father's military achievements should appeal to him more than his political distinctions. Further, Robert had been brought up in the country and his one recreation of which there is record was riding. He loved a good horse and a good hunt. Therefore a career which would keep him in the open and in the saddle was to him attractive. In 1825 when he was eighteen he entered the United States Military Academy at West Point.

If the schools of Virginia were, during Lee's youth, to seek, the training at West Point was altogether admirable, and could indeed challenge comparison with any contemporary military school in the world. Its prime purpose was, of course, to provide officers for the Army of the United States, but many fathers sent their sons to the Academy on the Hudson for the sake of the education it afforded, and numbers of those sons did not follow a military career. As the cadets were from all classes and from schools of all kinds, specialisation was not attempted. Drill, discipline, the use and care of arms and of equipment were the chief subjects of military instruction, the education being general in character. A high standard of drill was exacted and no smarter body of youths on parade were to be found anywhere. The discipline was strict; throughout the course of four years a rigid process of selection was applied. Rejections were numerous, and to have passed through the course with credit was a certificate both of character and ability. The training at West Point stood triumphantly the severe test of four years of war, for every successful commander of an army from 1861 to 1865 was a graduate of the Military Academy.

Robert Lee went through his course with distinction, attaining the post of adjutant, coveted by every cadet, and passing out second of his class to become a lieutenant in the engineers. When the handsome youth came home on leave in his smart uniform, he won the heart of a fair neighbour, Mary, the daughter of George Washington Custis of Arlington, and great-granddaughter of Martha Washington. She was the heiress both of Arlington and of the White House on the Pamunkey. Not unnaturally the father demurred at giving his daughter to a portionless younger son who had nothing to look to but the uncertain prospect of a soldier's life. The devotion of the young people overcame his objections and they were married when Lee was but twenty-four years old. The marriage was for Lee fortunate beyond the position and the possessions which it brought to him. It opened to him the houses of the leading men of the State, men in whose hands the future of their country lay to a great degree; it gave him eventually control of great estates, but it gave him what he needed more, a loving and a devoted companion. Lee was never what is called 'a man's man.' He did not drink, he did not smoke, he had no taste for the ordinary amusements and weaknesses of the male sex. While he had a limited number of professional friends and loved the companionship of service, he opened his heart to no man. He needed some outlet for his natural reserve and it was to a woman he turned when he felt that need. His deep affection for his mother had given him an unbounded respect for womanhood and that respect was added to his love for his wife. He chaffed her at times upon her little failings. 'The Mim, the dear Mim considers herself a great financier. Consult her about the expenditure of money, but do not let her take it shopping, or you will have to furnish her with an equal amount to complete her purchases. She has such a fine eye for a bargain.'

But he treated her in all the serious events of his life as an intellectual equal. After almost every crisis of the war, we find that his first thought is to write to his wife, and to write to her as he would have written to a trusted soldier comrade, assuming a knowledge of technicalities and telling her simply what his purpose and intentions had been. In many of these letters is to be found the key to his military mind.

It happened that Mrs. Lee the wife, like Mrs. Lee the mother, became an invalid and she was for years confined to her chair by rheumatism. The husband lavished on her the same tender care which the son had expended on the mother. 'To my mother, who was a great invalid from rheumatism for more than ten years,' writes their son Robert, 'he was the most faithful attendant and tender nurse. Every want of hers that he could supply he anticipated. His considerate forethought saved her from much pain and trouble. During the war he constantly wrote to her, even when on the march and amidst the most pressing duties. Every summer of their life in Lexington he arranged that she should spend in the neighboring mountains, as much that she might be surrounded by new scenes and faces, as for

[1] John William Jones: *Life and Letters of General Robert E. Lee*, p. 122.

the benefit of the waters. Whenever he was in the room, the privilege of pushing her wheeled chair in to the dining-room was yielded to him. He sat with her daily, entertaining her with accounts of what was doing in the college and the news of the village and would often read to her in the evening. For her his love and care never ceased, his gentleness and patience never ended.

'This tenderness for the sick and helpless was developed in him when he was a lad. His mother was an invalid and he was her constant nurse. In her last illness he mixed every dose of medicine she took and was with her night and day. If he left the room, she kept her eyes on the door till he returned. He never left her but for a short time.'[1] Such was he at home, whose 'characteristic fault' in the field was said by his comrade Longstreet to be 'headlong combativeness.'[2]

The Lees were a sturdy stock and Robert became the father of seven children. He took his duties as a parent as he took life, very seriously. His letters to his children smack rather of the heavy father, but it is clear that they do not give us the true picture of the family life, for all his children were devoted to him. He could not put his feelings upon paper, and behind the father's tendency to preach in the letters, preaching which was borne more

[1] Robert E. Lee: *Recollections and Letters of General Lee*, p. 325.
[2] H. D. Longstreet: *Lee and Longstreet at High Tide*, p. 83.

patiently by the young in the middle of the nineteenth than it is in the twentieth century, we must see the man's tender love, his beautiful and kindly smile, and a humorous twinkle often in his eye, if but rarely in his pen. The young people, and his wife, too, for that matter, found his insistence on military punctuality sometimes a little trying, and a daughter-in-law once said of him that she did not believe he could have an entirely high opinion of any one, even of George Washington, if he could return to earth, who was not in time for family prayer.[1] But there is no doubt that the home life was happy.

I have said that Lee's one recreation was riding. That does not mean that he set no value upon other manly exercises, and he took pains to see that his sons were taught not only to ride, but to skate and shoot. His methods with his children are charmingly indicated by his son Robert: 'I went to a day-school at West Point and had always a sympathetic helper in my father. Often he would come into the room when I studied at night, and, sitting down by me, would show me how to overcome a hard sentence in my Latin reader or a difficult sum in arithmetic, not by giving me the translation of the troublesome sentence, or the answer to the sum, but by showing me, step by step, the way to the right solution. He was very patient, very loving, very good

[1] Robert E. Lee: *Recollections and Letters*, p. 330.

to me, and I remember trying my best to please him in my studies. When I was able to bring home a good report from my teacher, he was greatly pleased, and showed it in his eyes and voice, but he always insisted that I should get the "maximum," and that he would never be satisfied with less.' [1] I cannot but think that Lee would have taken more pleasure in this homely tribute than in all the praises lavished on his generalship.

Such, then, was one side of Lee's private life, but there was another at which I have as yet barely hinted, a side more dominant than even his love of wife, children, and home, and that was his love of God. He believed in the Living God, the Father, the Judge of the earth. He had not the smallest doubt but that to God all things are possible, that by faith mountains might be moved. He had been brought up and remained an Episcopalian, but for him dogmas had no attraction. He abhorred religious controversy because, he said, it led to unchristian feeling, and he had a deep respect for the religious convictions of others. J. W. Jones, in his 'Christ in the Camp,' gives us a striking example of this tolerance: 'An application of a Jew soldier for permission to attend certain ceremonies of his synagogue in Richmond was endorsed by his captain: "Disapproved. If such applications were granted, the whole army would turn Jews or shaking

[1] Robert E. Lee: *Recollections and Letters*, p. 14.

Quakers." When the paper came to General Lee, he endorsed on it, "Approved and respectfully returned to Captain ——, with the advice that he should respect the religious views and feelings of others.'" Wellington once said that it was not possible to apply Christian principles to war. Lee thought otherwise. He fought because he thought he was fighting for the right, not with any bitterness against his enemies. Once to one who said to him of the Northerners, 'I wish all these people were dead,' 'How can you say so?' answered Lee. 'Now I wish they were all at home attending to their own business and leaving us to do the same.' [1] After the war he devoted himself to the task of reconciliation. Frequently importuned by those who wished to hear his voice in the many controversies arising out of the war, he refused all their requests, though acceptance would have relieved his straitened circumstances. His reason he gave in 1866 to the wife of Jefferson Davis: 'I have never seen Mr. Colfax's speech and am ignorant of the statements it contained. Had it, however, come under my notice, I doubt whether I should have thought it proper to reply. I have thought, from the time of the cessation of hostilities, that silence and patience on the part of the South was the true course, and I think so still. Controversy of all kinds will, in my opinion, only serve to continue excitement and passion, and will prevent the

[1] J. W. Jones: *Personal Reminiscences, Anecdotes, and Letters of General R. E. Lee.*

public mind from the acknowledgment and acceptance of the truth.'

To a clergyman who had allowed himself to give way to tirade against the iniquities of the North, Lee answered, 'Doctor, there is a good old book which says, 'Love your enemies."' [1]

There are signs that as he drew to the end of his life he thought that after all Wellington was right, and that it was hard to make war compatible with the spirit of Christ. 'For my own part,' he wrote to his old comrade Ewell, 'I much enjoy the charms of civil life, and find too late that I have wasted the best part of my existence'; [2] and he is said to have sighed, 'The great mistake of my life was taking a military education.' If Robert E. Lee, soldier, and Christian, was such 'as every man in arms would wish to be,' he was not a 'happy warrior.' At any time in his life it would have given him more joy to have won a soul to God than to have gained a victory. I agree with Mr. Gamaliel Bradford that Lee had one intimate friend — God. [3]

Such were in outline the circumstances of the private life of Robert Lee as son, husband, father, and gentleman of Virginia. His career as a soldier ended in disaster and behind his life as a citizen there lurked the shadow of tragedy. Stout democrat as he was, he, his family, and

[1] J. W. Jones: *Reminiscences*, p. 196.
[2] J. W. Jones: *Life and Letters of General Robert E. Lee*, p. 430.
[3] Gamaliel Bradford: *Lee the American*, p. 220.

the friends of his family were members of a ruling caste, which drew power to itself as definitely and as completely as any ruling caste in Europe. Not without good reason was the Virginia of the first half of the nineteenth century called the Mother of Presidents.[1] In the hands of her sons had rested to a predominant extent the shaping of the government of the Federated States which had won their independence. Neither was this due solely nor even chiefly to the prestige which she gained as the home of the victor of the War of Independence and the first President. The free life and independent means of the gentlemen of Virginia, the management of large estates, if they brought with them temptations to which not a few succumbed, produced men with a natural aptitude for government, men who in their day rendered great services. But their day was brief. During the boyhood and manhood of Robert E. Lee, they reached and passed the zenith of their power. New forces, so far removed from their sight, so far beyond their traditional outlook as to escape their observation, were at work. In the North industry began to develop rapidly, bringing with its development increase in population and in wealth. The flow westward grew steadily in volume, and neither

---

[1] We have Mr. Birdofredom Sawin's authority that:

'in order to be Presidunt
It's absolutely ne'ssary to be a Southern residunt;
The Constitution settles thet, an' also thet a feller
Must own a nigger o' some sort, jet black, or brown, or yeller.'
LOWELL: *The Biglow Papers.*

the farmer of the West nor the industrialist of the North found his needs and difficulties to be understood by the landowners of the South. As the States multiplied, the variety and complexity of their problems increased and it became more and more necessary for each to sacrifice something of its independence for the good of the whole. But they who had done so much to create the system of Federated Government were loath to give up control of power which they and their fathers had conferred. Their products either sufficed for their own wants or were in the main exported to Europe, and the need for intimate coöperation with other States, which the increased development of transport facilities was making daily more evident to the North and West, was not to them obvious. So it came about that a humble pioneer of the Middle West could look into the future with clearer eye and truer perception than could the gentleman of Virginia. So, too, it happened that Robert E. Lee became that pathetic figure, the noble champion of a lost cause.

CHAPTER II

THE TRAINING OF THE SOLDIER

ROBERT E. LEE completed his course at West Point in 1829 and was commissioned second-lieutenant in the Corps of Engineers. The army he joined was a very small one; at the outbreak of the Civil War the regular military forces of the United States numbered less than nineteen thousand men, about half the strength of one of the divisions which the United States sent to Europe for the Great War, and when Lee first became an officer the army was not nine thousand strong. Further, the greater part of this little body of troops was scattered over an immense stretch of country in small detachments, and it rarely happened that the officer of the regular army in time of peace saw one thousand soldiers assembled together. It is therefore remarkable to find how wide and varied was the experience which Lee gained during his military service before the Civil War, and how exactly that experience was of the kind to fit him for the work to which fate was to call him.

There were in the Civil War, as there have been in other wars, men who had no military training or education, who yet proved themselves to be admirable commanders in the field. Generals Logan and Terry on the Northern and Generals Forrest and Gordon on the

Southern side are notable examples. Equally there were in the Civil War, as there have been in every war, many men who have received military education and training and yet proved to be quite unfitted for command in war. Courage, physical and moral, common-sense, readiness to accept responsibility, the power to grasp quickly the essentials of a situation, and to form speedy decisions, these are not gifts which are confined to regular soldiers, nor have many regular soldiers possessed all or even most of these gifts. The possession of them will make any man a leader whether in peace or in war. So there have been men who, without any previous study or experience, have distinguished themselves greatly in the command of troops in the field. I have always thought that For-rest's rough common-sense enabled him to get more quickly and more truly than many profound students of the military art at the secret of success in war. To one who once asked him to what he attributed his victories he answered, 'I get there fustest with the mostest men.' There we have in eight words the gist of many volumes of Jomini and Clausewitz. But I have never read of a man who has distinguished himself in supreme command against an active and enterprising enemy who had not fitted himself for the test to which he was put both by long study and varied experience.

Julius Cæsar is sometimes cited as one who began the campaigns which placed him in the front rank of the

great commanders in history with little previous knowledge or experience of war. Now we do not know a great
deal about Cæsar's early life, but we do know that, in
order to gain military experience, he, as a young man,
took service in the operations against the pirates who
were ravaging the Eastern Mediterranean and that at
the storming of Mitylene he won the oaken crown, the
Roman's highest reward for valour. We know also that
before he became consul, and therefore some time before
he began his famous conquest of Gaul, he had had an
independent command in Spain and had completed the
Roman conquest of that country. As with Cæsar so with
others. A great commander is born, not made, but no
one has yet successfully shouldered the responsibility of
supreme control in the field who has not had and used
opportunities both for study and for testing the results of
study.

Given the circumstances of his country at the time,
the opportunities for both which came in the way of the
young soldier were exceptional. Naturally he began by
learning the technical duties of his profession, and his
first years as a young engineer were spent in helping in
the improvement of the defences of the Southern Ports.
The authorities of Washington, remembering the lessons
of the War of 1812, had set afoot some time previously
a considerable scheme of coast defence, and in the development of this scheme Lee gained his first experience

of military engineering; experience which was to be of peculiar value to him, for thirty years later one of the first tasks which fell to him as a general in war was the supervision of the very defences upon which he had been employed as a lieutenant. In 1834, Lee was transferred to the headquarters of his corps at Washington and there obtained some insight into military administration. The service at Washington was for a time interrupted by duty with a commission appointed to define the boundary between Ohio and Michigan, but he returned to Washington and was able to live at his wife's home, Arlington, whence he rode most days to his office and back.

I have in my opening chapter given a somewhat solemn portrait of Lee, and it cannot, I think, be doubted that he was by nature austere. But he was certainly not a kill-joy and was ready for an occasional lark with other young men. The young engineers of Washington had a mess of which Lee's greatest friend at West Point, J. E. Johnston,[1] was a member. Lee used the mess only when work or bad weather prevented him from going home to his wife, but he was on intimate terms with most of its members. His military secretary and biographer, General Long,[2] tells that one day Lee was starting for home on horseback when he saw one of his messmates,

[1] Afterwards the distinguished Confederate General.
[2] A. L. Long: *Memoirs of Robert E. Lee*, p. 37.

Lieutenant Macomb, and invited him to get up behind him. The two young men then caracoled down Pennsylvania Avenue and, meeting the Secretary of the Treasury in front of the White House, saluted him, to his amazement, with more than usual solemnity.

In 1837, Lee was sent to St. Louis to make plans and estimates for the improvement of the navigation of the Mississippi; his plans were approved and he was placed in charge of a difficult and highly important piece of engineering. As is usually the case there were plenty of people who knew a great deal more about how the job should be done than did the expert. Croakers predicted failure and even disaster, and Lee's methods and plans were freely criticised in the public press. He took not the smallest notice of this criticism and went quietly on with his work. But the press had gravely disturbed the mind of a section of the citizens of St. Louis who really thought that their interests were endangered by the blunders of a stupid soldier, and they threatened to drive away his workmen by force. The unruffled calm and quiet determination of the engineer caused them to change their minds, and the work went through to complete success.

In 1840, Captain I ee, as he had become, returned to purely military services and was engaged upon the planning and construction of the defences of the harbour of New York. While he was engaged on this duty the compliment was paid to him of appointment to the board of visitors to the Military Academy at West Point.

This brings us to 1845, when the long-standing dispute with Mexico as to the frontier between that country and the United States and as to the ownership of Texas flamed up into war. The annexation of Texas became a party question and opinions were widely divided, but in 1845 the advocates of a forward frontier policy won their way and General Zachary Taylor was sent with a force to protect the new territory and to insist on the Rio Grande being the frontier. The next year the Mexicans invaded Texas, and were defeated by Taylor who promptly followed them across the Rio Grande and war became a fact. There is no record that Lee expressed an opinion on the rights and wrongs of a quarrel in which Grant thought his country had behaved unjustly; indeed, from the ardour with which he threw himself into his work it is probable that the excitements and adventures of active service occupied his mind to the exclusion of considerations of policy. Lee was employed with Taylor's invading force, his immediate commander being General Wool under whom he won distinction in the operations which led up to the battle of Buena Vista. Taylor by his victories had secured a stretch of country, which, though considerable in itself, was but a mere strip of the territory of Mexico and these victories had not weakened the determination of the Mexicans to resist. The peace proposals of the United States were rejected and their old opponent of 1836, General Santa Anna, was raised to power. The American Government then decided to strike home; but distance and the nature of the country made a march into the heart of Mexico from the Rio Grande impossible, so General Scott was appointed to command a combined naval and military expedition against Vera Cruz while Taylor with a reduced force continued to keep the Mexicans in the North occupied.

Scott at once drew Lee to him for employment on his staff. At that time picked officers of the Engineers' Corps, itself a *corps d'élite*, performed many of the functions which to-day are assigned to the General Staff. They made reconnaissances, undertook the selection of positions, and prepared plans and orders for their general. In this work Lee speedily gained the confidence and won the admiration of Scott, becoming a member of what the Commander-in-Chief termed his 'little cabinet.' In that coterie Lee gained intimate and first-hand knowledge of the working of the headquarters of an army in the field; he naturally had many opportunities of making a name for himself, and he used them all. The first of these came in the siege of Vera Cruz which gave scope for the employment of his qualities as an engineer and he was constantly at work siting batteries

and designing approaches. Santa Anna had gone northward to try to overwhelm Taylor and in his absence the
siege was not prolonged. With Vera Cruz in his hands
Scott had gained the best line for the advance on Mexico
City. But if it was the best it was by no means easy, for
the road to the capital from the sea wound through
difficult mountainous country. Santa Anna hurrying
back from the North was able to occupy the first of the
passes at Cerro Gordo before Scott could seize it. Lee
has left us an account of the battle for the pass:

'*Perote, April* 25, 1847. The advance of the American
troops, under General Patterson and Twiggs, were en-
camped at the Plano del Rio, and three miles to their
front Santa Anna and his army were entrenched in the
pass of Cerro Gordo, which was remarkably strong.
The right of the Mexican line rested on the river at a
perpendicular rock, unscalable by man or beast, and
their left on impassable ravines; the main road was
defended by field-works containing thirty-five cannon;
in their rear was the mountain of Cerro Gordo, surrounded by entrenchments in which were cannon and
crowned by a tower overlooking all — it was around
this army that it was intended to lead our troops. I
reconnoitred the ground in the direction of the ravines
on their left, and passed around the enemy's rear. On
the 16th a party was set to work in cutting out the road;
on the 17th I led General Twiggs's division in the rear of

a hill in front of Cerro Gordo, and in the afternoon, when
it became necessary to drive them from the hill where
we intended to construct a battery at night, the first
intimation of our presence or intentions were known.
During all that night we were at work in constructing
the battery, getting up the guns, ammunition, etc., and
they in strengthening their defences on Cerro Gordo.
Soon after sunrise our batteries opened, and I started
with a column to turn their left and get on the Jalapa
road. Notwithstanding their efforts to prevent us in
this, we were perfectly successful, and the working
party, following our footsteps, cut out the road for the
artillery. In the meantime our storming party had
reached the crest of Cerro Gordo, and, seeing their whole
left turned and the position of our soldiers on the Jalapa
road, they broke and fled. Those in the pass laid down
their arms. General Pillow's attack on the right failed.
All their cannon, arms, ammunition, and most of their
men fell into our hands. The papers cannot tell you
what a horrible sight a field of battle is, nor will I, owing
to my accompanying General Twiggs's division in the
pursuit, and being since constantly in the advance. I
believe all our friends are safe. I think I wrote you that
my friend Joe Johnston was wounded the day before I
arrived at the Plano del Rio while reconnoitring. He
was wounded in the arm and about the groin; both balls
are out, and he was doing well and was quite comfortable

when I left; the latter wound was alone troublesome. Captain Mason, of the Rifles, was badly wounded in the leg, and General Shields was wounded in the chest; I have heard contradictory reports that he was doing well and that he was dead. I hope the former. Jalapa is the most beautiful country I have seen in Mexico, and will compare with any I have seen elsewhere. I wish it was in the United States, and that I was located with you and the children around me in one of its rich, beautiful valleys.

'I can conceive nothing more beautiful in the way of landscape or mountain scenery. We ascended upward of four thousand feet that morning, and whenever we looked back the rich valley below was glittering in the morning sun and the light morning clouds flitting around us. On reaching the top, the valley appeared at intervals between the clouds which were below us, and high over all towered Orizaba, with its silver cap of snow. The castle or fort of Perote is one of the best finished that I have ever seen — very strong, with high, thick walls, bastioned fronts, and deep, wide ditch. It is defective in construction and is very spacious, covers twenty-five acres, and although there is within its walls nearly three thousand troops, it is not yet full. Within the fort is a beautiful chapel, in one corner of which is the tomb of Guadalupe Victoria. There are various skulls, images, etc., in the sanctuaries. This morning I attended the Episcopal service within the fort. It was held on the parade. The minister was a Mr. McCarty, the chaplain of the Second Brigade, First Division. Many officers and soldiers were grouped around. I endeavored to give thanks to our Heavenly Father for all his mercies to me, for his preservation of me through all the dangers I have passed, and for all the blessings which he has bestowed upon me, for I know I fall far short of my obligations. We move out to-morrow, toward Pueblo. The First Brigade — Duncan's battery, light infantry and cavalry — form the advance. I accompany the advance. General Worth will remain a day or two with the remainder of his division, till the Second Division, under General Twiggs, shall arrive. General Scott is still at Jalapa, Major Smith with him. I have with me Lieutenants Mason, Tower, and the Engineer Company. In advance, all is uncertain and the accounts contradictory. We must trust to an overruling Providence, by whom we will be governed for the best, and to our own resources.' [1]

In this letter he, with that modesty which we shall find in him again and again, does not say that it was mainly owing to the skill and enterprise with which he guided the turning movement through an approach hidden from the enemy's view that the pass was secured at small cost. For his work at the Cerro Gordo he won

[1] Fitzhugh Lee: *Robert E. Lee*, p. 63 *et seq.*

his first mention in his chief's despatches and the brevet of major.

Scott was now hampered by a difficulty with which later every one of the Federal commanders during the Civil War was to be confronted. The little regular army of the United States had been expanded by enlisting volunteers for short terms of service. After Cerro Gordo many of these volunteers, whose term of engagement had expired, demanded their release, and it cost time to replace them. The delay gave Santa Anna opportunity to collect an army largely outnumbering Scott's and further reënforcements were needed. It was therefore nearly three months before Scott could resume an advance which, if it could have been prompt, would have ended the war in a few weeks. So the United States had to pay a stiff price for a bad system of enlistment. But this experience was forgotten by the authorities at Washington, and at the outset of the Civil War, when Scott himself was the chief military adviser of the Administration, the mistakes made in Mexico were repeated in the belief that the conflict would not be prolonged. There seems to be with civilian ministers of democratic states an ineradicable tendency to optimism in the early days of a war, and in 1914, after the Battle of the Marne, many of the Allied statesmen believed that the war would be over by Christmas.

The artificial defences of Mexico City were strong, but

the protection which nature afforded was even stronger. Mountains, lakes, and marshes limited the lines of approach to three, one from the southeast, and two from the South.   Scott coming by the southeastern route passed the mountains from which his men looked upon a rich plateau and the fair city, glistening in the brilliant sun, the goal of their labours.   But between them and it lay many an obstacle.   The Mexicans were found to be barring the road by which they were moving in a strong position, protected in front by marsh, its flanks covered by lakes.   So by a toilsome march Scott moved round their left to the nearest of the roads from the South. Having reached it, he was little better off than before. On his left lay a stretch of rough and barren foothills of rock and lava called the Pedregal, on his right a lake, and the narrow space between the two was occupied by a force of Mexicans firmly entrenched.   Again the only feasible course was to turn the enemy's left, and for that a way had to be found across the Pedregal.   Lee found a rough track which was rapidly improved, and by it half of Scott's force, crossing the Pedregal to the second of the southern roads, seized the village of Contreras, whence the enemy, blocking the other road, could be attacked in flank and rear.   But the Mexicans were quick to discover what was afoot.   A force came up from the direction of the city and endeavoured to drive the Americans back into the Pedregal.   These attacks were repulsed, but daylight might bring the enemy further reënforcements and the position of the detached force was far from secure. A council of war was held in Contreras church at which Lee, who had guided the column through the Pedregal, was present. He suggested a bold plan, a plan of the very type which later he was often to carry through successfully on a greater scale and against a more equal foe. He proposed that the force should be divided and that a detachment should be left to hold the attention of the enemy opposite Contreras while the remainder marched by night to a position from which the Mexican entrenchments could be attacked in rear. His plan was adopted, but for it to be successful Scott on the other side of the Pedregal must know what was to be done and keep the enemy opposite him engaged. The Commander-in-Chief had been racked with anxiety for news of his detachment, and sent no fewer than seven officers to find their way across the Pedregal, all of whom had returned to confess that they had failed to get through. Scott had resigned himself to wait for daylight when Lee arrived with the precious information. He had found his way with one orderly, through the wild country, which was believed to be teeming with Mexicans, in the darkness and through torrential rains. Coöperation between the divided forces was insured and the victory of Contreras was complete. Scott's gratitude was unbounded. He said in his evidence before the Court of

Enquiry into the war: 'Captain Lee, Engineers, came to me from Brigadier-General Smith, I think about the same time (midnight), he having passed over the difficult ground by daylight, found it just possible to return to St. Augustine in the dark — the greatest feat of physical and moral courage performed by any individual in my knowledge, pending the campaign.' In his despatch he said, 'The brilliant victory of Contreras on the following morning was made possible by Captain Lee's services that night,' and he recommended his staff officer for the brevet of lieutenant-colonel.

After this battle, in which the bulk of Santa Anna's forces had been met and beaten, Scott, hoping for an early peace, proposed an armistice which the wily Mexican accepted and proceeded to use to rally his forces and strengthen his defences. Scott, discovering this breach of faith, sent him an ultimatum which was rejected and hostilities were resumed. After an action at Molino del Rey, the American army found itself in front of the hill of Chapultepec, the site of Montezuma's palace, crowned by the strongest of the forts defending the capital. Both in the preparation for and the conduct of the attack on the fort Lee was again conspicuous. Again he was mentioned in his chief's despatches as 'constantly conspicuous, bearing important orders till he fainted from a wound and the loss of two nights' sleep in the batteries.' The wound was slight, and from it he recovered quickly. His work at Chapultepec was rewarded with a third brevet.

No matter how sure a man may be of his nerves, he is the better soldier when those nerves have been tested under fire and found reliable, and the better leader from the confidence in himself which such experience provides. With this confidence and with much useful experience the Mexican campaign furnished Lee. He had also an ample opportunity for gaining knowledge of the men who were to be his comrades and his foes within a few years. His position in Scott's headquarters brought him into personal touch with most of the officers of the little army and he was able to observe them under the testing conditions of active service. McClellan, Gustavus Smith, and Beauregard served with him on Scott's staff. Magruder commanded the battery in which Jackson served. Bragg, Sedgwick, A. P. Hill, Porter, Reno, all served in the artillery. Lee's greatest soldier friend, J. E. Johnston, was twice wounded and made himself conspicuous for his dash and courage. Grant served as a lieutenant in the infantry both with Taylor in the early operations of the war, and later with Scott's advance on Mexico City. Meade too served on both fronts as an engineer. McDowell was aide-de-camp to Wool, Lee's first general in the campaign. Shields commanded a brigade. Hooker and Pope both served on the staff. Burnside arrived with reënforcements while the march from the sea was in progress. Ewell proved himself to be a dashing dragoon. D. H. Hill and Early both won distinction, and by a prophetic association Longstreet and Pickett were together conspicuous for gallantry in the attack on Chapultepec. Within fifteen years of the close of the Mexican War these comrades in glory were to be arrayed in opposing ranks. All of them had had with Lee the close association of service against a common foe to add to the intimacy which arises from training in a common school and the links of their small circle. None of them made such use of the knowledge so gained as did Lee.

During the continuance of active service, Lee used all his energies, physical and mental in the exacting service in which he was employed, but when the occupation of the City of Mexico gave him leisure to look around him he showed that he could see his way beyond the bounds of his profession to the larger issues of the future and his correspondence from the captured town displays those broad views which distinguished him as a commander-in-chief, indicating that they were the product of a mind capable of surveying great questions with understanding and humanity. In February, 1848, he wrote to his wife: 'You will doubtless hear many speculations about peace. The boundary is said to be the Rio Grande giving us Texas, New Mexico, California, for which we pay twenty million dollars — five millions to be reserved for liquidation of claims of her citizens. These are certainly not hard terms for Mexico, considering how the fortune of war has been against her. For myself I would not exact more now than I would have taken before the commencement of hostilities, as I should wish nothing but what was just, and that I would have sooner or later. I can readily see that the terms said to be offered on the part of Mexico may not prove satisfactory to a large part of our country who would think it right to exact everything that power and might would require. Some would sacrifice everything under the hope that the proposition of Messrs. Clay, Calhoun, etc., would be acted upon, and save what they term the national honor. Believing that peace would be to the advantage of both countries I hope that some terms just to the one and not dishonourable to the other may be agreed on and that speedily.' [1]

Lee returned from Mexico with a reputation established at the age of forty-two. How widespread that reputation had become is shown by an incident which occurred not long after he had resumed his duty as an engineer, and taken up work on the defences of Baltimore. Representatives of the Cuban junta called upon him there and offered him the command of an expedition to overthrow the Spanish control of the island. The proposal was accompanied with very tempting financial

[1] Fitzhugh Lee: *General Lee*, p. 42.

terms. The question of the acquisition of Cuba had for some time been a political issue in the United States and there were many who favoured such a transaction. In such circumstances a man to whom notoriety was an inducement might well have persuaded himself that he was serving at once his own interests and those of his country in accepting the offer. Lee did not hesitate; he went at once to Washington to see Mr. Jefferson Davis, then Secretary of War, not to consult him as to whether he should undertake the mission, but because he held it his duty to inform his political chief of what had passed, and he told him he could not accept any proposition for foreign service against a government with which the United States was at peace.

There followed three years as superintendent at West Point. How valuable a training for high command is the supervision of military education is shown by the fact that Foch first made a name for himself as lecturer and later as chief of the French War College; while in the British army, Lord Rawlinson, one of our most successful commanders of armies, Sir William Robertson and Sir Henry Wilson, who both became Field Marshals and Chiefs of the General Staff, all served as commandants of the British Staff College. True, the education at West Point was less purely military in character than that of the military colleges of France and England, but the advantage to a future commander which the direction of

such an institution affords does not lie so much in the
nature of the instruction given as in the opportunities
afforded of judging men of very varied character and
attainments. A commander in the field must, to be
successful, be an accurate judge of the characters both
of his subordinates and of his opponents, and there is
clear evidence that Lee's experience at the head of the
United States Military Academy helped him greatly to
develop his judgment of men.

The great extension of the territory of the United
States due to the Mexican War made it necessary to
increase the regular army, and in 1855 Congress passed
a measure authorizing the formation of two regiments of
infantry and two of cavalry. The first of the new cavalry
regiments was commanded by Colonel E. V. Sumner,
with Brevet-Colonel J. E. Johnston as second in command. The command of the second regiment was given
to Colonel A. S. Johnston, with Brevet-Colonel R. E.
Lee as his lieutenant-colonel. Thus, as in the Mexican
War, we find a group of men brought together, all of
whom became famous in the Civil War. The first business of the senior officers was the creation of the regiments and in this work Lee gained some very useful
practical experience in military organization. The
Second Cavalry had an exceptionally fine body of
officers. Hood, Fitzhugh Lee, Stoneman, Kirby Smith,
and Field, all of them destined to become generals of

distinction, were among the subordinates. Its organization completed, the regiment was ordered to the country
of the Comanche Indians which lies between the Ar-
kansas River and the Rio Grande. The Comanches were
daring freebooters who lived by raiding impartially the
territories belonging to Mexico and the United States.
The method of controlling them was the establishment
of a chain of small military posts from which constant
forays were made to punish the Comanches when they
offended.

The service was arduous and exhausting, and Lee
did not find it particularly interesting. In April, 1856,
he wrote: 'We are on the Comanche Reserve with the
Indian camps below us on the river belonging to Catumseh's band, whom the Government is endeavoring
to humanize. It will be uphill work, I fear. Catumseh has
been to see me, and we have had a talk, very tedious on
his part and very sententious on mine. I hailed him as a
friend as long as his conduct and that of his tribe de-
served it, but would meet him as an enemy the first moment he failed to keep his word. The rest of the tribe
(about a thousand, it is said) live north of us and are
hostile. Yesterday I returned his visit, and remained a
short time at his lodge. He informed me that he had six
wives. They [1] are riding in and out of camp all day, their
paint and "ornaments" rendering them more hideous

---

[1] Presumably the Comanches, not their wives.

than nature made them and the whole race is extremely uninteresting.' [1]

For a man of Lee's tastes the life must have been dull to a degree. The posts were surrounded by uninteresting, almost desert country, and there were rarely more than two companies at any one of them. Mails were irregular, and it took several weeks for a letter to come from Virginia. The leading of the small punitive expeditions was usually in the hands of the junior officers and the seniors had very little society of any kind and small outlet for their energies. While Lee was not in his letters enthusiastic about the charms of this life, he made no complaint and regretted only the separation from his family. His father-in-law, Mr. Custis, died in 1859, and Lee obtained an extension of the usual furlough to settle up the estate. So it happened that in October, 1859, he was at Arlington when John Brown's raid on Harper's Ferry took place. The Secretary of War placed him in charge of the force hastily assembled to repress the raiders, and in this enterprise Lee was accompanied by J. E. B. Stuart, then a good-looking young lieutenant of cavalry, who acted as his aide-de-camp. This unpleasant duty accomplished, Lee returned to the Texas border to be summoned to Washington in February, 1861, to meet the crisis of his life.

For thirty-two years Lee had served his country with

[1] A. L. Long: *Memoirs of Robert E. Lee*, p. 78.

honour and distinction. He had during those years mastered the technicalities of his own arm of the service. He had as an engineer in the field been brought into close touch with the artillery, and he had been in command of a body of cavalry scattered over a great extent of country under very trying conditions. He had been employed on the staff both in peace and in war and he had held administrative positions of importance. His capacity had, therefore, been tested in many ways and he had passed every test triumphantly. He had given proofs of physical and moral courage and had won the confidence both of superiors and of subordinates. Such, then, was the equipment with which he entered the arena of history.

CHAPTER III

THE CRISIS OF 1861

As I have said, Lee, when in his family circle, was accustomed to meet men who held responsible positions in the governments both of their States and of their country and to hear questions of the day discussed with knowledge and authority. Though during his long isolation in Texas he was removed from such associations, he used all the means at his disposal to keep in touch with the political development of his country, and ever since the Compromise of 1850, he had watched closely the growth of the crisis which resulted in the secession of the Southern States. He had served the United States loyally and faithfully, but he had been brought up to hold that his first duty was to his State. It was in that spirit that he decided to resign his commission in the Army of the United States and to throw in his lot with Virginia.

It was natural that, in the heat and passion aroused by civil war, he should have been held up to obloquy as a traitor to the flag under which he had served, and the country to which he had sworn allegiance. But it is curious that such sentiments should have endured in the minds of some responsible writers long after Robert E. Lee had gone to meet his God. This is the account which so distinguished an historian as John G. Nicolay gives of Lee's action in April, 1861:[1] 'Whether because of family ties (he was a Virginian) or of property interests or of more alluring overtures from the South, Lee on April 20th tendered his resignation to General Scott. On April 22d, before that resignation had been accepted, he was formally invested by the Virginia Convention with the command of the Virginia troops, hostile to the United States.' It would, I think, be difficult to compress into a similar number of words a greater misrepresentation of fact.

Even a cursory examination of the evidence should have convinced any one that this is so. I will take Lee's property interests first: His principal estates lay in the valley of the Potomac on the frontier between the contending powers. From his house at Arlington could be seen the capital of the United States. No one will deny that in April, 1861, Lee was an experienced soldier, and that he must have known that his property would inevitably suffer in the event of war. It is probable that his modesty prevented him from assessing his capacity as high as did General Scott, who said that the accession of Lee to the South was worth the addition of twenty thousand men to their forces, but he could not but have been aware that the prospect of shortening the war and thereby reducing the risk to his property would be im-

[1] *Cambridge Modern History*, vol. VII.

proved both by the offer of his own services to the North
and by the effect of the example of such action at that
time upon others. He must equally have been aware that
his chances of protecting his property would be greater
if he were in command at Washington than they would
be if he were at Richmond. In the excitement of the
crisis there were many Southerners who believed that
the war would be short and that the South would soon
wring from the North recognition of their claim to independence. There were in the North many who thought
that it would be a simple task to bring the recalcitrant
States to reason. Lee was amongst the very few who saw
from the first that the war would be long. Within a few
days of reaching Richmond, after resigning from the
Army of the United States, he was writing to his wife at
Arlington: [1] 'I think you had better prepare all things for
removal from Arlington — that is, plate, pictures, etc.,
and be prepared at any moment. Where to go is the
difficulty. When war commences no place will be ex-
empt, in my opinion; indeed, all the avenues into the
State will be the scene of military operations. I wrote to
Robert [2] that I could not consent to take boys from their
schools and young men from their colleges and put them
into the ranks at the beginning of the war when they are
not needed. The war may last ten years. Where are our
ranks to be filled from then?' [3] It is abundantly clear

[1] April 30, 1861.   [2] His son.   [3] Fitzhugh Lee: *General Lee*, p. 93.

that Lee, more than most men in those critical days, risked by his decision the security of his property and the comfort of those dear to him. Consideration of property did not influence his judgment for a moment.

It is not less preposterous to suppose that he was influenced by more alluring offers from the South. I have already referred to the opinion that General Scott, then in control of the military forces of the United States, had formed of him. As soon as it became clear that a rupture was imminent, Scott induced Lincoln to make every effort to retain Lee's services for the cause of the Union, and the President sent Mr. Francis Preston Blair to offer to him the command of the active army of the United States. What must such an offer have meant to Lee? It realized what is the honourable ambition of every soldier who enters the service of his country. He would be associated with his old chief and close friend, Scott, himself a Virginian. Ties dear to all soldiers, but especially dear to the officers of a small army such as that of the United States, almost all of whom had passed through one school, would be continued. Lee wrote more than once that the comradeship of service was to him the chief attraction which the army had to offer. It was not possible that the South should have made him an offer more alluring than that conveyed to him from President Lincoln, and it is in fact evident that no offer, prior to his decision, was made. When Lee

sent in his resignation to Scott, he had made no provision for his future. Here is his own statement: 'I never
intimated to any one that I desired the command of the
United States Army, nor did I ever have a conversation
but with one gentleman, Mr. Francis Preston Blair, on
the subject, which was at his invitation, and, as I understood, at the instance of President Lincoln.

'After listening to his remarks, I declined the offer he
made me to take command of the Army that was to be
brought into the field, stating, as candidly and courte-
ously as I could, that, though opposed to secession and
deprecating war, I would take no part in the invasion
of the Southern States. I went directly from the interview with Mr. Blair to the office of General Scott, told
him of the proposition that had been made to me and
my decision. Upon reflection, after returning home, I
concluded that I ought no longer to retain any commission I held in the United States Army, and on the
second morning thereafter I forwarded my resignation
to General Scott.

'At the time I hoped that peace would have been preserved — that some way would be found to save the
country from the calamities of war; and I then had no
other intentions than to pass the remainder of my life as
a private citizen.

'Two days afterwards, on the invitation of the Governor of Virginia, I repaired to Richmond, found that the

convention there in session had passed the ordinance withdrawing the State from the Union, and accepted the commission of commander of its forces, which was tendered to me. There are the simple facts of the case.' [1]

Lee thus became Major-General of Virginia, but it happened that on the very day when the Convention of Virginia confirmed his appointment, it was proposed that the State should join the Confederacy. In order to facilitate this, Lee at once resigned his commission without making any attempt to bargain as to his future position. As late as June 9, 1861, that is, nearly two months after he had sent in his resignation to Scott, he wrote to his wife from Richmond: 'You may be aware that the Confederate Government is established here. Yesterday I turned over to it the command of the military and naval forces of the State, in accordance with the proclamation of the Government, under an agreement between the State and the Confederate States. I do not know what my position will be. I should like to retire into private life, so that I could be with you and the children, but if I can be of service to the State and her cause I must continue.' [2] At that time the Federal forces had already crossed the Potomac and were in occupation of the heights of Arlington. Lee was actu-

[1] A. L. Long: *Memoirs of Robert E. Lee*, p. 93.
[2] Fitzhugh Lee: *General Lee*, p. 98.

ally preparing to enlist as a private in the cavalry when in June, 1861, he received from the Confederate Government the commission to command its forces in the State of Virginia. But as will be seen the positions he at first occupied were inferior to that which Lincoln had offered. Ambition had not, any more than considerations of property, influenced Lee's decision.

It is, of course, true that family ties were to Lee a matter of great concern. 'I had to meet,' he said, 'the question whether I should take part against my native State. I have not been able to make up my mind to raise my hand against my relations, my children, my home.' Such sentiments, natural as they are, might have induced Lee to resign his commission, and to separate himself from the North, but they do not account for the devotion with which he served the South, nor for his repeated and obviously sincere appeals to his troops to fight for, and if need be die for, a just cause. He certainly did not believe slavery to be an institution for which men should fight and die. He had released his own slaves. In December, 1856, he had written to Mrs. Lee from Fort Brown, Texas:

'The steamer has moved from New Orleans, bringing full files of papers and general intelligence from the "States." I have enjoyed the former very much, and, in the absence of particular intelligence, have perused with much interest the series of the "Alexandria Gazette" from the 20th of November to the 8th of December inclusive. Besides the usual good reading matter, I was interested in the relation of local affairs, and inferred, from the quiet and ordinary course of events, that all in the neighborhood was going on well. I trust it may be so, and that you and particularly all at Arlington and our friends elsewhere are well. The steamer brought the President's message to Congress and the reports of the various heads of the departments, so that we are now assured that the Government is in operation and the Union in existence. Not that I had any fears to the contrary, but it is satisfactory always to have facts to go on; they restrain supposition and conjecture, confirm faith and bring contentment. I was much pleased with the President's message and the report of the Secretary of War. The views of the President on the domestic institutions of the South are truthfully and faithfully expressed. In this enlightened age there are few, I believe, but will acknowledge that slavery as an institution is a moral and political evil in any country. It is useless to expatiate on its disadvantages. I think it, however, to be a greater evil to the white than to the black race, and while my feelings are strongly interested in the latter my sympathies are stronger for the former. The blacks are immeasurably better off here than in Africa, morally, physically, and socially. The painful discipline they are undergoing is necessary for their instruction as a race, and, I hope, will prepare and lead them to better things. How long their subjection may be necessary is known and ordered by a wise and merciful Providence. Their emancipation will sooner result from a mild and melting influence than from the storm and contests of a fiery controversy. This influence though slow is sure. The doctrines and miracles of our Saviour have required nearly two thousand years to convert but a small portion of the human race, and even among Christian nations what gross errors still exist! While we hope that the course of the final abolition of slavery is onward and we give it the aid of our prayers and all justifiable means in our power, we must leave the result in His hands, who sees the end and who chooses to work by slow things, and with whom a thousand years are but as a single day. Although the abolitionist must know this and must see that he has neither the right nor the power of operating except by moral means and suasion; and if he means well to the slave he must not create angry feelings in the master; that although he may not approve the mode by which it pleases Providence to accomplish its purposes, the result will be the same; that the reasons he gives for interference in what he has no concern holds good for every kind of interference with our neighbors when we disapprove their conduct. Is it not strange that the descendants of those Pilgrim Fathers who crossed the Atlantic to preserve the freedom of their opinion have always proved themselves intolerant of the spiritual liberty of others?' [1]

The arguments in this letter are involved; not all of them are based on sound premises, and they are heavily expressed, but they make it clear that while Lee thought slavery to be an evil, he believed that more harm than good would result from the attempt to eradicate the evil by force, and there were in 1861 in the North very many who agreed with him in this. It is evident that he would not have resigned his commission in the United States Army, still less have opposed the Union in arms if in his mind the retention of slavery had been the chief issue.

Neither did Lee think secession a cause to fight for. He wrote from Texas on January 23, 1861, to his son: 'The South, in my opinion, has been aggrieved by the acts of the North, as you say. I feel the aggression and am willing to take every proper step for redress. It is the principle I contend for, not individual or private benefit. As an American citizen, I take great pride in my country, her prosperity, her institutions, and would defend any State if her rights were invaded. But I can anticipate no greater calamity for the country than a dissolution of the Union. It would be an accumulation of all the evils we complain of, and I am willing to sacrifice everything but honour for its preservation. I hope, therefore, that all constitutional means will be ex-

[1] Fitzhugh Lee: *General Lee*, p. 63.

hausted before there is a resort to force. Secession is nothing but revolution. The framers of our Constitution never exhausted so much labour, wisdom, and forbearance in its formation, and surrounded it by so many guards and securities, if it was intended to be broken by every member of the Confederacy at will. It is intended for "perpetual union," so expressed in the preamble, and the establishment of a government, not a compact, which can only be dissolved by revolution or the consent of all the people in convention assembled. It is idle to talk of secession. Anarchy would have been established, and not a government, by Washington, Hamilton, Jefferson, Madison, and all the other patriots of the Revolution. . . . Still a Union that can only be maintained by swords and bayonets, and in which strife and civil war are to take the place of brotherly love and kindness, has no charm for me. I shall mourn for my country and for the welfare and progress of mankind. If the Union is dissolved and the government dispersed, I shall return to my native State and share the miseries of my people and save in defence will draw my sword no more.' [1]

[1] A. L. Long: *Memoirs of R. E. Lee*, p. 88.

Mrs. Lee's views, expressed almost at the same time, were even stronger. On February 9, 1861, she wrote a friend, Mrs. W. H. Stiles: 'Has all love for and pride in their country died at the South, that they are willing to tear her in pieces and *some* even to *exult* to see her glorious flag trailing in the dust? It should rather have drawn tears from their eyes. We have lived and fought and *prospered* under this flag for so many years, and though the South has suffered much from the *meddling* of Northern fanat-

So four months before Lee resigned from the Army of the United States he made up his mind how he would act when and if Virginia left the Union. His decision was therefore no hasty one, and it happens that the concluding words of his letter of January 23, 1861, recur in his letter of April 20th to General Scott, by which he severed his connection with the service he had adorned.[1]

ics, yet do they expect to fare better now? Are there no rights and privileges but those of negro slavery? You by your situation are removed from any *active* interference, whereas *we* in the border States are so much annoyed that our slaves have become almost useless. In our own family we have lost numbers who have been decoyed off, and after my father's death we were preserved from an outbreak excited by two abolitionists who were constantly over here (as we learned afterwards, one of whom I am happy to say is now in the penitentiary for fourteen years) — we were preserved I say by the *special* mercy of God. The *Tribune* and New York *Times* published the most *villainous* attacks upon my husband by *name* and upon my father's memory in language I would not pollute my lips by repeating, and yet after all these wrongs I would lay down my life could I save our "Union." What is the use of a government combined as ours is of so many parts, the *Union* of which forms its strength and power, if any *one part* has the right for any wrong, real or imaginary, of withdrawing its aid and throwing the whole into confusion as Carolina, who refuses all overtures for peace and imagines the world will admire her independence, whereas they laugh at her folly which is perfectly suicidal. You know my feelings are all linked with the South and you will bear with me in the expression of my opinion, but while there are many of the Northern politicians who deserve no better fate than to be *hung* as high as Haman, believe me that those who have been *foremost* in this Revolution will deserve and meet with the reprobation of the world, either North or South, for having destroyed the most glorious Confederacy that ever existed.'

[1] GENERAL: — Since my interview with you on the 18th inst. I have felt that I ought not longer to retain my commission in the army. I, therefore, tender my resignation, which I request you will recommend for acceptance. It would have been presented at once, but for the struggle it has cost me to separate myself from a service to which I have devoted the best years of my life and all the ability I possessed. During the whole of that time — more than a quarter of a century — I have experienced nothing but kindness from my superiors and a most cordial friendship from my comrades. To no one, General, have I been as much indebted as to yourself for uniform kindness and consideration, and it has always been my

His mind was torn and anguished. He had grave doubts as to whether his State would be right to secede. 'Secession is nothing but revolution.' His was not one of those easy consciences which can dissolve all doubts in crises between states and between nations with the cry: 'My country right or wrong!' He was more critical of the action of the 'Cotton States' than many Northerners. On December 12, 1860, he wrote to his son from Texas: 'General Scruggs yesterday entered on the duties of the office, but he desires to remain till Major Nichols arrives. I go there in the morning to see what is to be done. He thinks the Union will be dissolved in six weeks, and that he will then return to New Orleans. If I thought so I would not take the trouble to go to Mason, but return to you now. I hope, however, the wisdom and patriotism of the country will devise some way of saving it, and that a kind Providence has not yet turned the current of his blessings from us. The three propositions of the President are eminently just, are in accordance with the Constitution, and ought to be cheerfully assented to by all the States. But I do not think

ardent desire to merit your approbation. I shall carry to the grave the most grateful recollections of your kind consideration, and your name and fame will be dear to me. Save in defence of my native State, I never desire again to draw my sword. So, please to accept my most earnest wishes for the continuance of your happiness and prosperity, and believe me truly yours,

R. E. LEE

ARLINGTON, VA.
        April 20, 1861

His resignation was officially accepted on April 25th.

the Northern and Western States will agree to them.'[1]

Yet Lee held it to be his bounden duty to defend Virginia if she were attacked. That his intention in the first months of 1861 was to do nothing more than resist aggression is, I think, made clear by a letter which he wrote to his sister who lived at Baltimore and was a supporter of the Union. The letter was penned on the same day as that to General Scott. It runs: 'I am grieved at my inability to see you. I have been waiting for a more convenient season, which has brought to many before me deep and lasting regret. Now we are in a state of war, which will yield to nothing. The whole South is in a state of revolution, into which Virginia, after a long struggle has been drawn; and, though I recognize no necessity for this state of things, and would have forborne and pleaded to the end for redress of grievances, real or supposed, yet in my own person I had to meet the question whether I should take part against my native State. With all my devotion to the Union and the feeling of loyalty and duty of an American citizen, I have not been able to make up my mind to raise my hand against my relatives, my children, my home. I have, therefore, resigned my commission in the army and save in defence of my native State, with the

[1] The reference is to President Buchanan's message to Congress of December 4, 1860. In it runs the phrase, 'Secession is neither more nor less than revolution,' which Lee adapted in his letter of January, 1861. The message certainly did not please the North and West and was not generally popular even in the Sout'

sincere hope that my poor services may not be needed, I hope I may never be called on to draw the sword.'

The suspicion that this last sentence is mere verbiage must occur to any one reading it in the light of Lee's career as a soldier, but the evidence of his sincere modesty is so ample that I am convinced that it was written in all good faith. In the anguish of the crisis he had no thought but to go to his State and to suffer with her children. At the back of his mind was his father's: 'Virginia is my country. Her I will obey, however lamentable the fate to which it may subject me.'

But when Lee got to Richmond and breathed the atmosphere of enthusiasm for a cause which pervaded his State, his attitude of mind changed gradually. He became convinced that Virginia was fighting for the right and said so again and again to his soldiers. Here I need do no more than quote the closing words of the pronouncement which he issued to his troops when he became Commander-in-Chief of the armies of the Confederacy, for it expresses, with a dignity and emotion unusual in one whose military utterances were as a rule plain to the verge of bluntness, what was his mind: 'Let us oppose constancy to adversity, fortitude to suffering, and courage to danger, with the firm assurance that He Who gave freedom to our fathers will bless the efforts of their children to preserve it.' [1]

[1] General Order No. 2, February 11, 1865.

Lee fought as a man fights who acts on conviction. What, then, was his conviction? There have been critics of his career who, while expressing every sympathy with him in the terrible situation in which he was placed in April, 1861, have been unable to explain to themselves with any satisfaction his breach of his oath as a regular officer of the Union and his enthusiasm for a cause which, as they say, he must have known to be based on slavery. As to the first of these criticisms, I would say that Lee did not break his military oath. He resigned his commission and the acceptance of that resignation released him from that obligation. It is true, as Nicolay says, that he went to Richmond before the formal notification that he had ceased to be an officer of the Army of the United States reached him. He assumed that his resignation would be accepted,[1] and he had reason for that assumption, for in the United States, it was recognized that in the event of civil strife the State should permit those in its service who had family ties with the participants in a rebellion to obtain release from service if they so desired. To act otherwise and to force men to fight those near and dear to them would be to make military service an unendurable tyranny. This

[1] On May 2d he wrote to Mrs. Lee: 'I have just received Custis' letter inclosing the acceptance of my resignation. This stated it will take effect on the 25th of April. I resigned on the 20th and wished it to take effect on that day. I cannot consent to its running on further, and he must receive no pay if they tender it beyond that day, but return the whole if need be.'

implicit right to resignation does not relieve those who
act upon it from the pains and penalties attaching to
them as rebel citizens, but does absolve them from the
charge of having broken a military oath. The fact that
the authorities at Washington accepted Lee's resignation and also accepted wholesale resignations of other
regular officers who were of Southern blood shows that
this was so.

Those who maintain that Lee must consciously have
been fighting for the maintenance of slavery would make
of him a casuist. My reading of his character is different.
I have said that his upbringing and associations made
him take a real and serious interest in political affairs,
and I hope to show that in his part in the conduct of the
war he displayed a statesmanlike grasp of situations
which is rarely found in soldiers. But for all that, Lee
was not a politically minded man. His praise of Buchanan's weak and time-serving message of December, 1860,
is sufficient to prove that. He could not follow political developments to their conclusion with the logic and
perspicacity of Lincoln. He could not foresee the out-
come of the struggle between those who advocated
limitation and those who pressed for the extension of
slavery. Be it remembered that in 1861 abolition was the
creed of a comparatively small number in the North.
The Lee I see was essentially a simple-minded man, with
a keen sense of duty and a perfect trust in God's provi-

dence. His nature was not such as to make him eager to investigate the complexities of involved political questions, and his military training was calculated to strengthen his natural distaste for such investigations. He followed Calhoun in believing the great and leading principle of the political life of the Union to be that 'the general government emanated from the people of the several States forming distinct political communities and acting in their several and sovereign capacity, not from all the people forming one aggregate political community.' He regarded the Union as a great possession, but only so long as it was a free association of free States.

The picture of Lee pacing his chamber at Arlington on the night of April 19, 1861, has been drawn by many and skilful pens. To me it is one of the sad pictures of history. He had, I am convinced, but one thought, 'What is my duty?' No motive of self-interest entered his mind. For duty he was prepared to make any and every sacrifice, and he prayed God to help him to answer rightly the question he had put to himself. The answer to it depended not upon the rights and wrongs of slavery — upon that, as I have shown, his mind was clear — but upon the answer to another question which is still perplexing us in Great Britain, and many in other countries in Europe. 'How far should the principle of self-determination be carried?'[1] Lee attempted to an-

---

[1] For Lee's considered opinion on this point after the war see the Appendix to this chapter.

swer that question honestly according to the light which was vouchsafed him. If history has shown that he was wrong and Lincoln right, that the future of his great country depended upon the development of the Union in ways and forms of which he did not approve, we need not, therefore, stint our admiration for the man's honesty of purpose and for his brave sacrifice for what he believed to be right. Lee was a rebel, as he himself admitted, but, as a generous opponent has said, in that category 'he stands awaiting sentence at the bar of history in very respectable company. Associated with him are, for instance, William of Orange, known as the Silent; John Hampden, the original Pater Patriæ; Oliver Cromwell, the Protector of the British Commonwealth; Sir Harry Vane, once a Governor of Massachusetts, and George Washington, a Virginian of note.' [1]

APPENDIX

R. E. LEE TO LORD ACTON, DECEMBER 13, 1866

Amid the conflicting statements and sentiments in both countries, it will be no easy task to discover the truth or to relieve it from the mass of prejudice and passion with which it has been covered by party spirit. I am conscious of the compliment conveyed in your request for my opinion as to the light in which American politics should be viewed, and had I the ability I have not the time to enter upon a discussion which was commenced by the founders of the Constitution and has been continued to the present day. I can only say

---

[1] Charles Francis Adams: *Lee Centennial Address.*

that while I have considered the preservation of the constitutional power of the General Government to be the foundation of our peace and safety at home and abroad, I yet believe that the maintenance of the rights and authority reserved to the States and to the people not only essential to the adjustment and balance of the general system but the safeguard to the continuance of a free government. I consider it as the chief source of stability to our political system, whereas the consolidation of the States into one vast republic, sure to be aggressive abroad and despotic at home, will be the certain precursor of that ruin which has overwhelmed all those that have preceded it.

I need not refer one so well acquainted as you are with American history to the state papers of Washington and Jefferson, and representatives of the Federal and Democratic Parties, denouncing consolidation and centralization of power as tending to the subversion of State Governments and to despotism. The New England States, whose citizens are the fiercest opponents of the Southern States, did not always avow the opinions they now advocate. Upon the purchase of Louisiana by Mr. Jefferson they virtually asserted the right of secession through their prominent men, and in the convention which assembled at Hartford in 1814 they threatened the disruption of the Union unless the war should be discontinued. The assertion of this right has been repeatedly made by their politicians when their party was weak, and Massachusetts, the leading State in hostility to the South, declares in the preamble to her Constitution that the people of that Commonwealth 'have the sole and exclusive right of governing themselves as a free, sovereign, and independent State, and do and forever hereafter shall exercise and enjoy every power, jurisdiction, and right which is not or may hereafter be by them expressly delegated to the United States of America in Congress assembled.' Such has been in substance the language of other State Governments, and such the doctrine advocated by the leading men of the country for the last seventy years. Judge Chase, the present Chief Justice of the United States,

as late as 1850 is reported to have stated in the Senate, of
which he was a member, that he 'knew of no remedy in case
of the refusal of a State to perform its stipulations,' thereby
acknowledging the sovereignty and independence of State
action.

CHAPTER IV

THE PROBLEMS OF THE CONFEDERACY

BEFORE I attempt to look at the story of the Civil War through the eyes of Lee, I must pay a tribute,which as an old student of the history of that war I have long felt to be due. The official histories of European wars are very rarely satisfying. The official military historian works in manacles. He cannot for obvious reasons speak his mind freely on the actions or inactions of the statesmen and soldiers of his own country, who are still alive. Often political considerations prevent him from criticising freely even the doings of the enemy. So official histories often tend to be either partisan propaganda, or are somewhat colourless narratives which rarely give the historian all the information he wants. For these reasons I have always admired the course adopted by the United States in publishing without comment, in as complete a form as possible, the documents relating to the Civil War. The heavy volumes of the Official Records, together with the admirable collection of contemporary opinions to be found in the Century Company's 'Battles and Leaders of the Civil War' and in the numerous papers of the Military Historical Society of Massachusetts and of the Southern Historical Society, supply the student with such a wealth of well-arranged

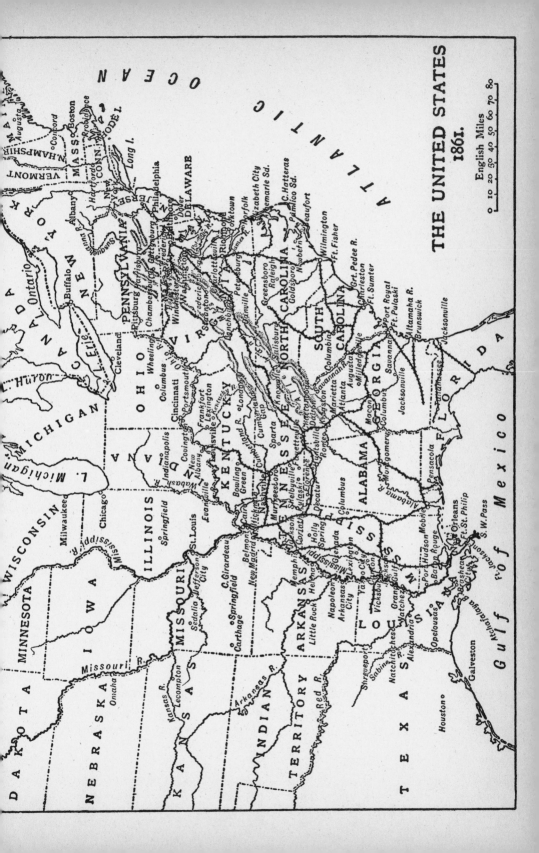

THE UNITED STATES
1861.

English Miles
0 10 20 30 40 50 60 70 80

and easily accessible material as is, in my judgment, un-
equalled in respect of any other war.

When the Confederate Government was transferred
from Montgomery to Richmond, Lee became its military
assistant, standing in relation to Jefferson Davis in the
position held in Europe by the Chief of a General Staff.
His business was to advise his Government as to the
strategy of the war, and to direct the organization of the
Confederate forces. Therefore, like the king of old, he
had first to sit down and consider whether 'he be able
with ten thousand men to meet him that cometh against
him with twenty thousand.' That is no unfair comparison of the general resources of the Union and of the
Confederacy. But that does not mean that on every
battlefield the North outnumbered the South by two to
one. There has been much controversy as to the strength
of the opposing forces on various battlefields of the
Civil War. McClellan's well-known tendency to exag-
gerate, sometimes almost fantastically, the strength of
his enemy has led some Southern writers to err in the
opposite direction. A witty Northerner has said, 'A few
more years, a few more books, and it will appear that
Lee and Longstreet, a one-armed orderly, and a casual
with a shot-gun fought all the battles of the Rebellion
and killed all the Union soldiers except those who ran
away.' The fact is that controversy about the strength
of armies in battle is as old as military history. In every

army, and in every battalion of infantry, battery of
artillery, and regiment of cavalry of every army, there
are men whose names are on the rolls, but who are
absent either from illness or because they are employed
in temporary duties away from their units. There are
many others who are required for various services
which do not normally take them into battle as fighters.
As in most armies the system of accounting for the
various categories of men varies, the opportunities
for argument on the subject are almost infinite. Speak-
ing generally, one may say that there is a tendency, on
the part of those who wish to make the best possible case
for the side they favour, to give the actual number of
fighting men in battle on that side and to oppose to
them all the men on the rolls of the other army. That is
a tendency which is particularly marked in many books
on the Civil War. None the less, it is, of course, beyond
dispute that in general resources, and above all at sea,
the North was vastly superior to the South, and Lee's
immediate task was to consider how that superiority
could be countered.

We are all of us more attracted by stirring events in
the field than by the patient work of organization. We
like to read of commanders teaching the 'doubtful battle
where to rage,' and to few of us is the administrator a
hero. Yet without the administrator and the organizer
there would not be many successful campaigns, and it

may well have happened that if there had been no Lazar Carnot there would have been no Napoleon. Bonaparte might, in that case, have gone down to history as the hero of 'the whiff of grapeshot.' Little has been said of Lee's work as an organizer, yet it had a great influence on the course of the war. I have already said he was one of the very few who from the first saw that the war would be long. The fact that the enlistment of the first volunteers in the North was for ninety days is sufficient evidence of the authoritative view held on that side. Lee endeavoured to persuade Davis to make enlistment compulsory and for the duration of the war, and though the Confederate Government was not at first prepared for so drastic a measure, he did succeed in getting it to accept the enlistment of volunteers without limit as to numbers, for the duration of the war, after a first enactment limiting service to twelve months had been adopted. In April, 1862, he persuaded the authorities of Richmond to get a Conscription Act passed, nearly a year before such a measure was adopted at Washington. In three other respects his plans of preparation seem to have been from the first superior to those adopted in the North. His own experiences had convinced him of the importance of having an efficient staff, and he took special pains to make this provision from his exiguous resources; he was equally convinced of the importance of having what in modern armies is called an 'order of battle' scientifically arranged; as a cavalry officer he attached a high value to that arm, for which the landowners and farmers of the South furnished splendid material. Until a late stage in the war the staff work of the Southern armies, if very far from perfect when judged by present standards, was better than that of the Northern forces; the organization of the Confederate troops in brigades and divisions and the establishment of a hierarchy of command were more adapted to the requirements of war than was the system first devised at Washington, that is to say, the Confederate order of battle was superior to the Federal until Hooker reorganized the army of the Potomac in January, 1863; the Southern cavalry was, until the middle of 1863, superior not only in its personnel, as was in the circumstances natural, but in its organization and methods. So for the first half of the period of the war, Lee's capacity as a military organizer conferred definite advantages on the South.

But Lee's most pressing concern at the beginning of the war was with the defence of Richmond. Not only was it necessary for the South to act defensively until at least the nucleus of an army was prepared, but the cause of State Rights to which the Confederacy was pledged, imposed extreme caution in invading the territory of Maryland without the explicit consent of that State, which it was hoped to induce to join the

Southern cause. There were three avenues of approach to Richmond; by the Orange and Alexandria Railroad to Manassas Junction and thence across the Rappahannock; by Harper's Ferry and up the Valley of the Shenandoah; and by sea through Fortress Monroe and the Yorktown Peninsula. Lee, as he had told his wife, expected that 'all the avenues into the State' would be the scene of military operations, and he prepared to meet attack in each of the three. He early predicted that Manassas would be the scene of one of the first battles, and there he assembled the chief Southern force. Jackson first, and then J. E. Johnston, were sent to Harper's Ferry, and defensive lines covering Richmond were prepared on the Yorktown Peninsula. It is evident that the South owed much to these timely dispositions. Not a little of the Confederate success at the first battle of Manassas was due to the familiarity of the troops with the ground on which they fought, while a rich return was to be gained for the familiarity with the Valley which Jackson early acquired.

Such were Lee's preoccupations during the first months of war, throughout which he worked in close accord with President Davis. The Confederate President had, for a statesman, an unusual degree of military experience. He was a West Pointer, and had been at the Military Academy at the same time as Lee. He had served both in the United States infantry and dragoons, and then resigned his commission. When the Mexican War broke out, he volunteered for service and became colonel of a Mississippi regiment, while he was Secretary of War in Mr. Pierce's administration. He had then had excellent opportunities for getting to know the small band of regular officers of the United States Army and he showed himself to be not only a good judge of men, but to have the firmness of character not to be moved from his judgment either by popular clamour or by temporary failures on the part of those in whose qualities he had convinced himself he had good reason to believe. It happened that the first performances of both Lee and Jackson in the field were unsuccessful, and the Press of Richmond was free with criticisms, particularly of the former, but Davis never wavered in his support of Lee either then or at any other time, while Lee was consistently loyal to the President, and there is no word of criticism of the statesman to be found throughout the soldier's correspondence. The Constitution of the Confederacy followed that of the Union in making the President Commander-in-Chief of its forces, and Lee had no desire to oust him from that position. In July, 1861, Lee wrote to his wife: 'I have never heard of the assignment to which you allude — of Commander-in-Chief of the Southern Army — nor have I any expectation or wish for it. President Davis holds that position.'

This was written when Davis's conduct of the war was

perhaps more open to criticism than at any other time. It cannot, I think, be disputed that the South had never again so favourable a chance of invading Maryland as occurred a few weeks after the first battle of Manassas. Both J. E. Johnston and Beauregard pressed the President to reënforce them by withdrawing troops allocated to the protection of the coast and to allow them to cross the Potomac. Jackson was almost passionately in favour of such action. It happened, as will be seen, that at this critical moment Lee was withdrawn from the President's councils and the President refused to listen to his generals. It has been generally believed that this was due to Davis's unwillingness to leave the Southern shores exposed to the depredations of the Federal fleet, and he certainly said that he could not provide the reënforcements for which the generals were clamouring without depriving some parts of the South of necessary protection. But the Federal fleet was not, in August, 1861, the menace it became later. At the outbreak of the war the Union had but 42 ships in commission, a number increased in 1864 to 671. I believe that Davis was influenced rather by political than by military considerations, and that those political considerations were the same which imposed a defensive attitude upon the South at the outbreak of the war. Davis was, it seems, indisposed to invade Maryland until there was evidence of a strong desire amongst the people of that

State for the appearance of Southern troops on their soil,
or until Maryland had more definitely espoused the
cause of the Union.

Davis's difficulties, in fact, sprang from the very
nature of the Southern cause, and are the best arguments in favour of a State having the power to place
unquestioned and supreme authority in one hand in a
great national emergency. The Confederate President
throughout the war showed a tendency to disperse his
resources in an attempt to secure too much, and an unwillingness to run great risks for great gains. But he
was bound by his contract with the States which formed
the Confederacy to give the utmost consideration to
their views, and each State, when threatened with invasion, naturally clamoured for protection, and was
unwilling to send more of its sons to fight on distant
fields. From the beginning of 1862, Davis was faced by
two bugbears. There was first the bugbear of the
Federal fleet, to attack from which the long Atlantic
coast-line of the South was exposed. The services of
that fleet in retaining forces from battles which Lee
hoped to make decisive have been somewhat obscured
by the still greater effect of the strangle-hold of its
blockade, a strangle-hold every whit as effective as that
of the fleets of the Allies in the Great War, but those
services were very real. At the time of the beginning of
Lee's second invasion of Maryland, which was defeated

at Gettysburg, no less than 59,000 Confederate troops were engaged in defending the coast. The second bug-bear was the danger that a Federal advance down the Mississippi would cut the Confederacy in two, and halve its already exiguous resources for the conduct of the war. In such circumstances it would have required quite exceptional courage, character, and prescience to have risked all upon the chance of winning a decisive victory in Maryland. Further, both Davis and the South generally believed that time was on their side, and that if they endured Europe would intervene and put an end to the struggle. Davis's task was supremely difficult, and criticism which does not take account of his difficulties is of little value. He at least showed that he possessed one of the great qualities required of a statesman in war, the capacity to select good generals and the courage to support them against popular pres-sure. His one failure in that respect is that he allowed himself to quarrel with J. E. Johnston, who does not seem to have been a very easy man to deal with; and in this case Davis, who later showed himself to be a some-what pompous and cantankerous controversialist, was to blame for not curbing his temper in the interests of the cause for which he stood.

There is no war which has yet passed into history which throws more valuable light than does the Civil War upon the grave problem of what should be the na-

ture of the relation between the statesman and the soldier in a modern democracy at war. The claim sometimes advanced that the soldier should be left in free
and complete control is ridiculous. War, such as the
Civil War, requires the employment of all the resources
of the contending States, and the tendency in great
nations since the Civil War has been to increase the
number and variety of those resources. In modern war
it is necessary not only to coördinate the employment
of military naval and air forces, but to decide also how
industrial, financial, diplomatic, and moral resources
can best be developed and used. These are tasks
which no soldier charged with the conduct of military
operations can possibly undertake. There is no better
proof of this than is to be found in von Ludendorff's
own memoirs of the consequence of his attempts to ar-
rogate to himself powers which he was from his very
position unfitted to wield. The general direction of a
war should be in the hands of one man, and in democratic countries that man must be a statesman. It is
very necessary that he should distinguish between direction and interference, and know what are the matters he should leave entirely to his soldiers and sailors.
That requires careful thought and study, and unfortunately statesmen do not often give it either until war is
upon them. Davis failed to see that he could not at
one and the same time direct the policies of the Con-

federacy and achieve in his own person effective unity of command. Lincoln, who had not had Davis's opportunities for getting to know the officers of the Army of the United States, was in the first years of the war less successful than Davis in choosing his generals, and when he found that his generals had failed him he took upon himself to give military directions which were sometimes very far from judicious. But in all Lincoln's remarkable career, nothing is more remarkable than the way in which he learned by experience, and his conduct of the latter part of the war seems to me to be a model of what the action of a statesman of a democratic country in war should be. The problems of the United States during the Great War were less complex than those of Great Britain. Towards the end of 1915 great Britain had seven theatres of war, the United States had never more than two — the Western Front and the sea — and a smaller call was made upon America's greater resources. None the less, the fact that the United States were less vexed by this question of the relations between soldiers and statesmen than were the Allied powers is, I think, attributable, firstly, to the fact that its Constitution, as confirmed by the result of the Civil War, permits the establishment of a dictatorship automatically, and, secondly, to the tradition established by Lincoln.

If Lincoln's conduct from March, 1864, to the end of the war should be a model for the statesman in the direction of war, Lee should be no less an example to the soldier. There is nothing in his generalship which is more striking than the manner in which he grasped the problems of the Confederacy and, without ever intruding into the sphere of the statesman, adapted his strategy both to the cause for which the South was fighting and to the major political conditions of the time. Though the North was in population and in wealth preponderately superior to the South, the contest was far from being so unequal as it appeared to be from a first glance at the resources of the combatants. In the first place, the South was fighting for the right to secede, the North to preserve the Union. Given that the Confederates were convinced that they were fighting for their rights and were ready to die for their cause — and of that Lee, once he was involved in the struggle, had not the smallest doubt — the Federals, to obtain their end, had to conquer the people of the South. That was an enormous undertaking. The distances were vast. Fifteen hundred miles separate the Potomac from the Rio Grande, Charleston lies a similar distance east of El Paso. Distances less serious had caused the defeat of Napoleon at the height of his power. Railways in the Southern States were few, roads were not numerous, they were at no season good, and in the winter all but impassable. The subjection of a hardy and determined population, scattered over such an area, was a military task which no power had proposed to undertake in one or even in a few campaigns. The territory which comprised the Confederate States was nearly ten times as large as that occupied by the Boer Republics, and if the frontiers of the North were contiguous with those of the South, while Great Britain lies at a distance of six thousand miles from South Africa, the Union had no army ready for a prompt invasion.

The mere movement of an army through great distances of country inhabited by a hostile population is, even if no organized resistance is opposed to its advance, an enterprise requiring careful thought and prolonged preparation. But in 1861 neither North nor South possessed an army. The organization of the small regular army of the United States had been disrupted by the departure of a large number of its officers to join the Confederacy, and much of such part of it as remained efficient was needed for the task of watching the Mexican frontier and controlling the Indians. The conditions out of which the war arose imposed on the Union an offensive policy, but attack requires a far higher degree of military training than defence, and the Southerners, with a white population accustomed to the saddle and the chase, could count on being able to withstand attack while their forces were being organized and trained, the more so because the nature of the theatre of war made attack difficult and defence, in comparison, easy.

The approaches by land from the Northern States into the Southern can be classed in four groups. The first of these, which led into Eastern Virginia from Washington and Maryland, I have already indicated. The second group passed through the rough hills of Western Virginia from the Valley of the Ohio and were hard to open, easy to close; the third group traversed Tennessee by Nashville and Chattanooga and, passing the Alleghanies to the South, led to Atlanta. Between the second and third group the Alleghanies blocked the approaches from Kentucky and Northeast Tennessee. The fourth group led down the valley of the Mississippi by Cairo and Corinth to Vicksburg. Forces operating on these four lines could not be in direct communication. The Federals moving along them would be, as it were, coming down the spokes of a wheel of which the Confederates held the hub. The South in fact, like the Central Powers in the Great War, enjoyed the advantage of having interior lines of communication and could transfer troops from one line of invasion to another far more quickly than could the North. Even the long stretch of coast, which on the map looks so exposed to attack by a power with command of the sea, was by no means all of it vulnerable. Great marshes and wild forests reduced the number of possible landing-places which required protection.

Then in Eastern Virginia, that part of the theatre of

war with which Lee was almost entirely concerned, the facilities for defence were numerous. The direct road to Richmond from Washington crossed four rivers, the Bull Run, the Rappahannock, the Mattapony, and the Pamunkey. Numerous subsidiary rivers fed these in their upper reaches, and in wet weather these became formidable obstacles. Between the rivers lay stretches of dense forest, the trails through which were almost impossible for traffic for a considerable part of the year. West of the plain of Eastern Virginia ran the Blue Ridge, an eastern range of the Appalachian system, which, with the Alleghany Mountains on its farther side, formed a trough-like valley for the Shenandoah. The course of the Shenandoah is generally northeast; so for a Northern army using it as a line of invasion it bore away from Richmond, while for a Southern army it formed an invaluable approach into Maryland, Pennsylvania, and, more important still, into the District of Columbia and toward Washington which lay on the very frontier of the Union and Confederate States. The gaps through the Blue Ridge by which practicable roads led from the Valley into Eastern Virginia were not numerous, and could readily be blocked. When these gaps were held, the Valley became a covered way leading toward the exposed heart of the Union. The topography of Eastern Virginia offered, therefore, many opportunities for skilful manœuvre to a commander defending Richmond who knew how to make military use of its features. The rivers gave him natural means for delaying an advancing enemy, the Blue Ridge provided him a screen to cover movements against that enemy's flanks. So the attackers in such country needed a considerable preponderance of force to overcome the resistance of a stout-hearted and expert opponent.

In fact the numerical preponderance of the North was for the purposes of the war far less than would appear from an examination of the census returns. The population of the twenty-three States of the Union was in 1860 in round numbers 23,000,000, and that of the eleven Confederate States 9,000,000, of whom nearly three and a half millions were negroes. But many of the Northern States were far removed by distance and by interest from the seat and causes of the conflict. Railway communication was still in its infancy and it was no easy matter in some of the more remote of the States which adhered to the Union to obtain men for the army and to transport them to the theatres of war when obtained. Further, in the States bordering upon those which formed the Confederacy there were numbers of sympathizers with the cause of the South. Maryland, Western Virginia, Kentucky, and Missouri all furnished many recruits to the Southern flag. Actually, as Colonel Thomas L. Livermore's careful calculations show,[1] the

[1] Thomas L. Livermore: *Numbers and Losses in the Civil War in America.*

number of enlistments in the Union army was 2,898,304 and in the Confederate army approximately 1,200,000. That is to say, the men who put on the Federal uniform outnumbered those in the Confederate by more than two to one. But the superiority in the field was not as great as that. For the North had until a late stage in the war a very faulty system of enlistment, and the Federal soldiers who had joined for short terms were continually claiming their discharge. Livermore, by an elaborate calculation, reduces the periods of service to a common term which he takes as three years, and arrives at the conclusion that the equivalent of 1,556,778 Union soldiers served for that period against 1,082,119 Confederates. This would make the ratio of strength three Northerners to two Confederates. But some allowance must be made for the effect of the strain of war upon the men who served the longer term, particularly as the Southern troops during the latter half of the war suffered considerably from undernourishment, and I think that a ratio of five Northerners to three Confederates would be a fairer estimate of the actual proportion between the numbers employed. This compares with a ratio of white population of about three to one, and was certainly not a greater superiority than the nature of the problem which confronted the North required.

On the other hand, the South had a task which was, from the soldier's point of view, simpler than that of the

Noīth. There could not be any question of the conquest of the Union States or of the subjection of their people. These were both militarily and politically out of court. The object of the Southerners was to convince the Northerners that it was not worth while to force them to remain in the Union. The majority of those who lived south of the Potomac thought at first that that would not be a very hard task, and there were certainly many Northerners, who, while convinced of the justice of their cause, were doubtful whether it was right to proceed to extremes on its behalf. Lee, who knew the real temper of the Northern people, was under no such delusion, but he believed the task was one which the South could and should undertake. I have never been able to find any evidence that he, or any one on either side, foresaw in the early days of the war what the effect of sea power on its course would be. He, like Davis, appreciated the danger to the coast of the South, and made preparation accordingly, but neither seems to have foreseen the effect of the blockade, which many Southerners, indeed, regarded as a double-edged tool. These persons expected that, if Europe were deprived of cotton and tobacco, it would intervene to stop the war, and that the blockade would be a means of obtaining for them the independence which they sought. But if Lee did not understand at first the importance of the economic weapon which the command of the sea had placed in the hands of the

North, the other considerations which I have here sum-
marised were duly pondered by him. Stated in the way
I have put them, in the light of after knowledge, it is easy
to see the reasons why the war was long. Lee saw them
and grasped their import, at the time when to do so was
of use to him, and to the cause for which he fought,
and it was not light-heartedly nor as a lucky guess
that he foretold a struggle that would last for years.

We find that Lee in his strategy employed three
methods, each admirably adapted to the means available and to the political situation at the time. In the
first period his policy was, as I have said, purely defensive. He was seeking time to prepare the means for
bolder courses, for no one knew better than he that defence by itself is but a sorry weapon. In the second
period he was seeking every opportunity to attack, not
merely on the battlefields of Virginia, but in the territory of his enemy. He never forgot that he had seen
from the heights of Arlington the domes of Washington.
He believed that the surest way to cause the North to
abandon the attempt to impose union by force of arms
would be to seize the seat of the Federal Government,
or at least to isolate it from the rest of the Union. So
while defending Richmond he had always an eye upon
Washington. Military critics are agreed that Napoleon's
mastery of the art of war was never more completely displayed than in his first great campaign in Italy. Lee's

campaigns of 1862 are also supreme in conception, and
have not been surpassed, as examples of strategy by any
other achievement of their kind by any other commander
in history. Both men had, when they were called to
positions of responsibility, a complete grasp of the fundamental principles of war. There are in war few com-
parisons more striking than that between the inaction of
the Southern forces after the first battle of Manassas and
Lee's energy, promptness, decision, and boldness in action after the second battle at the same place. True, as
I have shown, Davis must take his share of blame for
the loss of opportunity in 1861, but in 1862 the President
was the same, it was the soldier who was different. One
is forced to the conclusion that his absence from Davis's
side at this time was fraught with consequences. The
evidence is clear that the hastily formed levies of the
Confederacy at Manassas were almost as much disor-
ganized by victory as were the Federal troops by defeat,
and Davis had made out for himself a good answer to
the charge that he was responsible for stopping an immediate pursuit.[1] But when order had been restored and
the unreadiness of the Union was revealed, it is hard to
believe that Lee, if he had been given the chance, would
not have galvanized the leaders of the Confederacy into
action before the winter set in. The troops flushed with
victory needed no spur.

[1] Davis: *The Rise and Fall of the Confederate Government*, vol. I, chap. VII.

The third period of the war, reckoned from the point of view of a consideration of Lee's strategical methods, dates from the failure at Gettysburg. After that battle Lee saw that the growing power of the North and the increasing determination of its people made it impossible to force them to abandon the struggle by an offensive campaign in the border States, even if that campaign were successful. Henceforth the policy for the South was to endeavour to convince the North that the subjugation of the Confederacy was either a task beyond their means or one which would bring them more loss than gain. Lee's procedure was then, not as in the second period to seek to force a decision by boldness and enterprise, but to avoid decision and to cause delay. The Campaign of the Wilderness, of Spottsylvania, and the North Anna is a classical example in military history of how these objects should be sought. In method it was fifty years ahead of the times, and I believe that if the Allies in August, 1914, had applied Lee's tactical methods to the situation which then confronted them the course of the World War would have been changed.

Between the first and second periods in which Lee inspired the strategy of the South, he was employed on other duties. On July 28, 1861, a week after the first battle of Manassas he left Richmond for Western Virginia. In a letter to his wife on the eve of his departure he said, with that complete absence of self-seeking which marked his whole career: 'The battle will be repeated in greater force. I hope God will again smile upon us, and strengthen our hearts and arms. I wished to partake in the former struggle, and am mortified at my absence. But the President thought it more important that I should be here. I could not have done as well as has been done, but I could have helped and taken part in a struggle for my home and neighbourhood. So the work is done I care not by whom it is done.'[1] So while Johnston and Beauregard, the victors of Manassas, were being hailed as the heroes of the Confederacy, Lee went off to undertake a minor and unpleasant mission.

When Lee reached Western Virginia the fortunes of the Confederacy in that field were at a low ebb. McClellan had won the successes which had caused the Northern Press to dub him 'the young Napoleon,' and which had earned for him the command of the Army of the Potomac. The main Southern force under Garnett had been defeated, and its leader killed. Lee found his men despondent and suffering from sickness, the weather was vile, the roads were few and bad, and the country mountainous. The chances of making rapid and successful combinations, even with well-trained troops and trusted leaders, were therefore not great. But the troops were raw, the leaders inexperienced. Soon after his arrival Lee wrote to his wife: 'It is so

[1] Fitzhugh Lee: *General Lee*, p. 112.

difficult to get our people, unaccustomed to the necessities of war, to comprehend and promptly execute
the measures required for the occasion.' None the less,
by September 11th, Lee had all his plans ready for a
combined attack on a force of Federals commanded by
Reynolds. The several Confederate columns reached
their assigned positions and the prospect of surprising
Reynolds was excellent. The signal agreed upon for
attack was to have been the opening of fire by one of the
detached forces. The commander of that detachment,
finding the enemy's position to be stronger than he
anticipated, did not give the signal and the enterprise
failed. It is characteristic of a quality in Lee, which he
carried almost to a fault, that in his report to the Governor of Virginia there is not a word of reproach against
any one. Well-laid plans had gone agley, and his only
comment after narrating the events was: 'It is a grievous
disappointment to me, I assure you. But for the rain-
storm I have no doubt it would have succeeded. This,
Governor, is for your own eye. Please do not speak of it.
We must try again.' But he was never to have on this
campaign a like opportunity for a successful coup. He
succeeded in blocking the approaches into the Shenandoah Valley against Rosecrans, who commanded the
Federal troops in Western Virginia, until winter stopped
operations in the mountains, but that was all. The
people of Richmond, who had looked to him for some

resounding reply to McClellan's success, were bitterly disappointed; the Press was vocal in criticism. Lee returned to Richmond under a cloud. The cynic will find opportunity for comment on the value of Press criticism of commanders in the field in the fact that at one and the same time the newspapers of the North were boosting McClellan, those of the South were decrying Lee.

Probably in order to let the feeling against Lee cool, Davis sent him off to supervise the coast defences of South Carolina, Georgia, and Florida. Thus he resumed in a position of authority, and in time of war, the very tasks upon which in his youth he had been engaged as a subordinate. His work was put to a severe test as the power of the Federal fleet grew, but the best tribute to it is that Charleston so long resisted attack from sea. While he was thus engaged, the Trent incident occurred. The Confederate envoys to Europe, Messrs. Mason and Slidell, were removed from a British ship by the captain of a Federal cruiser. Feeling in England ran high, and Palmerston was disposed to bluster, but the Prince Consort intervened with prudent counsels, and Lincoln's calm judgment was not disturbed. The incident is a striking example of how wise statesmanship may dissolve in laughter passionate international quarrels. When feeling was at its height, when the North was applauding loudly the action of Captain Wilkes and public opinion in England was boiling with indignation at the insult to the British flag, the British Government decided to send out reënforcements to Canada to prepare for the eventuality of war with the United States. The staff officers required were put on board a decrepit transport and made a very slow passage. By the time they reached the American coast, the dispute was adjusted, and, as there was then no through railway from Halifax to Montreal and they were needed urgently in Canada because of threats of a Fenian invasion, they were, by the courtesy of the Government with which when they left England they had expected to be at war, permitted to land at Boston and to proceed by American trains to their destination.

While the quarrel was at its height, many in the South had allowed their hopes to persuade them that the foreign intervention, for which they looked, was really come. Lee had no belief in intervention. He wrote to Mrs. Lee on Christmas Day, 1861: 'You must not build your hopes of peace on account of the United States going to war with England. Her rulers are not entirely mad, and if they find England is in earnest and that war or a restitution of the captives must be the consequence, they will adopt the latter. We must make up our minds to fight our battles and earn our independence alone. No one will help us.' [1]

[1] Robert E. Lee: *Recollections and Letters of General Robert E. Lee.* I have adopted the text of this letter given by Lee's son as the most probable. Fitzhugh Lee (*General Lee*, p. 129) makes Lee say 'our rulers.'

As the year 1862 opened, the South began to pay the penalty for the inactivity of the previous autumn. Forts Henry and Donelson in Tennessee fell before the Federal attacks, and a great stretch of that State was lost to the South. Nashville capitulated, the attacks upon Savannah from the sea were being pressed. More serious still, McClellan had justified his appointment by displaying considerable gifts as an organizer, and had assembled on the Potomac a well-equipped army far out-numbering any force which the Confederacy could bring against him. Johnston had retired before the menace which this army presented, and had taken up a position behind the Rappahannock. Everywhere the Confederate fortunes seemed to be at a low ebb. In this crisis Davis had the good sense and courage to call Lee to his side, and on March 13th gave him the conduct of all the military operations of the South under his direction. For the short space of time which intervened between Lee's investment with these functions and his assumption of the active command of the army defending Richmond, the South enjoyed something in the nature of unity of command, and it is strange that the benefits that obviously resulted from this should not have convinced Davis of the wisdom of continuing the system. If the South possessed but one Lee, it had generals capable of giving the President sound military advice, and saving him from blunders which were committed.

Lee took up his heavy burden with a full consciousness of its weight, but with a firm trust in God's mercy and with the determination to arouse his countrymen to greater efforts. Just before he left the Atlantic Coast for Richmond he wrote to his daughter: 'I hope you are all well and as happy as you can be in these perilous times to our country. They look dark at present, and it is plain we have not suffered enough, repented enough, to deserve success. But they will brighten after a while, and I trust that a merciful God will arouse us to a sense of our danger, bless our honest efforts, and drive back our enemies to their homes. Our people have not been earnest enough, have thought too much of themselves and their ease, and, instead of turning out to a man, have been content to nurse themselves and their dimes and leave the protection of themselves and their families to others. To satisfy their consciences they have been clamorous in criticising what others have done, and endeavoured to prove that they ought to do nothing. This is not the way to accomplish our independence.' [1]

[1] R. E. Lee: *Recollections*, p. 65.

CHAPTER V

THE DEFENCE OF RICHMOND

THE day after Lee resumed his duties as the chief military advisor of Jefferson Davis he wrote to Mrs. Lee:[1] 'The enemy is pushing us back in all directions and how far he will be successful depends much upon our efforts and the mercy of Providence.' His task was, indeed, formidable. McClellan controlled well-equipped and well-organised forces assembled in the neighbourhood of Washington and on the borders of Virginia numbering not less than 180,000 men.[2] On the Confederate side Magruder, with less than 13,000 men, held the lines of Yorktown five miles in extent, which protected Richmond against a force landed at Fortress Monroe. Jackson was at Woodstock in the middle of the Shenandoah Valley with a force which did not total 5000; E. Johnson with less than 3000 was at the southern end of the Valley, where he barred the approaches from Western Virginia against superior Federal forces; the main Confederate army, some 50,000 strong, under J. E. Johnston, was behind the Rappahannock. How in these circumstances was the Confederate capital to be defended? The answer which he

[1] March 14, 1862.
[2] As I am not in this book concerned with tactical details, I have given throughout the nearest round number of the opposing forces.

POSITION MID-MARCH 1862.

found to that question is among Lee's chief titles to a place among the great commanders in history. The first step was obvious. When McClellan had disembarked at Fortress Monroe and had begun preparations for the attack on Magruder's entrenchments, the bulk of Johnston's army was brought back to the neighbourhood of Richmond, a small force being left at Fredericksburg and 8000 men under Ewell on the Upper Rappahannock. J. E. Johnston was placed by Davis in command of the troops in the Yorktown Peninsula in addition to those whom he had brought South. What was to be done next? Johnston examined the positions held by Magruder, found that the Confederate troops were suffering much from sickness, and recommended that no more men should be sent into the Peninsula, but that the policy should be to concentrate immediately around Richmond as large a Confederate force as could be collected, for the purpose of offering McClellan a battle which he hoped would decide the campaign.

If Richmond could be saved by defeating McClellan, there was much to be said for this plan. By hanging on in the Peninsula the Confederates would lose many men owing to the unhealthy climate, and they could afford such losses far less than could the Federals. Then the process of retreating up the Peninsula would be demoralising. A retreat is exhausting, wasteful to the most experienced troops, and no general, who knows his

business, lightly places his army where it must fall back.
In a newly formed army, in which the bonds of discipline are not firmly tied, a retreat is always exceptionally wasteful. But Lee saw that the greatest danger to
Richmond was not McClellan's army advancing up the
Yorktown Peninsula, formidable as that army was,[1]
but in the possibility that other Federal armies should
move against Richmond by the land routes through
Eastern Virginia, and that these, acting in coöperation
with McClellan, should approach the Confederate capital from the north and west while Johnston was busy
fending off the Army of the Potomac, as McClellan's
command was named. When McClellan embarked for
Fortress Monroe, President Lincoln relieved him of the
command of all the Federal forces other than the Army
of the Potomac, and took upon himself, with the aid of
his Secretary of War, Mr. Stanton, the general direction
of the troops around Washington and on the borders of
Eastern Virginia.

In the middle of April, 1862, the situation in Eastern
Virginia was, from the point of view of the strategist,
very similar to that which I have already described as
governing the major problem of the whole theatre of
war. Richmond was the hub of the wheel of the Virginian theatre of war and many Federal forces were prepar-

On April 30, 1862, McClellan's total strength in the Peninsula was
112,400 men.

ing to move towards it along the spokes. After the Army of the Potomac had left the waters of the river which was its godfather, Lincoln appointed General McDowell to the command of an army which had the double duty of guarding the approaches to Washington east of the Blue Ridge and of coming down upon Richmond from the northeast. McDowell's army soon numbered 30,000 men and was preparing to advance by the most direct land route to Richmond, which crossed by the Rappahannock at Fredericksburg. By the middle of April, McDowell's leading troops had reached Falmouth opposite Fredericksburg, at which place they were opposed by quite a small Confederate detachment. General Banks controlled the northern end of the Shenandoah Valley with close on 20,000 men, and General Frémont, who commanded in Western Virginia with 15,000, had already set his advanced guard under General Milroy in motion for the upper end of the Shenandoah Valley. The one hope of saving Richmond from the danger of simultaneous converging attacks from the north, east, and west lay in misleading and confusing the Federal generals; that is to say, in manœuvre first and in battle second.

The way to keep McDowell from Richmond was by playing upon the fears of the Federal Government for the safety of Washington; the way to arouse anxiety in Washington was to frighten Banks, who, from his

position in the lower Shenandoah Valley, guarded the
fords which led across the Potomac into Maryland. For
manœuvre time was necessary, and Lee therefore desired
that McClellan's movement on Richmond should be delayed by every possible expedient. There was a factor
in the problem which made it probable that McClellan
could be delayed, provided that the Confederates
occupied the Yorktown lines in strength. If he, as he
seems to have hoped, could have advanced up the
Peninsula with Federal ships of war upon both flanks in
the York and James Rivers, and therefore with the
power both to draw his supplies from and to operate on
either bank of these rivers, it is possible that he could
have manœuvred the Confederate army away from
Richmond, even if he was not able to defeat it decisively.
But when he arrived at Fortress Monroe he found the
James River commanded by a new type of armoured
vessel, the Merrimac, against which the Federal cruisers
were powerless, and as long as the Merrimac remained
afloat the James was closed to McClellan. Lee knew Mc-
Clellan well, and anticipated rightly that he would be
slow and cautious if the only prospect open to him was
to deliver frontal attacks upon positions prepared for
defence. Therefore it was of great importance that he
should be denied the use of the rivers as long as possible.
Now the existence of the Merrimac depended upon the
Confederates holding Norfolk, the one naval base from

which she could operate, and the safety of Norfolk in turn depended on the safety of the Yorktown lines. Lee wanted time—time for manœuvre against McDowell — time to strengthen the lines around Richmond — time to improve the forts closing the rivers, and the best way to gain time would be to delay McClellan before Yorktown. Further, after his recent experience on the Atlantic Coast and his experiences of the activities of the Federal fleet, he was loath to withdraw troops from Savannah and Charleston, as Johnston desired, in order to strengthen the Confederate force around Richmond. Therefore he urged that Johnston should be sent into the Peninsula to reënforce Magruder.

Davis held a conference of his generals to decide between the conflicting plans of Johnston and Lee and supported Lee's view. So Johnston with the bulk of his army went into the Peninsula. Johnston has left us an account of this conference,[1] and it is true that in his account of it Lee made no mention of the views which I have here ascribed to him. At the meeting Lee confined himself to stating his objections to denuding the Atlantic Coast. This was natural and in accordance with his methods. If the Federal generals were to be deceived, secrecy was essential, and the last place to divulge a plan for outwitting opponents would be, in his mind, a mixed conference of generals and statesmen.

[1] J. E. Johnston: *Narrative of Military Operations*, pp. 113–16.

But a reference to the Official Records of the war proves, I think conclusively, that such a plan was in Lee's mind at the time when the debate took place, whether Johnston should go into the Peninsula or not. For just after the conclusion of this conference, Lee wrote, on April 21st, to Jackson: 'I have no doubt that an attempt will be made to occupy Fredericksburg and use it as a base of operations against Richmond. Our present force there is very small [1] and cannot be reënforced except by weakening other corps. If you can use General Ewell's division in an attack on Banks and to drive him back, it will prove a great relief to the pressure on Fredericksburg.'[2] Here, then, is the genesis of Stonewall Jackson's famous Valley Campaign, and here the first move in Lee's consummate plan for the defence of Richmond. It has all the fascination to the amateur of chess of a game played by a master. Banks, the bishop, was to be forced back in order that the king, at Washington, might be checked and retain the castle, McDowell, to cover him; the bishop and castle were to be kept busy in order that the queen, McClellan, might be removed from the board. The two players for the Confederacy, Lee and Jackson, knew that they were not using boxwood pieces, but were manœuvring men of flesh and blood, with human limitations and weaknesses,

---

[1] Twenty-five hundred men under General Field.
[2] O.R., vol. xii, part iii, p. 859.

that their board was no polished work from the cabinet-maker's hand, but a rough and broken country full of obstacles, the effect of every one of which had to be studied and calculated.

On the other side, however, the attempt was made by Lincoln and Stanton to move troops as if they were pieces on a chessboard. There Lincoln stepped over the limits which a statesman should impose upon himself in conducting the policy of a war. There are few studies more instructive to those who would learn the principles which should guide the minds of the director at a distance and the executant on the spot than are furnished by a comparison between the correspondence of Lee and Jackson at this period, with that which took place between Stanton and his perplexed generals. In the one hand, we find timely suggestion of the best course to be adopted in the general interest, every suggestion being for action which is possible, given the conditions of time and space, yet made always without any attempt to hamper the initiative of the executant or to prescribe to him details of execution of the suitability of which only the man on the spot could be the judge. On the other side we find the statesmen planning strategical combinations and issuing orders to their generals without any exact knowledge of the condition of the troops or of the state of their supplies; making calculations as if miles of rough tracks through the mountains were to be

covered as easily as similar distances on a level turn-
pike.

Toward the end of April the Confederate numbers
were increasing, and it is a remarkable indication of
Lee's courage and vision that the increases were mainly
in those forces not engaged in the immediate defence
of Richmond. Jackson then had more than 6000 men,
E. Johnson 3500, the detachment at Fredericksburg,
now commanded by Anderson, had grown to 11,000.
Still McClellan's activities before the Yorktown lines
were too menacing to allow Lee to weaken Johnston.
So on April 30th, in reply to Jackson's request for
5000 men from Richmond, he wrote, amplifying the
suggestions he had made a week earlier: 'From the reports that reach me that are entitled to credit, the
force of the enemy opposite Fredericksburg [1] is repre-
sented as too large to admit of any diminution whatever of our army in that vicinity at present, as it might
not only invite an attack on Richmond, but jeopard the
safety of the army in the Peninsula. I regret therefore
that your request to have 5000 men sent from that
army to reënforce you cannot be complied with. Cannot you draw enough from the command of General
Edward Johnson to warrant you in attacking Banks?
The last return received from that army [Johnson's]
shows a present force of upwards of 3500, which it is

[1] McDowell's command.

hoped has been since increased by recruits and returned furloughs. As he does not appear to be pressed, it is suggested that a portion of his force might be removed temporarily from its present position and made available for the movement in question. A decisive and successful blow at Banks's column would be fraught with the happiest results, and I deeply regret my inability to send you the reënforcements you ask. If, however, you think the combined forces of Generals Ewell and Johnson, with your own, inadequate for the move, General Ewell might, with the assistance of General Anderson's army, near Fredericksburg, strike at McDowell's army between that city and Aquia with much promise of success, provided you feel sufficiently strong to hold Banks in check.' [1] Here then is a definite outline of the Valley Campaign. The prime object is to keep McDowell from Richmond. The defeat of Banks is suggested as the best means to that end, and the junction of Jackson with E. Johnson is indicated as the best preliminary to the defeat of Banks. Alternatively, if local conditions or the strength and movements of the enemy make the plan inapplicable, a movement by Anderson and Ewell against McDowell's communications with Aquia Creek is proposed. All the details of action are left to Jackson.

[1] R. E. Lee : *Recollections*, p. 72. A somewhat different version of this letter is given in O.R., vol. xii, part iii, p. 875. I am inclined to think that the one given by Lee's son is the later and more correct draft.

Now let us see what happened. On May 3d, Johnston, finding McClellan's preparations for attack on the
Yorktown lines to have become dangerous, began to fall
back upon Richmond, checking McClellan's not very
vigorous pursuit at Williamsburg on May 5th. On
May 10th, the Federal forces gained possession of Norfolk, and the next morning the homeless Merrimac was
blown up. As Johnston had foreseen, the stay of his
force in the Yorktown lines had sent many of his men
into hospital, and the retreat had lost him many more as
stragglers, but the result proved to be worth many times
the price paid. Lee had gained the time he needed,
and before Johnston was established in the lines covering Richmond, Jackson had begun to move. On May
5th, E. Johnson and Jackson had united their forces and
three days later had defeated Milroy at McDowell.[1]
The effect of this was to stop the movement into the Valley
of Frémont's force in Western Virginia, of which Milroy
led the advanced guard, a movement which endangered
Jackson's communications with Richmond. With Frémont at a standstill, Jackson was free to turn against
Banks, and he was back in the Valley on May 12th.
Lee then proposed to him the next step in the manœuvre.
On May 16th he wrote: 'The troops sent to Gordonsville
were ordered to report to General Ewell and can be

[1] A hamlet twenty-eight miles northeast of Staunton. Not to be con-
fused with the general of the same name.

POSITION MID-MAY 1862.

Martinsburg
Harper's Ferry
Romney
FREMONT
BANKS
Winchester
BALTIMORE
Moorefield
Strasburg
Front Royal B.
Rectortown
MILROY
SHIELDS
WASHINGTON
Franklin
Warrenton
Manassas Jn.
E.JOHNSON
New
Market
EWELL
Catlett's Sta.
JACKSON
Luraybg.
Harrisonburg
Swift Run Gap
Culpeper
McDowell
Mount Solon
Fredericksburg
McDowell
Staunton
Gordons-
ville
ANDERSON
Chickahominy
West
Point
Richmond
J. E. JOHNSTON
McCLELLAN
River
CHESAPEAKE BAY
Fort Monroe

Federals
Confederates

employed in making the movement on Banks. But you will not, in any demonstration you may make in that direction, lose sight of the fact that it may become necessary for you to come to the support of General Johnston, and hold yourself in readiness to do so if required. . . . Whatever movement you make against Banks, do it speedily, and if successful drive him back toward the Potomac, and create the impression as far as possible that you design threatening that line.' [1] The time had come to check the king; the movement toward the Potomac was designed to create alarm in Washington.

This letter of Lee's of May 16th was, in the circumstances in which it was written, a remarkable document. At that date the fortunes of the Confederacy had sunk even lower than they had been in the middle of March. McClellan's army was established within sight of the spires of Richmond. Daily it was unmasking new batteries against the lines covering the capital of Virginia. New Orleans had fallen before Farragut, Grant was in possession of a great part of Tennessee. Even Davis, whose stoutness of heart was unquestioned by his bitterest detractors, began to despair. The archives of the Confederacy were packed, and the President made arrangements for the removal of his family. J. E. Johnston, who may be taken as the type

[1] O.R., vol. XII, part III, p. 892.

of the good ordinary general, saw no alternative to
assembling the largest possible number of Confederate
troops around Richmond, and there hazarding all upon
the issue of a battle with McClellan. On May 10th he
had written to Lee: 'If the President will direct the
concentration of all the troops of North Carolina and
Eastern Virginia, we may be able to hold Middle Virginia at least. If we permit ourselves to be driven beyond Richmond, we lose the means of maintaining this
army. A concentration of all our available forces may
enable us to fight successfully. Let us try.'

Johnston was so completely convinced that this was
the only possible course that he unwittingly interfered
with Lee's plans. The limits of Johnston's command do
not seem to have been precisely defined, and he assumed
that he controlled certain detachments which he had
left behind when his army moved to Richmond and re-
enforcements which were on the way to him. Lee not
only proposed to unite Ewell and Jackson for the attack
upon Banks, but to strengthen Jackson by two brigades which were coming up from North Carolina.
Johnston sent orders to Ewell to move eastwards nearer
to Richmond and ordered the reënforcements to himself. Jackson at once telegraphed to Lee for instructions, the President supported Lee and the confusion
was put right. Johnston had, indeed, first approved of
the movement against Banks, but in the middle of

May the situation around Richmond appeared to him to be too desperate to allow of so hazardous an enterprise. He was a fine soldier, his men were devoted to him; it was on his representation that Davis agreed to leave Jackson in the Valley for the purpose of keeping the Federal forces in and west of it away from Richmond, at the time when the news of McClellan's move to the Peninsula first became known; as a commander on the battlefield he was possibly Lee's equal, but he lacked that wider vision, that power to look calmly beyond the dangers and perils of his immediate front to the situation in the whole theatre of war, that power, in short, which takes Lee out of the ranks of the good ordinary and places him in the select band of the supreme generals. The attitude and conduct of the two men in those critical days of May, 1862, seem to me to place beyond question Lee's superiority as a commander over Johnston. I am therefore surprised to find that Ropes, for whom, as an historian, I have the very greatest respect, after admitting that Lee possessed a combination of qualities, physical, mental, and moral, which marked him out among the leaders in the Civil War, says of him: 'In intellect it may be doubted whether he was superior to the able soldier whom he succeeded; indeed, Joseph E. Johnston possessed as good a military mind as any leader on either side.'[1]

[1] Ropes: *The Story of the Civil War. The Campaigns of 1862*, p. 158.

When McClellan was hammering at the gates of Richmond, Lee saw that the way to save the town was to make McDowell defend Washington; Johnston looked only to the prospect of a battle with McClellan. There we have a measure of the intellect of the two men.

On May 21st, Davis was trembling for the safety of Richmond; on the 24th, Jackson's march down the Valley had caused Lincoln to suspend McDowell's movement upon Richmond, and to employ the greater part of his force to take part in a combined movement to capture Jackson and Ewell. Thus the immediate purpose of Lee's manœuvre was achieved. On the 25th, Jackson had defeated Banks at Winchester, and occupied the town, and that evening the authorities in Washington were anticipating an attack upon the Federal capital. Stanton telegraphed to the Governors of the Federal States: 'Send forward all the troops you can, immediately. Banks completely routed. Intelligence from various quarters leaves no doubt that the enemy, in great force, are advancing on Washington. You will please organize and forward immediately all volunteer and militia force in your State.' It would be hard to find in the history of war so swift, so dramatic a change of fortune.

From Winchester Jackson sent to Lee for instructions, and answer came back at once directing him to press the enemy, to threaten an invasion of Maryland, and an attack upon Washington. Bold orders, but Lee knew both McClellan and the authorities at Washington. He was convinced that the Federal commander would not attempt an assault upon the Richmond lines without McDowell, and that Washington would not let McDowell move south as long as there was any prospect of Confederate troops crossing the Potomac. So Jackson made a feint at Harper's Ferry, a feint which was not particularly effective, for Lincoln and Stanton had set in motion all the troops who could be used against the daring raider and the net was closing round him. Shields with a portion of McDowell's army was closing on him from the east, while from the west Frémont was moving through the passes of the North Mountain to cut off his retreat. Jackson had to be moving speedily to escape the toils, but his task was for the time ended. McDowell's army was broken up, and there were no reënforcements for McClellan. So on May 31st, the long-expected battle was fought outside Richmond, but under conditions very different from those which a short time previously had seemed probable. McClellan, always expecting McDowell to come south from Fredericksburg, had thrown his right across the Chickahominy, so that he might join hands with him as he approached Richmond. Now McDowell was not coming, and McClellan found that a manœuvre which he had undertaken for good and sufficient reasons had put him in a difficult position. His army was divided by a broad marshy valley, liable to sudden floods. On May 31st, Johnston took advantage of this situation to attack McClellan in the battle of Seven Pines. The battle was well planned, but Johnston's direction of it was faulty, and though the Confederates gained some success, they were very far from causing McClellan to contemplate the abandonment of the attack on Richmond. Johnston's attack, however, kept the Federal army quiet for a month. In the battle he was wounded, and the next day Davis conferred the command of the Confederate Armies in Eastern Virginia and North Carolina upon Lee.

When he, for the first time, assumed the active command of a large army, Lee was far from possessing the general confidence which he soon won. The stigma of his failure in Western Virginia still clung to his name, and none save a few of the leading statesmen and soldiers of the Confederacy knew the part he had played in rolling away the heavy clouds which had gathered over Richmond in the beginning of May. The Press, unaware of his insistence that Johnston should reënforce Magruder in the Yorktown lines, gibed at him as the retreating strategist,[1] and Davis was accused of favouritism in placing him in high command. Unperturbed,

---

[1] The *Richmond Examiner* announced that 'Evacuating Lee, who has never yet risked a single battle with the invader, is commanding-general.'

Lee went on to complete the plan which had so far been brilliantly successful. A week after taking over his new command, he disclosed to Jackson the next manœuvre. On June 8th he wrote: 'Should there be nothing requiring your attention in the Valley, so as to prevent your leaving it in a few days, and you can make arrangements to deceive the enemy and impress him with the idea of your presence, please let me know, that you may unite at the decisive moment with the army around Richmond. Make your arrangements accordingly, but should an opportunity occur of striking the enemy a successful blow, do not let it escape you.' [1] On that very day Jackson was fighting the battle of Cross Keys. Retreating down the Valley to escape the Federal forces which were closing in on him, he had reached the neighbourhood of Port Republic where he found Frémont's army coming against him from the west, and Shields advancing from the east. Jackson, on June 8th, skilfully using his central position, had held Shields off on the Shenandoah and repulsed Frémont, and the next day turning against Shields had forced him to retreat.

On learning of these victories Lee wrote to Jackson on June 11th: 'Your recent successes have been the cause of the liveliest joy in this army, as well as in the country. The admiration excited by your skill and boldness has been constantly mingled with solicitude for your situ-

[1] O.R., vol. XII, part III, p. 908.

ation. The practicability of reënforcing you has been the subject of earnest consideration. It has been determined to do so at the expense of weakening this army. Brigadier-General Lawton, with six regiments from Georgia, is on the way to you, and Brigadier-General Whiting, with eight veteran regiments, leaves here to-day. The object is to enable you to crush the forces opposed to you. Leave your enfeebled troops to watch the country and guard the passes covered by your cavalry and artillery, and with your main body, including Ewell's division and Lawton's and Whiting's commands, move rapidly to Ashland by rail or otherwise, as you may find most advantageous, and sweep down between the Chickahominy and Pamunkey, cutting up the enemy's communications, etc., while this army attacks General McClellan in front. He will thus, I think, be forced to come out of his entrenchments, where he is strongly posted on the Chickahominy, and apparently preparing to move by gradual approaches on Richmond. Keep me advised of your movements, and, if practicable, precede your troops, that we may confer and arrange for simultaneous attack.' [1]

This was the complete project for driving McClellan from the Peninsula. For its full success not only must Jackson join the army defending Richmond, but McDowell must still be kept at a distance, since Jackson

[1] O.R., vol. XII, part III, p. 910.

would not be free to play his part if McDowell arrived on his heels. So reënforcements were sent off to the Valley and to give the impression that something serious was intended in that quarter Lee wrote formally to the Secretary of War requesting that any mention of this movement should be kept out of the newspapers. At the same time he took particular pains to insure that the Federals should know all about it. The troops were entrained openly and told where they were going. Federal prisoners were allowed to see their departure, and within a few days both McClellan and Lincoln were aware that considerable forces had joined Jackson.

In the meantime McClellan's army had also been strengthened. In the first half of June a division 9500 strong had joined him, and some 11,000 men had come to him from Baltimore and Fortress Monroe. Lee, therefore, on June 17th, ordered Jackson to suspend operations in the Valley and to come to Richmond, so that he might strike before McClellan's army was further increased. Jackson had anticipated such an order and not only concealed his departure with consummate skill, but left behind him the impression that he was preparing for a new offensive campaign in the Valley. So that at the very time that he was moving toward Richmond, Lincoln was telegraphing to McClellan that he could send him no more troops because Jackson was being heavily reënforced from Richmond.

Not until June 25th, when Jackson had joined Lee and
the Confederate orders for battle had been issued, did
Stanton, in Washington, come to the conclusion that
Jackson's real movement was toward Richmond. Thus,
when Jackson was bringing 18,500 men to the battlefield, Frémont, Banks, and McDowell remained in
other parts of Virginia or on its borders with no less
than 70,000 men guarding the approaches to Washington, and watched only by insignificant detachments.

Jackson's arrival brought Lee's army to a strength
of close on 87,000 men; McClellan's numbered 109,000,
but this superiority in numbers was more than counter-
balanced by the difficult situation in which it stood
astride the Chickahominy, a situation due, as I have
explained, to McClellan's justifiable expectation of the
arrival of McDowell, who never came. At the beginning of May, the Federal forces in the Peninsula had
outnumbered the Confederates by two to one, while elsewhere in Virginia their numerical superiority had been
overwhelming. Now Lee was about to join battle in
the Peninsula with a force nearly equal to that of his
opponent, who in fact believed himself to be hopelessly
outnumbered, and in circumstances which promised
great success. In other parts of Virginia, Federal
troops nearly equal in numbers to Lee's whole army
remained inactive while the fate of Richmond was
being decided. Truly Scott was right when he said that

Lee was worth 20,000 men; justly does Henderson say that 'only Napoleon's campaign of 1814 affords a parallel to this extraordinary spectacle.' [1]

I have told the story of these manœuvres deliberately from Lee's point of view, because, in England at any rate, Henderson's brilliant 'Life of Stonewall Jackson' has caused Lee's part in them to be somewhat obscured. That is clearly not the impression that Henderson intended to produce; he, like Jackson himself, who declared, 'Lee is the only man I know whom I would follow blindfold,' recognised the master mind, but he brought Jackson so skilfully into the limelight, and has presented him to us in so attractive a guise, that to many of his readers Jackson has become preëminently *the* hero of the Civil War. It is unnecessary for me to add my quota of praise of Jackson's conduct of the Valley Campaign. Without his tactical skill, fierce energy, and instant comprehension of what was in Lee's mind, Richmond could not have been saved in 1862. But save only in the retreat down the Valley, and in the battles of Cross Keys and Port Republic, the inspiration had in every case come from Lee. For that phase of the campaign the credit must be Jackson's alone. For the initiation of the enterprises which had kept McDowell from Richmond, and brought Jackson to fight McClellan, Lee was responsible, and his daring

[1] Henderson: *Stonewall Jackson*, vol. 1, p. 508.

yet measured planning in adversity displays a degree of enterprise and of strategical ability which has never been surpassed.

Lee's plan for the battle with McClellan was, like Johnston's, intended to take advantage of the Federal position astride the Chickahominy, but in a different way. He proposed to outflank McClellan's right, and to cut his communications with the York River, which, running eastwards to West Point, were only partially covered by the Federal troops north of the Chickahominy. So, before he completed his plan, and before he decided how he would use Jackson, he wanted exact information as to the direction of these communications and the way in which they were guarded. To get this information he sent off J. E. B. Stuart on June 12th with 1200 cavalry and a section of artillery to explore the Federal right. Stuart rode off northwards as if he were going to join Jackson; then, swerving eastwards down the Pamunkey Valley, he drove back parties of Federal cavalry, and by the 13th had gathered all the information Lee needed. He confirmed the report that the York River railway was McClellan's main line of communication, and that it was but lightly guarded. Fearing that, if he returned the way he had come, he would be intercepted, he boldly crossed the railway, made for the Lower Chickahominy, got over that river, and, riding clean round the Federal

army, came back into the Confederate lines from the
south. This enterprise amazed both armies, and set a
fashion which had pernicious results. Lee had used his
cavalry to get him information; the circuit of the Federal
rear had been merely Stuart's bold and original way of
bringing the information home. But the dramatic element in Stuart's ride so struck men's imagination that
the object of the expedition was forgotten, and the raid
behind the enemy's rear came to be regarded as something of value in itself. The damage which a body of
cavalry can do behind an army can be quickly made
good, and raids are of little advantage save when they
furnish information which can be quickly used, or can
create an effect which can be promptly exploited by
other troops. Where they take cavalry away from a
battlefield, they are definitely harmful, as Lee was soon
to find.

With the information he wanted to hand, Lee, as we
have seen, ordered Jackson to a position from which he
could sweep round McClellan's right flank. The greater
part of the Confederate army around Richmond was to
join Jackson in an attack on the Federal right. This involved some risk. Magruder was to hold the Richmond
lines with but 28,000 men against the 75,000 of McClellan's army south of the Chickahominy. But Lee was
certain that the Federal commander would not ven-
ture an attack. He soothed Davis's anxieties with the

assurance that should this happen 'I will be on Mc-Clellan's tail.' So on his chosen battlefield he had close on 59,000 men against the 34,000 under Porter, who were north of the Chickahominy. With a not inconsiderable inferiority of numbers around Richmond, and with a very marked inferiority in the Virginian theatre of war, he was about to attack with a superiority of nearly two to one. Strategy could do no more. It remained to gain the fruits of brilliant manœuvre in battle.

The fruits were not fully garnered, and for that Lee must bear a share of responsibility. As in West Virginia, on a small scale, so now on a large scale, Lee's plan entailed one of the most intricate operations in war, the exact combination of a number of columns in difficult country. For that his orders were too vague; too many of the movements prescribed were made to depend on the actions of other forces which might, and indeed did, turn out different to anticipation; his staff was not yet equal to so severe a test; he did not make sufficient allowance for the inexperience of his troops in the manœuvres of battle, and his right hand, Jackson, failed him.[1] On the 26th, in the battle of Mechanicsville, Jackson was late, with the result that only some 17,000 men of Lee's army were engaged, and A. P. Hill, attacking without the support he expected to find on his left, was repulsed. On the 27th, Jackson came up, and in the

[1] The orders referred to will be found in the Appendix to this chapter.

THE SEVEN DAYS

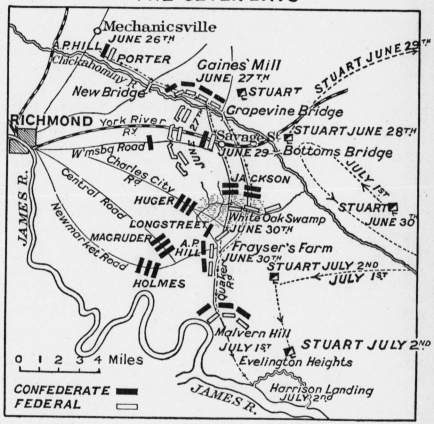

Mechanicsville
JUNE 26TH
A.P.HILL
PORTER
Chickahominy R.
New Bridge
RICHMOND   York River Ry.
W'msbg Road
Charles City Rd.
Central Road
Newmarket Road
HUGER
LONGSTREET
MAGRUDER
A.P. HILL
HOLMES
JAMES R.
Gaines' Mill
JUNE 27TH
STUART
STUART JUNE 29TH
Grapevine Bridge
STUART JUNE 28TH
Savage St.
JUNE 29
Bottoms Bridge
JACKSON
JULY 1ST
STUART
JUNE 30
White Oak Swamp
JUNE 30TH
Frayser's Farm
JUNE 30TH
Quaker Rd.
STUART JULY 2ND
JULY 1ST
Malvern Hill
JULY 1ST
Evelington Heights
STUART JULY 2ND
Harrison Landing
JULY 2nd
JAMES R.

0 1 2 3 4 Miles

CONFEDERATE
FEDERAL

fierce battle of Gaines's Mill, Porter, who was in command of McClellan's right and made a fine defence
against superior numbers, was defeated, but again opportunities were lost by defective combination. That
night the Confederates were in undisputed possession
of the north bank of the Chickahominy.

Lee was now in doubt as to what McClellan would do.
The Federals might retreat down the York River and
attempt to cross the Lower Chickahominy in order to
regain their base at Fortress Monroe, or they might, as
actually happened, establish a new base on the James
and move thither. This was the occasion for a dash by
Stuart, well placed for such a task on Jackson's flank,
behind the Federal lines in search of information.
Instead, on the 28th, Lee sent his cavalry off, supported
by Ewell's division, on a wholly useless expedition
against the York River railway from which Jackson had
already cut the Federal army. Having deprived himself
of his eyes, Lee lost valuable time, and with it the chance
of dealing McClellan a deadly blow. As soon as he discovered what McClellan was at, he ordered Magruder to
leave his lines and join with the remainder of the army
in a general advance on the 29th. But McClellan had by
this time got his men together and was conducting his
retreat with prudence and skill. To get to the James he
had to carry out a difficult flank march, and there remained the chance that he might be overwhelmed before

the movement was completed. Lee's movement in pursuit was well planned, but he was never able to regain the time lost on the 28th. On the 30th, McClellan had to stand in defence to give his baggage train time to get away. There resulted the battle of Frayzer's Farm, for which Lee designed a frontal attack by his main body combined with a movement by Jackson and D. H. Hill against the Federal flank and rear. But again the combination failed, again Jackson was late, while the frontal attacks were disjointed. The Federals were driven back, but such success as was won was far from being decisive, and was only obtained at a heavy loss.

On July 1st, McClellan had withdrawn to a stronger position on Malvern Hill, and there Lee promptly attacked him. The wisdom of that attack, as it was made, has been often and justly questioned. The situation of the Confederate troops after Frayzer's Farm made combination, even with the best staff work and the most experienced leaders, all but impossible. The justification for Lee's action is that he was engaged in a pursuit and he assumed that he had before him a demoralised enemy; but the Federal troops were as ready as ever to fight stoutly, and the attack was heavily repulsed. After the battle, McClellan withdrew without molestation into lines covering his new base on the James at Harrison's Landing, and so his great expedition against Richmond came to an inglorious end.

In this brief summary of the heavy fighting of the Seven Days I have been critical both of Lee and Jackson. Jackson showed a lack of enterprise so contrary to his character that it has been ascribed to physical exhaustion. This is probably one reason. He had followed the great strain of the Valley Campaign by riding the last fifty miles of his journey to meet Lee at Richmond on horseback in order that his arrival might be unobserved. That is not the best prelude to a long battle. But I think that another and perhaps a truer reason is that he was for the first time commanding in battle a considerable force, in intricate country and in circumstances of great responsibility. In the Valley he could set his little army in motion almost with a nod of his head, but to bring 20,000 men into battle in difficult country required thought and preparation of a different order. My impression is that Jackson underrated the difficulties of his task, and for that cause failed to do what was expected of him.

Lee was, too, for the first time commanding a large army in battle, and he, too, appears to have failed to appreciate the difficulties of obtaining combination in battle with an inexperienced staff and with leaders asked for the first time to work together in attack. The result was that the Confederate losses were far higher than they need have been. Lee had proved himself to be a brilliant strategist; he had yet to win his spurs as a tactician. He was himself far from satisfied with the result of the Seven Days, and as we shall see was quick to learn from the mistakes then made. On July 9th he wrote to his wife: 'I have returned to my old quarters and am filled with gratitude to our Heavenly Father for all the mercies he has extended to us. Our success has not been as great or complete as we could have desired, but God knows what is best for us.' [1] But if opportunities had been missed and McClellan's army was still intact, Richmond had been saved. May had opened in gloom for the Confederacy; with the beginning of July the sun of victory rose bright and cheering. Hopes in the South soared high, and those hopes were fixed on two men, Lee and Jackson.

APPENDIX

LEE'S BATTLE ORDERS FOR THE "SEVEN DAYS"

General Orders No. 75.

HEADQUARTERS
ARMY OF NORTHERN VIRGINIA
June 24, 1862

1. General Jackson's command will proceed to-morrow from Ashland toward the Slash Church and encamp at some convenient point west of the Central Railroad. Branch's brigade, of A. P. Hill's division, will also to-morrow evening take a position on the Chickahominy near Half-Sink. At three o'clock Thursday morning, 26th inst., General Jackson will advance on the road leading to Pole Green Church, communicating his march to General Branch, who will immediately cross the Chickahominy and take the road leading

[1] Fitzhugh Lee: *General Lee*, p. 171.

to Mechanicsville. As soon as the movements of these columns are discovered, General A. P. Hill, with the rest of his division, will cross the Chickahominy near Meadow Bridge and move direct upon Mechanicsville. To aid his advance the heavy batteries on the Chickahominy will at the proper time open upon the batteries at Mechanicsville. The enemy being driven from Mechanicsville and the passage across the bridge opened, General Longstreet, with his division and that of General D. H. Hill, will cross the Chickahominy at or near that point, General D. H. Hill moving to the support of Jackson, and General Longstreet supporting General A. P. Hill. The four divisions — keeping in communication with each other and moving *en échelon* on separate roads, if practicable, the left division in advance, with skirmishers and sharpshooters extending their front — will sweep down the Chickahominy and endeavor to drive the enemy from his position above New Bridge, General Jackson bearing well to his left, turning Beaver Dam Creek and taking the direction toward Cold Harbor. They will then press forward toward the York River Railroad, closing upon the enemy's rear and forcing him down the Chickahominy. Any advance of the enemy toward Richmond will be prevented by vigorously following his rear and crippling and arresting his progress.

2. The divisions under Generals Huger and Magruder will hold their positions in front of the enemy against attack, and make such demonstrations on Thursday as to discover his operations. Should opportunity offer, the feint will be converted into a real attack, and should an abandonment of his intrenchments by the enemy be discovered, he will be closely pursued.

3. The Third Virginia Cavalry will observe the Charles City road. The Fifth Virginia, the First North Carolina, and the Hampton Legion (cavalry) will observe the Darbytown, Varina, and Osborne roads. Should a movement of the enemy down the Chickahominy be discovered, they will close upon his flank and endeavor to arrest his march.

4. General Stuart with the First, Fourth, and Ninth

Virginia Cavalry, the cavalry of Cobb's Legion and the Jeff Davis Legion, will cross the Chickahominy to-morrow and take position to the left of General Jackson's line of march. The main body will be held in reserve, with scouts well extended to the front and left. General Stuart will keep General Jackson informed of the movements of the enemy on his left and will coöperate with him in his advance. The Tenth Virginia Cavalry, Colonel Davis, will remain on the Nine-Mile road.

5. General Ransom's brigade, of General Holmes's command, will be placed in reserve on the Williamsburg road by General Huger, to whom he will report for orders.

6. Commanders of divisions will cause their commands to be provided with three days' cooked rations. The necessary ambulances and ordnance trains will be ready to accompany the divisions and receive orders from their respective commanders. Officers in charge of all trains will invariably remain with them. Batteries and wagons will keep on the right of the road. The Chief Engineer, Major Stevens, will assign engineer officers to each division, whose duty it will be to make provision for overcoming all difficulties to the progress of the troops. The staff departments will give the necessary instructions to facilitate the movements herein directed.

By command of General Lee.

(Signed)

R. H. CHILTON
Assistant Adjutant General

CHAPTER VI
THE FIRST OFFENSIVE

THERE has been a disposition among many of those who have told the stirring story of the Civil War to suggest that Lee was helped to some of his more striking achievements more by good luck than by good judgment; that he was almost foolhardy in accepting risks and was more than once saved from merited disaster by timely turns of Fortune's wheel and by the blunders of his opponents. This is especially the case of that part of the war to which I now come — the latter half of the year 1862. I hope to show that the risks run were taken deliberately and after careful calculation, and that Lee, so far from being the darling of the Fates, had to meet his full share of those accidents and mischances which are inevitable in war, and to prove himself to be the master not the servant of Fortune.

As I have said, Lincoln and Stanton made, during the period which preceded the battles of the Seven Days, some grievous mistakes, but, as I have also said, no statesman has shown himself to be quicker than Lincoln in learning from experience. He saw that he had been wrong in attempting to direct military movements from the White House, and decided to place the troops required to cover Washington under the command of one man, and to have at his side a trained soldier responsible for the general direction of all the military operations of the Union forces. The measure was prudent, but the choice of the men to give it effect was unfortunate. For the command of the scattered forces in Northern Virginia he selected Pope, and for his military adviser at Washington, Halleck, men who had made reputations in the Western theatre of war. Pope's first step was to endeavour to relieve the pressure on McClellan by advancing southward down the Orange and Alexandria railways across the Rappahannock toward the Rapidan.

Lee, while watching McClellan in his lines round Harrison's Landing, still kept an eye looking northwards toward Washington. McClellan's army was, despite its reverses, in numbers superior to his own. The memory of Malvern Hill precluded any idea of an assault upon the lines drawn round Harrison's Landing, but a large Federal force which had proved its fighting qualities could not be neglected while it lay within a few marches of Richmond. Lee therefore remained in the Yorktown Peninsula ready to oppose McClellan. But Pope could no more be neglected than the Federal army on the James River, for his movement threatened to cut the railway which connected Richmond with the Shenandoah Valley. Therefore, on July 19th, Lee sent off Jackson to Gordonsville with his own and Ewell's divisions, together with some 11,000 men, to watch Pope. Pope controlled more than four times that number of men, but his troops were widely scattered; the leading troops of his central column under McDowell were nearing the Rapidan. One of his divisions lay forty miles to the east at Fredericksburg, another was forty miles behind at Warrenton. Banks and Sigel, who now commanded Frémont's corps, were another forty miles to the northeast about Luray and Sperryville where they watched the Valley. Pope made the mistake of coming forward without concentrating; his dispositions displayed uncertainty and the desire to guard too much. Jackson, seeing an opportunity, asked Lee for reënforcements, but before making up his mind Lee had to see what McClellan would do.

Just as the right *riposte* to Jackson's move on Winchester in the Valley Campaign would have been a prompt march by McDowell on Richmond rather than Lincoln's and Stanton's ill-judged attempt to cut off the daring raider in the Valley, so now the answer to Jackson's appearance at Gordonsville should have been a movement by McClellan on Richmond. McClellan saw that and urged Halleck to send him the necessary reënforcements. But Halleck, though he possessed certain military qualities, lacked the character and decision to take risks, and above all the keen sense of the value of time in

war which Lee possessed. Time was lost in discussion
and debate, and the opportunity slipped by. McClellan's
inaction gave Lee a hint as to doubts in Halleck's mind,
and he determined to help him to a decision. On July
27th, he wrote to Jackson: 'I will send A. P. Hill's
division and the 2nd brigade of Louisiana Volunteers to
you. .... A. P. Hill, you will, I think, find a good officer,
with whom you can consult, and, by advising with your
division commanders as to your movements, much
trouble will be saved you in arranging details, as they
can act more intelligently. I wish to save you trouble
from my increasing your command. *Cache* your troops
as much as possible till you can strike your blow, and be
prepared to return to me when done, if necessary. I will
endeavour to keep General McClellan quiet till it is over
if rapidly executed.' [1] Lee had seen the weak spot in
Jackson's conduct in the fighting of the Seven Days, and
here hinted to him plainly that he could not command
20,000 men as he had led 6000 in the Valley.

These reënforcements gave Jackson close on 24,000
men. They left Lee with but 50,000, to oppose McClellan
who had 90,000 effectives. The risk which Lee here took
was small. He was rightly confident of being able to
check McClellan, if he moved out of his lines in another
attempt upon Richmond, long enough to allow Jackson
to rejoin him, and for the speedy return of Jackson he

[1] O.R., vol. XII, part III, p. 918.

had prepared. Even this small risk quickly disappeared. The news that Jackson had been reënforced decided Halleck, and on August 4th, orders went out to McClellan that he was to reëmbark and bring the Army of the Potomac back whence it had come. While McClellan was still trying to get this order altered, Lee had divined its purport, and on August 7th, he wrote to Jackson that he now had no expectation that McClellan would move on Richmond.[1] A week later he learned that McClellan's troops were leaving the James for the Potomac. His mind was instantly made up. That evening the first of Longstreet's troops left by train for Gordonsville, and Lee followed with the greater part of his army, leaving only the divisions of D. H. Hill and McLaws to see McClellan off the Peninsula. Lee had decided to use his central position to overwhelm Pope before the Army of the Potomac had completed its circuitous voyage.

In the meantime Pope had brought his scattered forces nearer together, and on July 29th, had joined them with instructions to advance to the Rapidan to cover McClellan's movement to the Potomac. On August 9th, Banks, advancing only with some 8000 men, encountered, at Cedar Mountain, Jackson, who with 17,000 men had marched northwards across the Rapidan in the hope of finding an opportunity for striking at

[1] O.R., vol. XII, part III, p. 925.

Pope's flank. Banks's bold attack was heavily repulsed, but, on the evening of the 11th, Jackson, finding that Banks had been strongly reënforced, fell back to Gordonsville in the hope of drawing the Federals further from their base, which gave Pope and Halleck an excuse for proclaiming Cedar Mountain as a victory. Pope then moved forward to the Rapidan. On August 15th, Lee met his generals at Gordonsville. He had there, or ready to join him shortly, an army superior to Pope's troops immediately opposed to him. His plan was that Jackson should engage the Federal front while Longstreet, moving round their left front, cut their communications. Pope was in grave danger when an accident saved him. Stuart leading the advance was all but captured. He lost his famous plumed hat, a subject of much chaff on both sides, and, what was of greater importance, his despatch box containing a letter conveying the information that more troops from Richmond had joined Jackson. Pope, warned in the nick of time, fell back speedily and skilfully behind the Rappahannock. Again Lee planned to turn his flank; this time it was the right he aimed at; again Fortune intervened to save Pope. Heavy rains brought the river down in flood, and Jackson, to whom the turning movement had been entrusted, was unable to cross. But Fortune was not wholly unkind. Stuart got over the river and in a raid had his revenge, for he captured some of Pope's papers which disclosed the fact that part of McClellan's army had reached Aquia Creek, and that within a few days Pope's strength on the Rappahannock would be formidable. Lee, who now had with him 55,000 men, at once ordered up the remaining troops from Richmond. The arrival of part of the Army of the Potomac had brought Pope's numbers to over 70,000.

On August 24th, Lee and Jackson met in consultation. If Pope was to be compelled to give ground there was little time to spare. To await attack would be useless, as Pope would naturally hold his hand until the reënforcements, of which he was assured, had come up. It would be equally useless to force him back toward his reënforcements by direct attack for this would almost certainly be a slow and costly process. The situation called for such a bold and original enterprise as would confuse Pope and create the opportunity for fighting him where he would be at a disadvantage. The solution found was so bold, so original, as to amaze many of the critics of the war. Lee decided to divide his army in the presence of the enemy, and to send nearly one half of them under Jackson along the eastern slopes of the Blue Ridge, to come down by a circuitous route upon Pope's communications with Washington. This manœuvre has been described as 'contrary to every rule of war,' and to the recognised principles of strategy. Ropes says of it: 'The disparity between this force

[Pope's 70,000] and that of Jackson [24,000] is so enormous, that it is impossible not to be amazed at the audacity of the Confederate general in thus risking an encounter in which the very existence of Jackson's command would be imperilled, and to ask what was the object which General Lee considered as warranting such an extremely dangerous manœuvre. The answer is not an easy one. Lee himself has said nothing in justification of his course.' [1] Ropes, however, has overlooked the fact that Lee, in reply to a similar comment, had answered this criticism before it was written. 'Such criticism,' he said, 'is obvious, but the disparity of force between the contending forces rendered the risk unavoidable.' [2] Lee had to take risks or to await attack by a force which he knew would before long be overwhelmingly superior. What were the risks which he chose to take?

There are no rules of war; there are certain general principles of strategy. One of these principles is that measures which may justifiably be taken against one general would be wholly unjustifiable against another, and that a task which may be safely entrusted to a man of proved capacity should in no case be given to one untried. Lee knew Pope and he knew Jackson. He was aware that Pope's first duty was to cover Washington, a

---

[1] Ropes: *The Story of the Civil War*, part 2, p. 262.
[2] Allan: *The Army of Northern Virginia*, p. 200. In making this statement Lee had, I take it, in mind the reënforcements coming to Pope from the Army of the Potomac.

mission which did not encourage enterprise. He cannot have been impressed by the Federal commander's foolish and bombastic pronunciamento to his army, for which Pope had been freely chaffed in the Northern Press.[1] He knew that Pope had openly declared that he would defend Washington by taking up flank positions against any force which should attempt to advance against the capital. Flank positions do not predicate bold offensive action. There were, therefore, good grounds for believing that Pope would not be prompt in attempting to overwhelm one or the other of the divided parts of the Confederate army. Lee knew, too, that relations between the Federal commanders were at this time none too harmonious, and that Pope's forces consisted of parts of three armies,[2] of which all had suffered heavy reverses. They were, as Ropes justly says, rather an 'agglomeration of troops' than an army. The army confronting Pope was, in fact, in spite of its inferior numbers, superior in fighting power. Lincoln's Administration had made a mistake not infrequently made by a civilian ministry in war. They had permitted themselves to give way to the tendency to count heads and to ignore those elements which are of greater importance to an army than numbers. They had very unwisely

---

[1] Pope began his address: 'I have come to you from the West, where we have always seen the backs of our enemies; from an army whose business has been to seek the adversary and to beat him when he was found.' Not very flattering to the men of his new command.

[2] Banks's, Sigel's, and McDowell's.

stopped recruiting in April, 1862, and when it was re-opened had permitted, and even encouraged, the raising of a stream of new regiments instead of establishing a systematic recruitment, which would keep the veteran regiments up to strength. Thus, while the experienced regiments of the Army of the Potomac were dwindling from sickness and battle losses, new formations inspired with the valour of ignorance were coming in.

In the Confederate army, as I have shown, the contrary policy had on Lee's advice been adopted, and a definite if limited flow of recruits was assured to regiments justly proud of their achievements. The army, too, had profited much by the experience of the Seven Days. The generals had learned from their mistakes to work together as a team under a chief whom they trusted. For these reasons the risk which Lee took in dividing his army before Pope was far less than would appear from an examination of the respective strengths. There remained the important consideration of the character of the man to whom the task of marching round Pope was entrusted. Jackson had shown that his qualities of generalship were at their highest when he was entrusted with an independent and dangerous enterprise. He had proved that he could move secretly and swiftly, and carry boldness up to, but not beyond, the very limit of prudence. In the Valley he had extricated himself from dangers more perilous than were likely to confront him in his new task, and he knew every yard of the country he was to traverse. Indeed, the nature of the country into which he was about to advance greatly reduced the risks which Lee was taking. Each of the divided parts of his army was to skirt the Blue Ridge with the gaps leading into the Shenandoah Valley at their backs. If either part was in danger of being overwhelmed, both could slip through the gaps and unite in the Valley. In such an eventuality Pope would have escaped, but Lee's army, too, would have avoided danger. It is certain that Lee would not have sent half his army away under another leader than Jackson, nor indeed under him if he had not proved that he was fit for the responsibility put upon him. It is equally certain that Lee would not have done, in the face of Grant or Sherman, what he did in face of Pope. As things were, he calculated that the odds were in his favour, and the event proved that he was right. It is true that if he failed he would have been held up to obloquy as a foolhardy and ignorant general. It is the destiny of generals to take risks, and be condemned when they fail. But it by no means follows that they were wrong, even when they failed. If a bridge player holds the aces and kings of three suits, he is right in going 'no trumps.' If the player on his left has the seven top cards of the fourth suit, and says nothing, the contract will not be made, but that does not make the bid a bad one. Lee's aces and kings were the quality of his army, Jackson's skill and familiarity with the ground, Pope's character, the fact that the Federal army had been hastily flung together, his knowledge that he was about to do the last thing Pope would expect of him, and his confidence in himself. Still the risk was there. Pope might hold the other suit, an unlucky accident might delay Jackson, or disclose Lee's plans. The days while Jackson was away were of necessity days of poignant anxiety, but that anxiety was shown to no one. There is no better proof of Lee's high courage and firm character than his calm face between the night of August 24th, when Jackson left him, and that of the 30th, when the second battle of Manassas had been fought and won.

It is now time for a word about Lee's habits of life and methods of work in the field. Just before the opening of the campaign of Seven Days he sent, on June 22, 1862, a description of himself to his daughter-in-law, Mrs. W. H. Fitzhugh Lee: 'And now I must answer your enquiries about myself. My habiliments are not as comfortable as yours nor so suited to this hot weather, but they are the best I have. My coat is of gray, of the regulation style and pattern, my pants of dark blue, as is also prescribed, partly hid by my long boots. I have the same handsome hat which surmounts my gray head (the latter is not prescribed in the regulations) and shields my ugly face, which is masked by a white beard as stiff and wiry as the

teeth of a card. In fact, an uglier person you have never
seen, and so unattractive is it to our enemies, that they
shoot at it whenever visible to them; but though age
with its snow has whitened my head, and its frosts have
stiffened my limbs, my heart, you well know, is not
frozen to you, and summer returns when I see you.' [1]
The reader may judge of the truth of this description
from the portrait which forms the frontispiece of this
book. Almost the only luxuries, if they may be so
called, which Lee permitted himself on service were a
meticulous neatness of appearance and a good and well-
groomed horse. Of his horses his favourite 'Traveller'
was nearly as famous in the Confederacy as the rider.
Together they made a noble picture of the physical qualities which breeding can produce. After the war Lee
sent to a friend a pen portrait of his beloved companion
which reveals not only his affection for a tried comrade,
but the spirit of the true lover of horseflesh: 'If I were an
artist like you, I would draw a true picture of "Traveller," representing his fine proportions, muscular figure,
deep chest and short back, strong haunches, flat legs,
small head, broad forehead, delicate ears, quick eye,
small feet, and black mane and tail. Such a picture
would inspire a poet, whose genius would then depict
his worth and describe his endurance of toil, hunger,

[1] J. W. Jones: *Personal Reminiscences*, p. 185.

thirst, heat, cold, and the dangers and sufferings through which he had passed. He could dilate upon his sagacity and affection and his invariable response to every wish of his rider. He might even imagine his thoughts through the long night-marches and days of battle through which he has passed. But I am no artist, and can only say he is a *Confederate gray*. I purchased him in the mountains of Virginia in the autumn of 1861 and he has been my patient follower ever since, to Georgia, the Carolinas, and back to Virginia. He carried me through the Seven Days' battle round Richmond, the second Manassas, at Sharpsburg, Fredericksburg, the last day at Chancellorsville, to Pennsylvania, to Gettysburg, and back to the Rappahannock. From the commencement of the campaign in 1864 at Orange till its close around Petersburg, his saddle was scarcely off his back, as he passed through the fire of the Wilderness, Spottsylvania, Cold Harbor, and across the James River. He was almost in daily requisition in the winter of 1864–65, on the long line of defences from the Chickahominy north of Richmond to Hatcher's Run south of the Appomattox. In the campaign of 1865 he bore me from Petersburg to the final days at Appomattox Courthouse.' [1]

This description of the work done by the horse gives us some idea of the activities of the rider, and one can-

[1] A. L. Long: *Memoirs of Robert E. Lee*, p. 131.

not but wonder how Grant came to speak of Lee as 'a good deal of a headquarters' general.' [1] Lee's life in the field was intensely active and simple to austerity. The same tin mug and plates, which he took with him on his first campaign in Western Virginia, served him throughout the war. He lived habitually in a tent, though the people of Virginia were eager to have the honour of receiving him into their houses, and even when he was ill his staff had almost to compel him to take shelter under a roof. General A. L. Long, whose duty it was to arrange accommodations for headquarters, has left us a description of some of the difficulties which his chief's habits caused him: 'After a long and fatiguing search a farmhouse was discovered surrounded by a large shady yard. The occupants of the house with great satisfaction gave permission for the establishment of General Lee not only in the yard, but insisted on his occupying a part of the house. Everything being satisfactorily settled, the wagons were ordered up, but just as the unloading began the General rode up and flatly refused to occupy either yard or house. No one expected him to violate his custom by occupying a house, but it was thought he would not object to a temporary occupation of the yard. Being vexed at having to look for another place for headquarters, I ordered the wagons into a field almost entirely covered with massive stones. The boulders

[1] J. R. Young: *Around the World with General Grant*, vol. 2, p. 459.

were so large and thick that it was difficult to find space
for the tents. The only redeeming feature the location
possessed was a small stream of good water. When the
tents were pitched the General looked round him with a
smile of satisfaction and said: "This is better than the
yard. We will not now disturb those good people."" [1]
In such simple surroundings Lee planned and worked.
His staff was a small one; it rarely consisted of more than
eight or nine persons and its chief duty was to relieve
him of the routine of administration. [2] One of its special
functions was to keep from him the numerous appeals
against disciplinary actions with which his tender heart
hated to have to deal. His plans he kept almost entirely
to himself. Operation orders such as those for the Seven
Days were not issued regularly. Often he gave his instructions personally to the commanders of his corps and
divisions. This helped greatly to the preservation of
that secrecy which was one of his chief weapons, and was
probably necessary in a war in which both sides spoke
the same language and spying was comparatively easy.
But it had grave disadvantages, and on important occasions the misunderstandings which are the inevitable
sequence, sooner or later, of verbal orders had fatal consequences. Only with Jackson, who was the ideal sub-

[1] A. L. Long: *Memoirs of Robert E. Lee*, p. 227.
[2] Long (p. 501) gives a complete list of those who served on Lee's
staff throughout the war, including commissaries, ordnance officers, and
replacements, of which there were many. The number was thirty-four.

ordinate of such a chief, was this method completely successful.

Having a well-ordered mind and very methodical habits, Lee during his campaigns was able to get through an amazing amount of work. He was largely his own intelligence officer; he studied assiduously the files of the Northern newspapers and he read all the chief reports which came to the army of affairs in Washington and in Federal camps. In coming to the conclusions which he reached, he was, of course, helped greatly by his unique knowledge of the character and attainments of his opponents. It was on this knowledge, as I have said, he based his plan of campaign against Pope, to which I must now return.

On August 25th, Jackson in his march round Pope's flank reached Salem at the western foot of the Thorough-fare Gap; the next day his leading troops had come down behind the Federal army and had captured its advanced base at Manassas. During the forenoon of the 27th, he had his whole force there revelling in the vast accumulation of food and equipment which they found. Pope got early news of Jackson's march, and, thinking it to mean that the whole Confederate army was moving into the Valley, he decided presently to fall back on Gainesville. When he learned on the 27th that Jackson's whole force was at Manassas, he ordered a concentration on that place, designed, as he put it, 'to bag Jackson and his whole crowd.' But Jackson had no intention of waiting, isolated, athwart Pope's communications. The plan concerted with Lee was that he should draw Pope after him northward and away from the reënforcements disembarking in the Potomac. Jackson, therefore, slipped off northwards on the night of the 27th, and the next day had his troops concealed near the old battlefield of Bull Run in a position where he had, for use in case the junction with Longstreet failed to mature, a line of retreat behind him to Aldie Gap and into the valley. Throughout this apparently dangerous manœuvre Lee had had it in mind that it might be necessary to reunite the divided parts of his army in the Valley. Both he and Jackson were therefore careful to keep the gaps leading into the Valley at their backs. He knew too much of war to promise to engage in battle before he had seen the situation of his enemy and therefore his first purpose was to get Pope to retreat, while providing for the safety of his army. That this is so is shown by a letter he wrote to Davis from the very field of battle on August 30th. He said: 'The movement has as far as I am able to judge, drawn the enemy from the Rappahannock frontier and caused him to concentrate his troops between Manassas and Centreville. My desire has been to avoid a general engagement, being the weaker force, and by manœuvring to relieve the portion of the country referred to.'[1]

[1] *Lee's Confidential Despatches to Davis*, p. 56.

Lee had followed with Longstreet on August 26th the route Jackson had taken. On the night of the 28th Longstreet was in Thoroughfare Gap, and the distance between the extreme wings of the two Confederate forces was already less than that between the limits of Pope's scattered forces. For Pope, finding that Jackson was not at Manassas, was bewildered. For several hours he was uncertain where Jackson had gone, and then late on the afternoon of the 28th ordered all his army on Centreville several miles to the east of Jackson's actual position. These changes of direction entailed much marching and counter-marching on the Federal troops, who were beginning to feel the want of the supplies which Jackson had destroyed at Manassas. Weary men were therefore approaching the *dénouement* of these manœuvres.

While 'Stonewall' Jackson was resting his troops on the 28th near Groveton, within sight of the battlefield which had given him his nickname, some papers captured from a Federal train were brought to him. These disclosed Pope's orders for concentration on Manassas. Now the chief object of Lee's manœuvre was to force Pope back before he could be reënforced by McClellan's troops, and the second to bring him to battle in circumstances less favourable than were afforded by his strong position on the Rappahannock. If Pope got away eastwards, his junction with the Army of the

Potomac would be certain. To prevent that, Jackson decided to attack at once any Federal troops within his reach. It happened that King's division of McDowell's corps was marching, all unwittingly, down the road to Centreville across Jackson's front. He was promptly attacked by superior force, but his men fighting with skill and courage held their ground till far into the night, when he fell back on Manassas. This sharply fought action at Groveton told Pope where Jackson was, and still, with the one idea in his mind of crushing the hero of the Shenandoah Valley, he turned his whole army against him without making sufficient effort to hold off Lee and Longstreet. On the 28th, Lee had turned the one division under Ricketts, left to oppose him at Thoroughfare Gap by sending a detachment through Hopewell Gap round its flank, and before noon on the 29th, Longstreet was in touch with Jackson's right. The perilous manœuvre had been accomplished, and an opportunity highly favourable to the Confederates had been created. While Pope was bringing his corps up piecemeal to attack Jackson, Longstreet stood stretching well beyond the Federal left, ready to strike a deadly blow. On this day Jackson had to play the part of Wellington at Waterloo, and stand the pounding until Longstreet, in the rôle of Blücher, gave the *coup-de-grace*. But the *coup* was not given. Three times did Lee urge Longstreet forward, three

EVENING AUGUST 28TH 1862

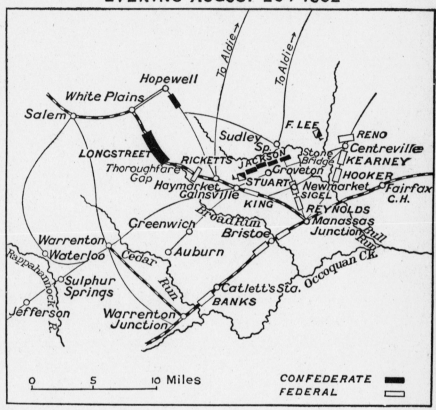

Hopewell

White Plains

Salem

To Aldie →

To Aldie →

Sudley Sp.

F. LEE

RENO

Centreville

LONGSTREET

RICKETTS

JACKSON

Stone Bridge

KEARNEY

Thoroughfare Gap

Groveton

HOOKER

Haymarket

STUART

Newmarket

Fairfax C.H.

Gainsville

SIGEL

KING

REYNOLDS

Greenwich

Broad Run

Manassas Junction

Bristoe

Bull Run

Warrenton

Waterloo

Cedar

Auburn

Occoquan Ck.

Rappahannock R.

Sulphur Springs

Run

Jefferson

Warrenton Junction

Catlett's Sta.

BANKS

0   5   10 Miles

CONFEDERATE

FEDERAL

times did Longstreet find reason, which seemed to him good, for not attacking. Longstreet was an obstinate man. It may be that the experience of Malvern Hill weighed heavily on him, but it is clear that he was obsessed by one idea. He believed the recipe for victory to be to manœuvre an army into a position such that the enemy would be compelled to attack at a disadvantage, and there await the blow. That belief of Longstreet's and consequent unwillingness to attack was later to be disastrous to the Confederate cause, and it is at least probable that it saved Pope's army from annihilation on August 29th. Longstreet had in front of him Porter with very inferior numbers, and was so placed that he could have speedily enveloped Porter's flank. Curiously enough, while Lee was pressing Longstreet to attack, Pope, who appears to have been unaware that Longstreet's whole force was in the field, was doing the same thing to Porter, who prudently refrained from so desperate a measure until he had more certain information of the force opposite him. After the battle Porter was dismissed for failing to do the very thing that Longstreet hoped he would do.[1] A share of the responsibility for Longstreet's inaction must be Lee's. One of the few defects of his generalship was a curious reluctance in battle to back his own judgment against that of his chief subordinates and to enforce his will upon them. It is a

[1] After a subsequent inquiry, Porter was absolved and reinstated.

hard thing for a commander to draw the line correctly between undue interference and excess of liberty. Lee once described the principles which guided his conduct in battle. 'My interference in battle would do more harm than good. I have then to rely on my brigade and division commanders. I think and work with all my power to bring the troops to the right place at the right time; then I have done my duty. As soon as I order them forward into battle, I leave my duty in the hands of God.' [1] This, as a system of command, is sound to a point. It is entirely applicable to the commander-in-chief of such huge armies as fought in the Great War, but in forces of the size which Lee commanded some more direct intervention when battle is joined is sometimes necessary. Lee was disposed to err on the battlefield in not asserting his authority enough. He suffered, as the French say, from the defects of his qualities, for it is probable that, if his character had allowed him to be more assertive, he would not have inspired in those he led the devotion which made them endure as men have rarely endured.

Having failed to get Longstreet to move on the 29th, Lee changed his plans for the 30th. He was aware that Pope would have taken advantage of the respite allowed him to bring all his troops within reach in due order to the battlefield. The reënforcements he had ordered from

[1] J. Scheibert: *Der Bürgerkrieg in den nordamerikanischen Staaten*, p. 39.

Richmond, numbering more than 20,000 men, were fast approaching. They had, in fact, crossed the Rappahannock. He therefore decided to await Pope's attacks, to place Longstreet in position to assault the Federal left, and to watch for an opportunity to strike back. Pope, who never throughout the battle grasped the situation, was deceived by some readjustments which Lee made in his line of battle into thinking that the Confederates were retreating. About noon he ordered an attack upon Jackson. Jackson stood firm and the Federals suffered severely from enfilading fire from Longstreet's guns. Pope then made the crowning mistake of taking troops from his left opposite Longstreet to support the attack on Jackson. The opportunity for the counter-attack had come, and Lee ordered a general advance. Longstreet, who was now fighting a battle after his own heart, had seen the chance and was already on the move. The Federal left was driven in. Their reserves behind Pope's centre and right were ordered to the left to meet the new danger, and Jackson's attack, crashing forward against troops who had already suffered a repulse, completed the Confederate victory.

The effect of Jackson's destruction of the stores at Manassas and of the marches to and fro which had preceded Pope's attacks had increased the strain of battle almost to breaking point. 'The complete prostration of his troops from hunger and fatigue' of which

Pope speaks [1] was the natural reaction from gallant
efforts made in adverse conditions. That prostration was
increased by a retreat at night. Jackson's men were,
however, too exhausted, Longstreet's too far off, for a
prompt and vigorous pursuit of Pope into the position at
Centreville to which he retreated. But on September 1st
Pope threw up the sponge and wrote to Halleck that the
army 'should draw back to the entrenchments in front
of Washington.' Halleck perforce agreed; the retreat
was continued, and on September 2d, McClellan was
placed in command of all the troops within the defences
of the capital.

Lee had made up his mind as to his next move before
the Federal retreat was ended. In nine weeks he had
transferred the front of battle from the outskirts of
Richmond to the neighbourhood of Washington. His
immediate purpose was to keep it there, if possible, until
the rains of winter made the active operations of an
invader so difficult as to be unlikely. He wished the
harvests of Virginia to be garnered without interference,
and the devastations of battle to be transferred beyond
the Potomac. These ends could not be reached by repeating the process of watching and waiting which had
followed the first battle of Manassas, but he had no
intention of knocking his head against the now formidable lines which had been drawn round Washington. A

[1] O.R., vol. XII, part II, p. 43.

success gained in Maryland might have the effect of making decisive the influence of those in the North who thought that the attempt to maintain the Union by force was not worth the cost, and would almost certainly bring considerable reënforcements from that State to the Confederate cause. Lee therefore asked Davis's consent to an invasion of Maryland, a consent this time promptly given, but before it was received, on September 2d, the Confederate army, which with the troops from Richmond now numbered some 60,000 men — for the reënforcements had more than made good the losses of battle — was set in motion for Leesburg above which lay an easy crossing over the Potomac. Though many in Washington were trembling for its safety, Lee had no illusions as to his chances of entering the city in triumph. 'The army,' he wrote to Davis, 'is not properly equipped for an invasion of an enemy's territory. It lacks much of the material of war, is feeble in transportation, the animals being much reduced, and the men are poorly provided with clothes, and in thousands of instances are destitute of shoes.' The effect of the blockade was becoming deadly, and it is not surprising that Lee pondered deeply and consulted both Longstreet and Jackson before deciding to enter hostile territory with his ragged army. A smaller man would have found ample reason for inaction, in the condition of the army, but Lee's plain statement of fact to Davis is followed by: 'We cannot afford to be idle, and though weaker than our opponents in men and military equipments, must endeavour to harass if we cannot destroy them.'[1] The bare feet of his men meant much to Lee, for like Napoleon he won his victories with his men's legs. None the less he started on another bold manœuvre, and in appraising that decision it is well to compare the correspondence between Lee and Davis which preceded it with that between McClellan and Halleck a few weeks later, when the former regretted that he could not move because the boots furnished for his troops were too large.[2]

From September 4th to 6th, Lee's troops splashed through the fords above Leesburg singing 'Maryland, My Maryland,' but Maryland showed little inclination to respond. On the 7th, Frederick City was occupied, and there Lee was well placed to threaten either Washington, Baltimore, or Philadelphia, and to cut the communications of the capital with the remainder of the Union. He thought himself also well placed to make a proposal upon which he had been meditating for some days. On September 8th he wrote to the President: 'The present position of affairs in my opinion places it in the power of the Government of the Confederate States to propose with propriety to that of the United

[1] O.R., vol. XIX, p. 590.
[2] Cf. Rhodes, vol. IV, p. 186, and O.R., vol. XIX, part I, pp. 22, 23, and 75.

States the recognition of our independence. For more than a year both sections of the country have been devastated by hostilities which have brought sorrow and suffering upon thousands of homes, without advancing the objects which our enemies proposed to themselves in beginning the contest. Such a proposition coming from us at this time could in no way be regarded as suing for peace, but being made when it is in our power to inflict injury upon our adversary would show conclusively to the world that our sole object is the establishment of our independence and the attainment of an honourable peace.' [1] But before the machinery of diplomacy could be set in motion, military events had put it out of gear. Lee's first care on entering Maryland was to consider his own communications. He could no longer use his line through Manassas Junction with safety and he wanted to open up the Valley. He had hoped that his movement across the Potomac would have caused the Federal troops at the head of the Valley to withdraw. But it did not. Harper's Ferry was strongly held, and Lee determined to take it. He also decided, in spite of Longstreet's protests, again to divide his army. Jackson with 25,000 men, nearly half the army, which was now rapidly diminishing as the footsore fell out, was sent to clear the Valley; with the remainder Lee moved north of Hagerstown in order to spread fear for the safety of

[1] O.R., vol. XIX, part II, p. 600.

Pennsylvania, draw McClellan away from Washington, and create a chance of accepting battle on favourable terms.

Jackson marched from Frederick City on September 10th, and, crossing the Potomac near Williamsport, drove a Federal detachment at Martinsburg into Harper's Ferry, and on the 13th had surrounded the place which now held 12,500 Federal troops. Meantime McClellan, who had pulled his army together with remarkable speed, began on September 5th an unexpectedly prompt advance from Washington with an army of about 70,000 men. On September 12th, he reached Frederick City and there received reënforcements which brought his strength to 85,000. On that day Lee with 30,000 men was about Hagerstown. Jackson's force of 25,000 in three groups was twenty-five miles away, approaching Harper's Ferry. If Harper's Ferry was promptly captured, one day's march would unite the Confederate wings, and McClellan's habits were so deliberate that there seemed no doubt that the junction could be made in ample time to meet him. Then two things happened. First, McLaw's and Walker's divisions of Jackson's force were longer in getting into position round Harper's Ferry than Lee had calculated, and the attack could not be begun on the 13th. Next, on that day a copy of Lee's orders, disclosing his entire plan and the separation of his forces, was picked up by a

Federal soldier and brought to McClellan,[1] who then had nearly three times as many men as had Lee, and was nearer to Lee than Lee was to Jackson. Fortune then thought it time to give her wheel a turn. McClellan believing, as always, that Lee's army outnumbered his own, took no advantage of her favours and did not begin to move until the 14th. The fickle lady had meantime smiled on Lee. A citizen favourable to the Confederacy had been present when the order was brought to McClellan, and on the night of the 13th Lee knew what McClellan knew. He at once sent troops to hold the gaps of South Mountain and to bring Longstreet to Boonsboro', where he could support them and be nearer Jackson. McClellan was not able to force one of the passes until late in the afternoon of the 14th, and the other till long after dark, and by that time Lee had been able to get his baggage trains away, and the fate of Harper's Ferry was sealed, though he did not know it. But with McClellan in possession of the passes, Lee either had to retreat across the Potomac or accept battle with the river at his back. At 8 P.M. on the 14th he had decided to retreat;[2] at 10.15, probably on getting news that Harper's Ferry would speedily fall, he changed his mind and issued orders to his army to take up a position behind Antietam.

[1] These orders will be found in the appendix to this chapter.
[2] *Battle and Leaders*, vol. II, p. 675.

Of all Lee's actions in the war this seems to me to be
the most open to criticism. He was only justified in
giving battle if retreat was impossible without fighting,
or if he had a good prospect, not merely of repulsing
attacks, but of beating his enemy soundly. He could
have got over the Potomac without difficulty on the
15th, and returned to Virginia, if not with all the results
he had hoped to obtain, with the prestige of the capture
of Harper's Ferry, many prisoners and quantities of
stores. The ground he chose for battle, while admirably
suited for defence, left him no opportunity for such a
counterstroke as Longstreet had delivered at the second
battle of Manassas. He could at best hope to beat off the
Federals. But at the end of such a battle, he would be
no better off than he was on the morning of the 15th.
The Antietam, the most desperately fought struggle of
the war, must be numbered among the unnecessary
battles.

Harper's Ferry fell at 7.30 A.M. on the 15th, and Jackson promptly marched with the greater part of his force
to meet Lee. McClellan moved slowly forward through
the South Mountain Gap, and spent the greater part of
the 16th in reconnoitring Lee's position. That evening
he began with his right what was little more than a
preliminary skirmish. Lee had counted, and with good
reason, on McClellan's slowness. Having made up his
mind, he was calmly confident. Walker, who joined him

from Harper's Ferry on the 16th, has happily left us an
account of his bearing: 'Anxious no doubt he was; but
there was nothing in his look or bearing to indicate it.
On the contrary, he was calm, dignified, and even cheer-
ful. If he had had a well-equipped army and a hundred
thousand veterans at his back he could not have appeared more composed and confident.' [1]

The battle began in earnest on the 17th. Owing to
detachments and stragglers Lee had never more than
50,000 men on the battlefield, and until the arrival of
the troops from Harper's Ferry many fewer. McClellan
attacked with some 75,000;[2] but Lee had chosen his
position with the eye of the engineer and the skill of the
practised tactician. His flanks were protected by the
Potomac, across his front ran the Antietam. McClellan
could therefore only make frontal attacks in difficult
conditions, and his superiority was not in the circumstances sufficient to ensure success even if the leadership
had been equal, which it was not. The Federal attacks
were made with supreme gallantry, but were disjointed.
Lee's conduct of the defensive battle was masterly, and
the timely arrival of A. P. Hill with the last of the troops
from Harper's Ferry destroyed McClellan's chance of

---

[1] *Battles and Leaders*, vol. II, p. 675.

[2] There has been more dispute about the strength of the opposing forces
at Antietam than about any other battle in the war. Lee's own statement
that he fought with less than 40,000 men is clearly an underestimate, but
I think that Colonel T. L. Livermore, in giving the Confederates 59,000,
has not made sufficient allowance for stragglers.

gaining a victory. Lee, not satisfied with repulsing attacks, proposed in the evening of the 17th and again on the morning of the 18th to hit back. But while the Potomac protected his flanks, it left no space, not swept by the superior Federal artillery, for such an operation against McClellan's right as he proposed, and he reluctantly abandoned the idea. On the night of the 18th, he crossed the Potomac and McClellan remained with the bulk of his army watching the passages over the river.

So ended in failure a remarkable campaign. Between June 25th and September 18th, Lee had defeated two armies and repulsed a third, each of them much larger than his own. He had cleared Eastern Virginia of all Federal troops save a few detachments. He had made two mistakes in battle: one in attacking at Malvern Hill; the other in standing on the Antietam. Both of them were, I believe, due to the same cause, his confidence in himself and in his men, and a tendency to believe that the effect of his victories on the Federal troops was greater than it was. But if he had not been confident, if he had not thought the Southern soldier a better man than the Northerner, he could not have ventured on the daring yet calculated strategy which had produced results so amazing. He knew, as Napoleon knew, that moral ascendancy is in war many times more valuable than material superiority. He believed that the moral ascendancy won on the first battlefields of the Seven Days would allow him to do what he liked with his enemy. He had entered Maryland to fight an army which he held to be 'much weakened and demoralised,' [1] and he had fought it rather than lose his moral ascendancy by retreat. In both cases he was wrong, but as Lincoln is reported to have said of Grant's whiskey, a little of that spirit in his opponents would have given the war a very different course. Despite these errors of judgment, Lee's campaign of 1862 is a remarkable example of calculated boldness and of imaginative strategy. No other commander has achieved with means so exiguous results more remarkable. And throughout the campaign Fortune had been almost uniformly unkind. The loss of Stuart's despatches and the sudden rising of the Rappahannock had twice saved Pope. The discovery by McClellan of the order of South Mountain deprived Lee of all chance of dealing with him in Maryland as he had dealt with Pope in Virginia. But Lee was above the rebuffs of Fortune. Napoleon believed in his star, Lee in his God. The courage founded on faith is more enduring than the courage founded on luck. [2]

[1] O.R., vol. XIX, part II, p. 590.
[2] I have been told that this remark is somewhat cryptic, seeing that the careers of both of these great commanders ended in disaster. Like Solon I look at the end of their lives. Lee died in his own land full of years and honour, having by his conduct won the respect of his former enemies; Napoleon died in middle age a broken exile.

APPENDIX

Extract from Special Order No. 191 of September 9, 1862, which was found by Private B. W. Mitchell of the 27th Indiana Volunteers of McClellan's Army, wrapped round three cigars.

The army will resume its march to-morrow taking the Hagerstown road. General Jackson's command will form the advance, and after passing Middletown with such portions as he may select, cross the Potomac at the most convenient point and by Friday night, September 12th, take possession of the Baltimore and Ohio Railway, capture such of the enemy as may be at Martinsburg, and intercept such as may attempt to escape from Harper's Ferry.

General Longstreet's command will pursue the road as far as Boonsboro', where it will halt. . . .

General McLaws with his own division and that of General Anderson will follow General Longstreet; on reaching Middletown he will take the road to Harper's Ferry and by Friday morning (September 12) possess himself of the Maryland Heights and endeavour to capture the enemy at Harper's Ferry and the vicinity.

General Walker with his division . . . will take possession of the Loudoun Heights, if practicable, by Friday morning (September 12).

CHAPTER VII

WAITING TO STRIKE

THE first consequence of Lee's withdrawal from Maryland had not been foreseen by him, nor indeed by any one not in the confidence of the Northern President. On September 23, 1862, Lincoln issued his first emancipation proclamation. This pronouncement, regarded not unnaturally in the South as an attempt to promote a negro rebellion which would increase the embarrassments of the Confederacy, was, apart altogether from its high political significance, a war measure of the first importance. It is unnecessary to insist upon the military value of enthusiasm for a cause. With it armies, inferior in every material respect to their opponents, have triumphed; without it, numerous and well-equipped hosts have failed. During the first years of the war the advantage of enthusiasm lay, as it seems to me, with the Southerners, who were convinced, in the mass, that they were fighting for liberty. In the North few besides Lincoln saw the vision of the future which lay before a great and united America, and toward the close of 1862 the maintenance of the Union was becoming more and more a party rather than a national question. The emancipation proclamation gave the Northern cause a moral fillip which it was beginning to need. Its effect was not immediate, for it was received with divided opinions in the Army of the Potomac, in which McClellan in particular did not accept it with joy, but its effect was certain and far-reaching. Its influence extended beyond the boundaries of the Federal and Confederate States and produced before long a great change of opinion in Great Britain, which had been irritated by the Trent and excited by the Alabama incident; and Lincoln soon had no more whole-hearted supporters than were to be found among the distressed cotton hands of Lancashire. I do not think it is too much to say that the proclamation saved the cause of the Union in the crises I am now about to describe.

Lee's first care when he had recrossed the Potomac, after providing for the possibility of a pursuit by McClellan, was to rest and, as far as might be, to refit his ragged army in the Valley around Winchester. He did not waver in his conviction that the one way to finish the war successfully for the South was to obtain a victory in Northern territory, but the sight of his men showed him that they were in no condition for such an enterprise. He had to wait and create the opportunity to strike as he wished to strike. On September 25th, he wrote to Davis: 'In a military point of view the best move, in my opinion, the army could make would be to advance upon Hagerstown and endeavor to defeat the enemy at that point. I would not hesitate to make it

even with our diminished numbers, did the army exhibit
its former temper and condition; but as far as I am able
to judge the hazard would be great and reverse disastrous.'[1] The reaction after the strain of three months
of hard marching and harder fighting was pronounced.
The tale of stragglers mounted ominously and the
number of absentee officers was remarkable. Lee's
correspondence at this time is largely concerned with his
efforts to remedy an evil from which McClellan's army
was suffering as greatly as his own, to restore the health
of his men and to provide them with adequate equipment. On September 13th, the fatal day when McClellan
discovered his plans, he wrote to Davis: 'I have received
as yet no official list of the casualties in the late battles,
and from the number of absentees from the army and
the vice of straggling, a correct list cannot now be
obtained. The army has been so constantly in motion,
its attention has been so unremittingly devoted to what
was necessary, that little opportunity has been afforded
for attention to this subject.'[2] Now that he was back
in the Valley, he had the time he needed for attention to
these matters and they were his chief concern. On
September 22d, he told the President: 'In connection
with the subject of straggling . . . the destruction of
private property by the army has occupied much of my
attention. A great deal of damage to citizens is done by

[1] O R., vol. XIX, part II, p. 627.   [2] *Ibid.*, p. 605.

stragglers, who consume all they can get from the charitable and all they can take from the defenceless, in many cases wantonly destroying stock and other property'; and on the same day he caused his adjutant-general to send a circular order to Longstreet and Jackson which begins: 'The depredations committed by this army, its daily diminution by straggling, and the loss of arms thrown aside as too burdensome by stragglers make it necessary for preservation itself, aside from considerations of disgrace and injury to our cause arising from such outrages committed upon our citizens, that greater efforts be made by our officers to correct this growing evil.'[1] On September 23d, he again wrote to Davis: 'The subject of recruiting this army is also one of paramount importance. The usual casualties of battle have diminished its ranks, but its numbers have been greatly decreased by desertions and straggling. This was the main cause of its retiring from Maryland.'[2]

I need not weary the reader with further quotations from the Official Records which abound with Lee's references to this subject. I have given examples of them because he has been criticised by foreign observers as being a poor disciplinarian. One of them has ascribed to him, 'an indifference to discipline and a too kindly consideration for incompetent officers.'[3] Discipline cannot

[1] O.R., vol. XIX, part II, pp. 617 and 618.   [2] Ibid., p. 622.
[3] Mangold: Der Feldzug in Nord-Virginien.

be learned in a day, and undoubtedly it was not learned in either army till a comparatively late stage of war. But Lee with the lessons of West Point in his mind certainly did not undervalue it; as early in the war as May 10, 1861, we find him writing to a Colonel D. Ruggles: 'You are desired to use all the means in your power to advance the instruction and discipline of your command. . . . You must establish rigid discipline and endeavour to place with each command competent officers as instructors, though they may be of inferior rank to the respective commanders.'[1] Almost the only recorded instances of loss of temper by Lee were over breaches of discipline. General Long tells us that, during the first invasion of Maryland: 'Lee was riding along a little in the rear of the lines when he came across a soldier who had stolen and killed a pig, which he was surreptitiously conveying to his quarters. Positive orders having been given against pillage of every kind, this flagrant disregard of his command threw the General into a hot passion. Though usually greatly disinclined to capital punishment, he determined to make an example of this skulking pilferer, and ordered the man to be arrested and taken back to Jackson with directions to have him shot.'[2] Jackson was just going into action, and he gave the culprit the chance of saving his life by showing his courage in battle, which he did.

[1] O.R., vol. II, p. 828.
[2] A. L. Long: *Memoirs of Robert E. Lee*, p. 222.

To one brought up under the methods of Continental armies, the discipline of the armies of the Civil War may well have seemed strange or even non-existent. The free chaff by the men in the ranks of any idiosyncrasies of manner or of dress in the officers must, naturally, have horrified a Prussian, who would, just as naturally, have been amazed at seeing the Commander-in-Chief of the Army of Northern Virginia, when riding with his staff past a prayer meeting, conducted by a humble private, halt, dismount, bare his head, and humbly take part in the simple service. Discipline to be of any value must be suited to the character of the men who are to be controlled. Lee knew well that the discipline of Frederick's grenadiers would break his army in pieces. He did not drive, he led his men; he led them and they followed, because he lived amongst them, because they knew of his constant anxiety for their welfare, because his honesty and complete lack of self-seeking were obvious to the least observant, and because his early victories had given him a prestige so high that it could not be lowered even by defeat. But not all the influence of Lee's character could overcome the evil of straggling. In a vast country, with as yet poor communications, inhabited by a people with little experience and no love of war, it was easy for men to escape at will. Many on both sides left the armies, in the intervals between the campaigns, from war weariness and homesickness to

come back again when active operations were resumed.
But many more stayed away hidden by their friends or
concealed themselves in the woods and mountains. Lee
could not stop desertions, but if he failed in this no other
commander on either side in the war ever succeeded.
Yet despite this grave defect, the discipline in neither
army was so bad as it appeared to the casual observer.
The object of discipline in an army is to give bodies of
men both cohesion and the instinct to suffer all for duty
in circumstances of great stress and danger. If this be so,
and I do not think it can be disputed, then there must
have been some value in the discipline which took
Pickett's men across the fire-swept ground up to the
ridge of Gettysburg, and Grant's soldiers to the assaults
of the 'Bloody Angle' of Spottsylvania. Armies which
stood the losses of the battles of the Civil War and kept
their spirit and cohesion had a discipline which, if *sui
generis*, was effective.[1] One foreign observer at least saw
this, Colonel Wolseley,[2] who had had wide and very
varied war experience in Burma, the Crimea, the Indian
Mutiny, and in China, and was at the time employed in
Canada, visited Lee's army in the autumn of 1862 and of
it he said: 'I have seen many armies file past in all the
pomp of fresh clothing and well-polished accoutrements,

[1] The percentage of casualties to numbers engaged at Gettysburg was
24, Chickamauga 27, Shiloh 20, the Antietam 17. At Waterloo it was 24,
Inkermann 15, Königgrätz 6, Wörth 13, Gravelotte 9.

[2] Afterward Field Marshal Viscount Wolseley. He first introduced the
study of the Civil War to British soldiers.

but I never saw one composed of finer men or that looked more like business than that portion of General Lee's army which I was fortunate enough to see inspected.'[1]

The General was in as much need of rest as his army. He had conducted the short Maryland campaign under great physical disabilities. Just before he crossed the Potomac, he had been standing by his horse with the reins over one arm when the animal gave a sudden plunge and threw him violently to the ground. Both his arms were injured and the bones in one hand broken. I have always attributed his failure to observe that the position of his army behind the Antietam did not lend itself to the counter-attack for which he pined to the fact that this injury prevented him from making a full personal survey of the battlefield. Soon after his return to Winchester he wrote to Mrs. Lee: 'I have not laid eyes on Rob [his son] since I saw him in the battle of Sharpsburg[2] going in with a single gun of his battery for the second time after his company had been withdrawn in consequence of three of its guns having been disabled. Custis has seen him and says he is very well and apparently happy and content. My hands are improving slowly and with my left hand I am able to dress and undress myself, which is a great comfort. My right is becoming of some assistance, too, though it is still swollen

[1] *Blackwood's*, vol. XLIII, p. 21.
[2] The Confederate name for the battle of the Antietam.

and sometimes painful. The bandages have been removed. I am now able to sign my name. It has been six
weeks since I was injured and I have at last discarded
the sling.'[1] One is in doubt whether to admire more the
constancy of mind which in such circumstances took the
decision to fight on the Antietam, or the devotion to
principle which would not admit the possibility of placing a beloved son in a position of more comfort and less
danger.

As the General recovered, so did his army, which early
in October had increased to more than 60,000 men.
These were now organised in two corps under Longstreet and Jackson. On the other side McClellan,
despite Lincoln's promptings, remained inactive on the
Potomac, and Lee began to be anxious as to what his
opponent was about. So on October 8th he ordered 'Jeb'
Stuart, with 1800 cavalry and four guns, into Pennsylvania to investigate. Stuart crossed the Potomac near
Williamsport on the 19th, rode to Chambersburg behind
the Federal right flank, and then repeated the feat he
had performed in the Peninsula by making a circuit of
McClellan's rear, and coming east of the South Mountain through Frederick City and Poolesville, back over
the Potomac on October 12th. This raid stirred the
Federal cavalry as ants are stirred to scurryings in all
directions when a stick is thrust into their nest. But

[1] Fitzhugh Lee: *General Lee*, p. 216.

excursions hither and thither failed to stop Stuart and wore out McClellan's horse, giving that commander yet another reason for inaction, and undermining the public confidence in him which the Antietam had in a great measure restored. But to Lee the main advantage of Stuart's enterprise was the knowledge that no preparations were being made for another expedition by sea to the Peninsula. He knew that the next Federal invasion would come by land. So Longstreet's corps was assembled round Culpeper Court-House, while Jackson remained in the neighbourhood of Winchester. Thus Lee was prepared, whether McClellan came down the Valley or along the Orange and Alexandria railway, to delay him with one part of his force while the other used the screen of the Ridges to cover a movement against the enemy's flank.

Toward the end of October, McClellan at length moved into Virginia and progressed slowly toward Manassas Junction. His army numbered then some 125,000 men with large reserves behind it, and on November 7th the bulk of it was in process of concentration around Warrenton. Lee, who had about 72,000 to oppose him, on November 10th explained his dispositions to the Secretary of War at Richmond: 'As long as General Jackson can operate with safety, and secure his retirement west of the Massanutton Mountains, I think it advantageous that he should be in a position to threaten the enemy's flank and rear, and thus prevent his advance southwards on the east side of the Blue Ridge. General Jackson has been directed accordingly, and, should the enemy descend into the Valley, General Longstreet will attack his rear and cut off his communications. The enemy is, apparently, so strong in numbers that I think it preferable to baffle his designs by manœuvring, rather than resist his advance by main force. To accomplish the latter without too great a risk and loss would require more than double our present numbers.' [1] Manœuvre continued to be Lee's recipe for victory.

But McClellan and Lee were not again to meet in battle. On November 7th, Lincoln, weary of the former's procrastination, displaced him and put Burnside in his place. Burnside's plan, approved by the President after some discussion, was to make a feint toward Culpeper and then to move rapidly on Fredericksburg, where he would base himself on Aquia Creek, thus removing his communications from the danger of attack from the Valley, while, if he got over the Rappahannock quickly, he would be between Lee and Richmond. The plan was sound, provided that it could be executed swiftly. As it turned out, the essential element of success was lacking, and not wholly through Burnside's fault. He had organised his command in three grand divisions under

[1] O.R., vol. XIX, p. 711.

Sumner, Franklin, and Hooker. Sumner reached Falmouth opposite Fredericksburg on November 17th; but the pontoons promised by Washington had not arrived, nor was the new line of communications ready, and so nothing was done, though the Confederate garrison of Fredericksburg was small. The opportunity of seizing the crossing of the Rappahannock passed quickly, for on the day of Sumner's arrival Lee sent part of Longstreet's corps to Fredericksburg, and on the 18th, finding that the whole of Burnside's army was moving east, he told Longstreet to follow with all his men, while Jackson on the 19th was ordered from the Valley to Orange Court-House.

Lee at this time had no intention of fighting Burnside on the Rappahannock. He still sought opportunity for manœuvre, and manœuvre which would enable him to strike at his enemy's flanks and communications. Now Falmouth is barely twelve miles from Aquia Creek, and there would be no opportunity for a blow at a line of supply so short. Therefore, he had it in mind to let Burnside come on and to oppose him behind the North Anna; therefore also, he was in no hurry to bring Jackson to join Longstreet. That these were the thoughts in his mind is shown clearly by his correspondence with Jackson to whom he wrote on November 19th; 'As to the place where it may be necessary or best to fight, I cannot now state, as this must be determined by circumstances which may arise. I do not now anticipate making a determined stand north of the North Anna,' [1] and on November 25th: 'I have thought that if we could take a threatening position on his right flank as a basis from which Stuart, with his cavalry, could operate energetically, he would be afraid to advance. . . . I believe now, if you take a position at Culpeper Court-House, throw forward your advance to Rappahannock Station, and cross the cavalry over the river, the enemy would hesitate long before making a forward movement.' [2] Lee's intention was to watch Burnside, whose plan he had divined as early as the 20th, with Longstreet, and threaten the Federal flank with Jackson. [3] This is merely a variation suitable to the changed circumstances of the plan of November 10th, and implied no danger to Longstreet, who was never intended to fight Burnside alone. But Jackson was not much longer to remain apart. Burnside's pontoons did not reach him till the 25th, and his inaction, a break in the weather, which made the roads bad and that rapid manœuvre necessary for a *coup* by Jackson impossible, together with Davis's desire that Burnside should not be permitted to make further inroads into Virginia, decided Lee to fight at Fredericksburg. So Jackson was brought in, and on November

---

[1] O.R., vol. XXI, p. 1021.   [2] *Ibid.*, p. 1031.
[3] Lee to Davis, Nov. 20th: 'I think Burnside is concentrating his whole army opposite Fredericksburg.' *Lee's Confidential Despatches to Davis*, p. 66.

30th the two armies stood facing each other across the Rappahannock. Burnside had available for battle 122,000 men, Lee 78,000, the largest and most efficient force he had yet controlled. A part only of the Confederates were assembled around Fredericksburg, Jackson's corps being strung out down the Rappahannock watching points of passage, and there during the first days of December it was kept in a state of activity by Burnside's demonstrations.

Lee had ample time to choose and prepare his ground. He determined to oppose the crossing of the river only with detachments, the function of which should be observation rather than fighting, and to accept battle on the wooded heights behind. These were not only tactically strong, but made concealment easy, and indeed the woods which screened Lee's plans were Burnside's undoing. The Federal Commander believed that he had kept Jackson at a distance down the river, and hoped by a sudden crossing at Fredericksburg to overthrow Longstreet and seize the heights west of the town. Lee was far too experienced to be taken in by so simple a plan. It was quite clear to him that a large army could not cross the river and deploy beyond it for attack very speedily, and he was confident that if Burnside attempted to rush Longstreet with a part only of his army, he could be held off long enough to allow Jackson to come up. But Burnside made no attempt to rush the position. His army began to cross during the night of December 11th, and the whole of the 12th was occupied with getting it into position. By noon Jackson had brought up the divisions of A. P. Hill and Taliaferro, and had hidden them in the woods, but not till then, when it became certain that the whole of the Federal army was crossing, were his remaining divisions, those of Early and D. H. Hill, summoned, and these were in position by dawn of the 13th. With Lee's whole army opposed to him, Burnside had not even a remote chance of success. He was attacking directly a naturally strong position, which had been artificially strengthened. Had his numbers been twice those of his enemy, the attempt would have been hazardous; with a superiority of only fifty per cent, he was asking of his men the impossible. The attack failed, as it was bound to do, and with very heavy loss. On the 14th the armies watched each other, both expecting attack, and on the night of the 15th the Army of the Potomac recrossed the Rappahannock.

Lee has been considerably criticised for his failure to exploit his victory. In the South there was bitter disappointment. As Rhodes puts it: 'The feeling in regard to Lee might have found expression in the words of Barcas, a Carthaginian, after the Battle of Cannæ. "You know how to gain a victory, but not how to use it." [1] This criticism, which is not Rhodes' but that of the

[1] Rhodes: *History of the United States*, vol. IV, p. 198.

Southern press, is amateur. One of the reasons Lee had not wished to fight at Fredericksburg was that he remembered the experience of the Antietam, and knew that the Rappahannock would be a bar to the kind of pursuit which makes victory decisive. Jackson had been of the same mind and for the same reason. 'I am opposed,' he told D. H. Hill when he reached the Rappahannock, 'to fighting here. We will whip the enemy, but gain no fruits of victory. I have advised the line of the North Anna, but have been overruled.' [1] It is true that a counter-attack might have been made on the evening of the 13th if Lee had realised that the Federal assaults had come to an end, but these had been so easily repulsed that the Confederates expected more to come, and to have left strong positions prematurely would have been foolish. To have attacked on the 14th would have been still more foolish, for Burnside had then re-formed his men, and on the Stafford Heights behind him had a great mass of guns which would have pounded the Confederates on the open ground. If Lee made a mistake at all, it was in not insisting with Davis on his plan of fighting on the North Anna, but Burnside's experience of the roads of Virginia soon after the battle in what is known as 'the mud campaign,' makes it probable that the weather rather than the Confederate President was the chief influence in Lee's mind.

[1] Dabney: *Life and Campaigns of Stonewall Jackson*, p. 595.

On December 16th, Lee wrote to his wife: 'I had supposed they were just preparing for battle, and was saving our men for the conflict. Their hosts crowned the hill and plain beyond the river, and their numbers are to me unknown. Still I felt a confidence that we could stand the shock, and was anxious for the blow that is to fall on some point and was prepared to meet it here. Yesterday evening I had my suspicions that they might return during the night, but could not believe they would relinquish their hopes after all their boasting and preparations, and when I say the latter is equal to the former, you will have some idea of the magnitude. This morning they were all safe on the north side of the Rappahannock. They went as they came, in the night. They suffered heavily as far as the battle went, but it did not go far enough to satisfy me.' [1] As in this letter, so in all Lee's correspondence about the war, there is a remarkable absence of that exaggeration common in the reports of generals in their victories, and no attempt to take any credit to himself. No one reading this letter and ignorant of the facts would imagine that the writer had just won a victory which had caused acute depression in the North.

Bad weather and worse roads imposed inactivity on the infantry, though on December 26th Stuart succeeded in making yet another of his daring raids behind

[1] Fitzhugh Lee: *General Lee*, p. 255.

the Federal lines, during which he sent a cheeky tele-gram to General Meigs, the Northern Quartermaster General, complaining of the quality of the mules sup-plied to the Army of the Potomac. Burnside's 'mud campaign' came to nothing, and on January 26, 1863, Lincoln replaced him by Hooker. So the winter passed with the armies still on either bank of the Rappahan-nock. It was a hard winter for the Confederacy. At Fredericksburg the meat ration was but a quarter of a pound, and the number of men without boots or blan-kets ran to thousands.[1] There was difficulty in forward-ing even the exiguous supplies authorised for the army, and to make the feeding of the troops easier, Lee con-sented early in 1863 that Longstreet with two of his divisions should go into the district south of the James River. He had agreed that Longstreet should make a prompt attack upon Suffolk, where there was a Fed-eral garrison of 15,000, increased soon to 24,000 and later to 32,000 men. But Longstreet, who had views of his own as to the strategy of the war, finding it hopeless to assault Suffolk, gained the ready assent of Davis and Seddon to his undertaking a prolonged, and as it turned out useless, siege of the place. Ransom's division had already left the Rappahannock to guard the railways from Wilmington and Charleston, to the security of

[1] 'One brigadier reported on Jan. 19, 1863, that of 1500 men reported for duty, 400 were totally without covering of any kind on their feet.' O.R., vol. XXI, p. 1097.

which Lee attached great importance, so that when the next crisis came the Army of Northern Virginia was weaker by nearly 20,000 men than it had been at the battle of Fredericksburg.

With the first breath of spring Lee began again to look northwards to the Potomac. On March 31, 1863, he wrote to General Jones: 'There is no better way of defending a long line than by moving into the enemy's country.'[1] A fortnight later he was telling Davis: 'I think it is all-important that we should assume the aggressive by the 1st of May.... If we could be placed in a position to make a vigorous advance at that time, I think the Valley could be swept of Milroy, and the army opposite[2] be thrown north of the Potomac.' The manœuvre here indicated was less than two months later to be the prelude to the campaign of Gettysburg. But without Longstreet, Lee could not move, and Longstreet was engaged on other plans; so it happened that the initiative fell to Hooker. Hooker's plan was evidently based on a study of Lee's strategy. He had reorganised his army of 130,000 men into a cavalry corps under Stoneman, and twelve infantry corps, of which seven were available for his plan, and he had done much to remove the depression caused by the defeat at Fredericksburg. Stoneman was to copy Stuart, make a wide

[1] O.R., vol. xxv, part ii, p. 680.
[2] Hooker's. O.R., vol. xxv, part ii, p. 725.

détour round Lee's left, and come down upon his communications with Richmond; Sedgwick with three corps [1] was to make a vigorous demonstration against Lee's front at Fredericksburg, while Hooker with three corps [2] marched up the Rappahannock and crossed it and the Rapidan, and came down behind Lee's lines of defence through the Wilderness to Chancellorsville. There he was to be joined by one of Sedgwick's three corps, [3] and as soon as the demonstration had been developed by another corps, [4] which had in the interval to act as a connecting link between the two bodies, and finally by yet another of Sedgwick's corps. [5] Thus Hooker was following Lee's example in dividing his forces, and, as we know, Lee succeeded in attacking the divided parts separately. Why, then, was what Lee did at the second Manassas right and what Hooker did at Chancellorsville wrong? Certainly not merely because the one succeeded and the other failed. In the first place, Hooker made, on a larger scale, the same mistake which Lee had made after Gaines' Mill. He sent his cavalry off on a distant raid when its absence would certainly be felt in the forthcoming battle. Stoneman started off on April 13th, but was delayed by swollen rivers and bad roads, and achieved very little. It is not true, as has been said, that if he had been at Chancel-

---

[1] Sixth, Third, and First.   [2] Eleventh, Twelfth, and Fifth.
[3] Third.   [4] Second.   [5] First.

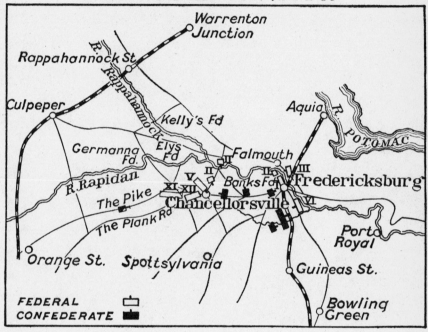

CHANCELLORSVILLE NIGHT APRIL 30TH

Warrenton
Junction

Rappahannock St.

R. Rappahannock

Culpeper

Kelly's Fd

Aquia R.

POTOMAC

Germanna
Fd.

Elys
Fd.

Falmouth

R. Rapidan

II

V

Banks Fd.

III

Fredericksburg

The Pike

XI XII

Chancellorsville

VI

The Plank Rd.

Port
Royal

Orange St.

Spottsylvania

Guineas St.

FEDERAL
CONFEDERATE

Bowling
Green

lorsville he would have altered the issue of that battle by discovering Jackson's movements. These movements were duly observed and reported to Hooker, who misinterpreted them, as we shall see, but the presence of a fine body of cavalry on the battlefield might well have made a material difference in the event. In the second place, it was not safe to try against Lee methods which might well be taken against Pope. But the third and cardinal difference between Lee's manœuvre before the second battle of Manassas and Hooker's at Chancellorsville was the difference in the ground. Hooker had no friendly mountains to screen his march, which was not only fully known to Lee almost from its inception, but its purpose was obvious. Pope had been in doubt as to what Lee was doing, Lee was in no doubt as to Hooker's plan, and 'in vain is the net spread in the eyes of any bird.' Hooker took all possible precautions for secrecy. He did not tell his corps commanders what their destination was until their troops had reached the fords of the Rappahannock; he began his movement under cover of darkness; but this was all in vain unless he could conceal his purpose till he was ready to strike, and that was not, in the circumstances, possible. Then Hooker selected for his deployment the tangled woods of the Wilderness which would make control difficult at the time when control would be most needed. Calculations of time and space, the character of the opposing

general and the quality of his troops, study of the ground
and of obstacles which may be met, the chances of the
object of the plan being discovered, these are all matters which must be weighed carefully before dividing
forces in the presence of the enemy. Lee had weighed
them carefully and correctly, Hooker did not.

The Federal infantry corps began to move on April
27th, and the next day Stuart had informed Lee of what
was up. More news dribbled in during the 28th and
29th, and Lee began to cast anxious eyes back to Longstreet on the James and to the troops about Richmond.
On the 29th he telegraphed to Davis: 'If any troops can
be sent by rail to Gordonsville under a good officer, I
recommend it. Longstreet's division had better come
to me and the troops for Gordonsville and protection of
railroad from Richmond and North Carolina if practicable.' [1] The defect of Davis's system of control was
becoming apparent. The President with all the cares
of the Confederacy on his shoulders could not be expected to deal promptly and effectively with military
problems of this kind, and, as we shall see, he did not.
A responsible military adviser at Richmond with the
courage and capacity to act promptly on his own initiative, if need be, was required to deal with such a situation as arose at the end of April, 1863.

Lee had already called up Jackson from the lower

[1] *Lee's Confidential Despatches to Davis*, p. 84.

Rappahannock to Fredericksburg and had sent Anderson's division to Chancellorsville. It was then clear that Hooker's object was to turn the Confederate left and the positions of the fords marked the lines by which he would move. It was equally clear that Sedgwick's noisy activity at Fredericksburg was a demonstration, and a demonstration which betrays its purpose has little value. When one of Jackson's aides on the 29th brought to Lee news that Sedgwick was crossing the Rappahannock, he answered quietly, 'Well, I heard firing and I was beginning to think that it was time some of you lazy young fellows were coming to tell me what it was about. Tell your good general he knows what to do with the army just as well as I do.' He knew that Sedgwick was feinting. Hooker had failed to mystify and mislead his enemy. Jackson at first thought of attacking Sedgwick at Fredericksburg, but Lee soon convinced him that the Federal guns on the Stafford Heights would be as formidable as they had been in the previous December, so a concentration was ordered in the direction of Chancellorsville, Early's division being left with some reënforcements to watch Sedgwick. On the 30th not only was the general direction of Hooker's turning movement clear, but it had become obvious that he was endeavouring to move through the Wilderness against the Confederate rear. Lee had his counter-plan ready. At noon on the 30th, he telegraphed to Davis:

'Learning, yesterday afternoon, that the enemy's right wing had crossed the Rapidan and his head had reached the position assumed on our extreme left [1] to arrest their progress, I determined to hold our lines in the rear of Fredericksburg with part of the force and endeavour with the rest to drive the enemy back to the Rapidan. Troops were put in motion last night and will soon be in position. I hear nothing of the expected reënforcements.' [2]

Hooker meantime had been moving fast, and late on the night of April 30th he had three corps and part of a fourth concentrated around Chancellorsville, and two others ready to support his left, so that he had some 52,000 ready to fall upon Lee's 46,000, who were not yet concentrated; another 30,000 only waited for his word to come and join him; while Sedgwick with 27,000 contained Early's 10,000. Hooker was delighted with his success, and proceeded to issue a recipe for the cooking of the hare before it was caught. The next day some of the defects of his plan became clear. During his circuitous march which Stuart had faithfully reported to Lee, he had had no certain information of what Lee was doing. Had Longstreet come back from Richmond? He did not know, and doubt is an evil counsellor in battle. So when on May 1st, Lee and Jackson did not

[1] A position near Chancellorsville.
[2] *Lee's Confidential Despatches to Davis*, p. 86.

'ingloriously fly,[1] but instead drove his pickets back into the Wilderness, he hesitated, fell back, decided to await the arrival of his remaining corps and to receive attack, under the impression that Lee must come and drive the Federals from their position to save his communications.

Lee was quite of opinion that this was necessary, but he proposed to do it in a way Hooker had not anticipated. That night he and Jackson, sitting on a couple of ration boxes, discussed the situation. If a direct attack on Hooker in the tangle of the Wilderness was out of the question, it was equally out of the question to sit still and do nothing. Sedgwick would before long discover Early's weakness, and turn him out of his position. So once more it was agreed to adopt the bold expedient of dividing the army in the presence of a superior force. Lee had strongly entrenched his position on the outskirts of the Wilderness, and with the help of these lines he proposed to hold Hooker in front with 15,-000 men, while Jackson with 31,000, including the bulk of Stuart's cavalry, marched round the Federal right, which Fitzhugh Lee, one of Stuart's brigadiers, had discovered was unprotected. The hazard in this plan was less than at first sight appears. Hooker's action on May 1st showed that he was unlikely to attack vigorously the next day. While Lee and Jackson were conferring, the

[1] See Hooker's order. O.R., vol. xxv, part 1, p. 171.

sound of the axes of Hooker's men felling trees for their breastworks could be heard, and the erection of breastworks is not a sign that early attack is intended. When Jackson was in position the distance between the Confederate armies would never be more than seven miles, and would be quickly reduced. Lee had to calculate whether if Hooker attacked him he could hold his lines until Jackson made himself felt, and he had good reason to suppose that he could do this. The danger to Jackson during his flank march was small, as the nature of the Wilderness made it very difficult for Hooker to execute a rapid change of front. Such a movement from an entrenched position is never easy, and when to entrenchments were added the thick woods and dense undergrowth of the Wilderness, it was an all but impossible manœuvre.

Jackson marched off at dawn on the 2d by a track which had been discovered for him during the night. The movement was observed and reported to Hooker, who construed it as the beginning of a Confederate retreat. By 3 P.M. Jackson had his leading troops in position on Hooker's flank, and deploying quickly he overwhelmed Hooker's right consisting of the Eleventh Corps, and threw the whole of the Federal flank into confusion. In the moment of victory Jackson, who had ridden ahead to reconnoitre, fell mortally wounded by his own men.

As soon as the sound of Jackson's guns was heard, Lee began to press Hooker's left front so as to prevent troops from being diverted against the turning movement. Hooker had still sufficient fresh troops at hand to retrieve the disaster, but he was morally overwhelmed.[1] By 10 A.M. on May 3d, the Confederates were in possession of Chancellorsville, and on the next morning, Hooker had fallen back to a defensive position with his back to the junction of the Rapidan and Rappahannock. Meanwhile Sedgwick, in response to an order from Hooker that he should come down on the rear of the retreating Confederates, had on May 3d attacked and carried Fredericksburg and the hills west of the town, but by then Hooker had already acknowledged defeat, and there was no combination between his wings. Leaving three divisions to watch over Hooker, Lee fell with superior numbers on May 4th on Sedgwick, who, finding himself in danger of being hemmed in, retired over the Rappahannock. By the morning of the 6th, Hooker had done the same, and so ended the battle which more than any other displays Lee's faculty for calculated daring.

Given the relative strengths of the opposing armies, Lee's achievement was truly wonderful. Hooker had begun his campaign with 133,000 men, but of these some

[1] He was partially stunned by a cannon shot which struck the verandah of the house in which he was standing.

11,000 of the cavalry under Stoneman had taken no part in the battle. Had that cavalry been in position on Hooker's left covering the exposed flank of his Eleventh Corps, such a movement as Jackson's must have failed and probably would not have been attempted. Reynolds's 1st Corps of 17,000 men, after taking part in Sedgwick's demonstration, marched off to join Hooker, but it arrived too late to affect the issue of the battle. It accomplished little at Fredericksburg and still less in the struggle between the Wilderness and the Rapidan. Like D'Erlon's Corps at Quatre Bras and Ligny, it was of no value on either battlefield. So some 28,000 of Hooker's men were not used. Lee on the other hand used every soldier. He had on the Rappahannock some 56,000 men, considerably less than half of Hooker's command, but in the action which won him victory he flung 31,000 against 13,000 of Howard's Eleventh Corps.

There has been some dispute as to whether the credit for the inception of the manœuvre of Chancellorsville should be given to Lee or to Jackson. In 1867 a Dr. Bledsoe put to Lee the specific question: 'Who originated the plan?' Lee replied: 'I have learned from others that the various authors of the "Life of Jackson" award to him the credit of the success gained by the Army of Northern Virginia when he was present, and describe the movements of his corps or command as independent of the general plan of operations, and undertaken at his own suggestion and upon his own responsibility. I have the greatest reluctance to do anything that might be considered as detracting from his well-deserved fame, for I believe no one was more convinced of his worth and appreciated him more highly than myself; yet your knowledge of military affairs, if you have none of events themselves, would teach you that this could not have been so. Every movement of an army must be well considered and properly ordered, and every one who knew General Jackson must know that he was too good a soldier to violate this fundamental principle. In the operations around Chancellorsville I overtook General Jackson, who had been placed in command of the advance as the skirmishers of the approaching armies met, advanced with the troops to the Federal line of defences, and was on the field until the whole army recrossed the Rappahannock. There is no question as to who was responsible for the operations of the Confederacy or to whom any failure would have been charged.' [1]

Mr. Gamaliel Bradford, in his admirable study of Lee's character, professes to find this letter incomprehensible.[2] I agree with Lee that to any one with a knowledge of military affairs it is as clear as daylight. A very similar controversy has raged in our time as to whether to Joffre or to Galliéni should be given the credit for

[1] A. L. Long: *Memoirs of Robert E. Lee*, p. 253.
[2] Gamaliel Bradford: *Lee the American*, p. 151.

victory in the first battle of the Marne. Joffre, who like Lee has kept aloof from all the controversies which follow war, is reported to have replied to an interviewer: 'Who was in command at the battle of the Marne? Upon whom would the responsibility for failure have devolved?' A reply very similar to Lee's and such as might be expected from a generous commander, who did not wish to detract from the credit due to an able and gallant subordinate. Lee was present at Chancellorsville, he concerted the details of his plan with Jackson on the spot, those details could not be settled until exact and timely information had been received, but the broad lines of the plan were determined long before, as Lee's telegram to Davis of April 30th, which I have quoted above, shows. He then proposed to 'drive the enemy back to the Rapidan.' He would not attack the Federal entrenchments in front as Hooker wanted him to do; he could not turn the enemy's left which rested on the river; it remained for him, therefore, to attack the Federal right, as he did. The plan was Lee's, the execution was Jackson's; both were admirable.

But as usual Lee was not satisfied with himself. He, like Nelson, found no victory great enough which did not end with the destruction of his enemy. He had hoped after driving back Sedgwick to return to the Wilderness and destroy Hooker, and was woefully disappointed when he learned that he had escaped. Had

Longstreet been with him on May 4th, he would almost certainly have been able both to deal faithfully with Hooker and to begin immediately the offensive campaign, for which since his return from Maryland he had been waiting. As he wrote to Seddon,[1] after Chancellorsville nothing could be gained 'by remaining quietly on the defensive.'[2] The consequence of Longstreet's delay at Suffolk had become serious.

I have never been able to convince myself that the effect of Jackson's disablement on the issue of Chancellorsville was as serious as it has, quite naturally, been taken to have been by some of his ardent admirers. It is not easy to see what more the Confederates, in the circumstances of ground and of numbers, could have achieved on the night of May 2d, or during May 3d, than they actually accomplished. Lee, as he said, had lost in Jackson his right arm, but the right arm had done its work at Chancellorsville. Within two months the Confederacy was to realise the truth of Lee's words, and the extent of its loss. Never again were there to be those bold and brilliant manœuvres which had neutralised superiority of numbers and turned doubtful situations into victory. Without Jackson's daring energy, tactical skill, and instant sympathy with and reading of Lee's mind, the combinations of the second

---

[1] J. A. Seddon, Confederate Secretary of War.
[2] O.R., vol. XXVII, part III, p. 868.

Manassas and Chancellorsville were impossible. The quaint prayer of the Confederate chaplain, 'When in Thine inscrutable decree it was ordained that the Confederacy should fail, it became necessary for Thee to remove Thy servant Jackson,' [1] had in it little of exaggeration.

[1] Field: *Bright Skies and Dark Shadows*, p. 294.

CHAPTER VIII

THE SECOND INVASION OF MARYLAND

On May 9, 1863, three days after Hooker had recrossed the Rappahannock, Longstreet rejoined Lee on that river. He had had precise instructions to be ready to move swiftly when the call came, but when it reached him he was occupied with his investment of Suffolk, had sent away his baggage trains, and was in no condition to march quickly. How differently would Jackson have acted in like circumstances! In Longstreet's absence Lee had neither the numbers nor the fresh troops to make an immediate campaign of an offensive character possible, and the victory of Chancellorsville, like that of Fredericksburg, yielded the Confederacy no substantial results. After the latter battle, Burnside, and after the former, Hooker, remained on the Rappahannock in superior force.

Lee was still convinced that the one way for the Confederacy to obtain the peace which it sought was to convince the public opinion of the North that the attempt to keep the South within the Union was not worth its cost, and that the surest way to bring that about was to win a victory on Northern territory. It has been suggested that, after Chancellorsville, he was disposed to seek a peace of accommodation, and that it was Davis who was then responsible for the continuance of the war. The only justification for this inference is Lee's letter to Davis of June 10th: 'We should neglect no honourable means of weakening and dividing our enemies. We should give all the encouragement we can, consistently with truth, to the rising peace party in the North. Nor do I think that we should in this connection make nice distinctions between those that declare for peace unconditionally and those who advocate it as a means of restoring the Union, however much we may prefer the former.' This letter is in fact a justification of the policy of the Gettysburg campaign, and is an example of Lee's far-sighted views. He saw clearly that defeat of the Northern armies was but a means to an end, and the end was the weakening of the *moral* of the people of the North. No commander has ever subordinated himself and his views to those of his political chief more loyally than did Lee, and but few commanders have seen more clearly what should be the political aim of his military operations. The remainder of this letter to Davis shows beyond possible doubt that he was opposed to any accommodation which would impair the independence of the Southern Confederacy, for he went on: 'When peace is proposed to us, it will be time enough to discuss its terms, and it is not the part of prudence to spurn the proposition in advance, merely because those who wish to make it believe, or affect to believe, that it will result in bringing us back to the Union. We entertain no such apprehension, nor doubt that the desire of our people for a distinct and inde-pendent national existence will prove as steadfast under the influence of peaceful measures as it has shown itself to be in the midst of war.' [1] What Lee most earnestly de-sired was that political and military strategy should go hand in hand. He had followed most closely political developments in the North, he was aware of Lincoln's embarrassments,[2] and he wished to turn them to ac-count in the prosecution of the war.

Unfortunately for the Southern cause, at the very time when the unity of political and military strategy was most needed, that unity was most conspicuous by its absence. Davis was looking to foreign intervention as the means of saving the South. He was aware that Napoleon III, personally in favour of such action, was only waiting upon England for a lead. He believed, not without some justification, that opinion in the ruling classes of England was steadily moving in the direction he wished, and his agents in London seem to have played the part, not unusual with such men, of supplying him with information which was pleasing rather than cor-rect. He did not grasp the fact that Lincoln's Emanci-

[1] O.R., vol. XXVII, part III, p. 881 *et seq.*
[2] Mr. C. L. Vallandigham, the Democratic candidate for the governor-ship of Ohio, had engaged in a 'stop the war' campaign. He was arrested somewhat arbitrarily by Burnside on May 5, 1863.

pation Proclamation had settled the question of intervention, and that no British Government could go
against the steadily rising tide of popular opinion in
favour of the Northern cause. So while he did not oppose, he had no very great enthusiasm for Lee's policy.
Nor was there greater unity amongst the military ex-
perts. While Lee was all for crossing the Potomac,
Beauregard was no less insistent upon concentrating
the efforts of the Confederacy on a summer campaign
in Tennessee and Kentucky; Longstreet was in favour of
a variant of this programme, and on his arrival on the
Rappahannock must have wearied Lee with his arguments, in which he finally agreed to an invasion of
Pennsylvania, provided that if the strategy was to be
offensive the tactics should be defensive. Torn by conflicting advice, and without a responsible military advisor at his side, Davis did not throw behind Lee either
the full support of his authority or all the available resources of the Confederacy. By June 1st, the arrival of
Longstreet's division and other reënforcements had
brought Lee's strength up to 73,000 men, but a careful
examination of the whole situation in the Confederacy
shows that without incurring any risks which should
not have been accepted with the prospect of winning a
great stake, the Army of Northern Virginia might have
been increased to 100,000 men. It is remarkable that
while Lee was preparing his 73,000 men for the decisive

campaign of the war, 193,000 Confederate field troops were scattered between the Mississippi and the Rappahannock. Lee was the only man in the Confederacy who at this time viewed the war as a whole and with clear eyes. He saw that foreign intervention was a broken reed, and that victory won in distant Tennessee, though it might compel Grant to abandon the siege of Vicksburg, would not affect opinion in Washington in the way he wanted it to be affected. He saw that the South could not wait. He told Davis on June 10th: 'Our resources in men are constantly diminishing and the disproportion in this respect between us and our enemies, if they continue united in their efforts to subjugate us, is steadily augmenting.' [1] He saw that time was on the side of the North, and he was therefore determined to dare all on a great effort, but divided opinions caused him to have smaller means than might and should have been furnished to him. As in the World War, so in the Civil War, while every one in authority was agreed on the principle of concentration at the decisive point, there was divergence of view as to where the decisive point was to be found; Lee held that it was to be found in Maryland,[2] Beauregard saw it in the West, and Davis looked for it in Europe.

[1] O.R., vol. XXVII, part III, p. 881.
[2] I am aware that, on the eve of the surrender of his army, Lee is reported to have said to General Pendleton: 'I have never believed we could, against the gigantic combination for our subjugation, make good

Lee's plan was that which he had outlined to Seddon in the previous March. He proposed to clear the Shenandoah Valley, to use it and the Cumberland Valley across the Potomac as covered avenues of approach into Pennsylvania, and to fight a decisive battle on Northern soil. To begin this plan he had, like Hooker in the Chancellorsville Campaign, first to move to his left in the presence of the enemy strongly posted across the river. This movement was obviously probable and Hooker had foreseen its probability. But in carrying it through Lee had advantages which Hooker had not, or of which he, in the campaign of Chancellorsville, had deprived himself. Lee used his cavalry to picket the crossings over the Rappahannock and prevent prying eyes from watching his columns. Then the Wilderness and the forests southwest of Culpeper Court-House provided him with an admirable screen. He had re-organised his army into three corps under Longstreet, Ewell, and A. P. Hill, much to the annoyance of Longstreet, who objected to the diminution of his own corps which this arrangement entailed, and to becoming one of three instead of one of the two corps commanders of the army. But a division of his army into three parts was, as will be seen, essential to Lee's scheme.

in the long run our independence, unless foreign powers should directly or indirectly assist us.' But again and again in his correspondence he showed that he did not believe that intervention was likely. *Cf.* Long: *Memoirs of R. E. Lee*, p. 416.

Longstreet marched off on June 3d, and Ewell followed during the next two days; both being assembled in the neighbourhood of Culpeper Court-House on the 8th. A. P. Hill was left in the trenches around Fredericksburg with some 20,000 men to convince Hooker, who had 105,000, that the Army of Northern Virginia was still there. Hill with his troops well concealed fulfilled his mission admirably, and on June 6th, Sedgwick, who had been ordered by Hooker to cross the Rappahannock and make a reconnaissance, reported that the Confederates were still in force around Fredericksburg. So it was not until the 10th that Hooker discovered that Lee was moving. The previous day there had taken place at Brandy Station, just northeast of Culpeper, the most considerable cavalry battle of the war, between the corps of Stuart and Pleasonton, who had taken Stoneman's place, in command of the Federal cavalry corps. The action brought Pleasonton more loss than it caused Stuart, and the information obtained by the Federals was somewhat nebulous, but it confirmed Hooker's suspicions and showed that the Union cavalry leaders were beginning to be a match for their formidable opponents. On the 11th, Hooker began to move up the Rappahannock. Lee has again been accused of rashness or of contempt of his opponent in leaving only Hill between Hooker and Richmond. But again examination shows that the risk he took was small. Had Hooker at-

tempted to cross at Fredericksburg in force, the operation must have taken some time, Hill could have fallen
back as slowly as might be behind the North Anna, and
Lee with the bulk of his army round Culpeper could
have attacked Hooker's flank. In fact, Lee would have
brought off, in more favourable circumstances, the manœuvre he had hoped to carry through before Fredericksburg. Hooker had, indeed, proposed to Lincoln that the
right answer to Lee's move would be to attack at Fredericksburg, but the President, with his usual acumen,
and in his racy language, had answered that he 'would
not take any risk of being entangled upon the river, like
an ox jumped half over a fence, and liable to be torn by
dogs in front and rear without a fair chance to gore one
or kick the other.' [1]

Not until he heard that Hooker had begun to move
northwards did Lee send Ewell off toward the Valley.
Then he did indubitably risk, not his army, but his
scheme; for Ewell crossed the Blue Ridge on the 12th,
Longstreet remaining at Culpeper and Hill about Fredericksburg, the distance between each part of the army
being then about twenty-five miles. From the 12th to
the night of the 13th, Hooker could have held Hill, attacked Longstreet, driven in the Confederate centre,
and brought Lee's plan to naught, if his instructions
from Washington had permitted him so to act. In that

[1] O.R., vol. XXVII, part I, p. 31.

JUNE 9TH 1863.

Federals ☐ V

Confederates ■ H.Hill L.Longstreet E.Ewell S.Stuart

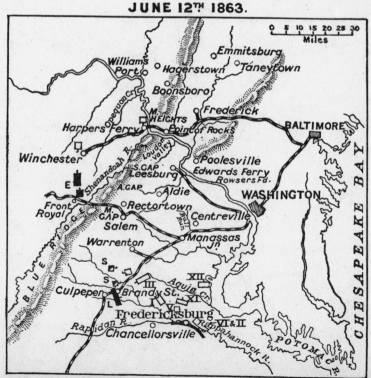

JUNE 12TH 1863.

Federals ☐ VI

Confederates ■ H.Hill L.Longstreet E.Ewell S.Stuart

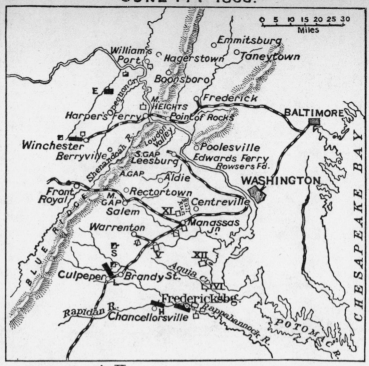

JUNE 14TH 1863.

Miles 0 5 10 15 20 25 30

Emmitsburg
Williams Port
Hagerstown
Taneytown
Boonsboro
E.
Frederick
M. HEIGHTS
Harper's Ferry
Point of Rocks
BALTIMORE
Winchester
Loudon Valley
Berryville
S. GAP
Poolesville
Leesburg
Edwards Ferry
Rowsers Fd.
A. GAP
Aldie
WASHINGTON
Front Royal
Rectortown
M. GAP
Salem
Centreville
XI
Warrenton
Manassas Jn.
Aquia Cr.
V
XII
Culpeper
Brandy St.
III
Fredericksbg
Rapidan R.
H
Chancellorsville
Rappahannock R.
POTOM CR. R.

CHESAPEAKE BAY

Federals ⬜ V
Confederates ◻ H. Hill L. Longstreet E. Ewell
S. Stuart.

JUNE 17TH 1863.

Miles 0 5 10 15 20 25 30

Emmitsburg
Hagerstown
E.
Boonsboro
Martinsburg
Frederick
E.
M. HEIGHTS
Harper's Ferry
Point of Rocks
BALTIMORE
Loudon Valley
S. GAP
Poolesville
Leesburg
Edwards Ferry
Rowsers Fd.
A. GAP
XI
Front Royal
S.
Aldie
XII
L.
Rectortown
I
S.
WASHINGTON
M. GAP
Salem
III
Centreville
Alexandria
Warrenton
II
VI
H.
H.
Culpeper
Brandy St.
H.
Fredericksbg
Chancellorsville
POTOM R.

CHESAPEAKE BAY

Federals ⬜ VI
Confederates ◼ H. Hill L. Longstreet E. Ewell S. Stuart.

case Longstreet would not have stood to be beaten, as some critics have assumed, but Lee would have had to fall back to Gordonsville to unite his army, and Hooker would have gained much territory at little cost. But Lee was aware that Hooker was based on Aquia Creek, and that he could not at once open a new line of supply down the Alexandria railway. He saw that the Federal movement portended a desire to cover Washington rather than a bold enterprise against Longstreet, while previous experience had led him to guess that Hooker would be pretty closely tied to the Capital. So even in this case he incurred no danger of disaster, and no great risk of having his plans upset. On the 14th, Early drove Milroy into Winchester, from which the latter escaped next day to Harper's Ferry, with the loss of half his troops. On the 14th, too, Lincoln wrote to Hooker: 'If the head of Lee's army is at Martinsburg and the rest of it on the Plank Road between Fredericksburg and Chancellorsville, the animal must be very slim somewhere. Could you not break him?' [1] A very reasonable suggestion if armies were without encumbrances and could be moved like chessmen on a board, but both Lincoln and Halleck had already directed Hooker [2] that, if Lee did what he was doing, the Army of the Potomac 'should follow on his flank and on his inside track, shorten-

[1] O.R., vol. XXVII, part I, p. 39.
[2] Lincoln to Hooker, June 10th. O.R., vol. XXVII, part I, p. 35.

ing your lines while he lengthens his,' and this meant a change of base which, when he received Lincoln's suggestion, Hooker was in the act of carrying out. While this was in progress, he could not suddenly attack the parts of Lee's army, and on the 14th he, too, had divided his army, about half of it being in process of concentration around Manassas Junction, and the other half, a tribute to the respect which Stuart raids had inspired, covering the evacuation of Aquia Creek.

From the 14th, then, Lee was for a spell in no danger of attack, while he was transferring his troops and his line of supply into the Valley. On that day Hill began his march from Chancellorsville to Culpeper, and on the 15th Longstreet was moved northward, east of the Blue Ridge as if to threaten Hooker's right, one of the objects of this threat being to cover Hill's march. On the 17th, Ewell's leading troops had crossed the Potomac at Williamsport, and Hill's rear detachment was still near Culpeper. Thus there were seventy-five miles between the head and tail of Lee's army, and the 'animal,' as Lincoln said, was 'very slim somewhere.' Hooker, with his line of supply established on the Alexandria railway, was now free to act. Could he have broken Lee? If any one has the curiosity to sit down with a large scale map and work out the possible combinations of the two armies, he will, I think, find that the answer is 'no.' Longstreet's movement on the 15th was not merely a demonstration against Hooker's flank; it was designed to secure Lee's old friends, the gaps through the Blue Ridge. By the time when Hooker was prepared to attack, Lee had these in his possession, with the single exception of that at Harper's Ferry, where the remnants of Milroy's command held the Maryland Heights on the north bank of the Potomac. It would have been a slow and dangerous movement for Hooker to have passed 100,000 men through the single gap at the Ferry, and Lee was in a position to hold the other gaps long enough to allow him to get his army together in the Valley. A resolute advance toward the gaps by Hooker would have stopped Lee's invasion of Pennsylvania, but it could not have cut the animal in half. I have dwelt at some length on these movements by Lee, because, while they appear at first sight to be foolhardy, and to have been successful only on the assumption that Hooker was incompetent, as he was not, they are in fact a fascinating example of Lee's calculation of risks, and it will be found that for every possible movement by the Army of the Potomac, there was an answering movement which would have removed the apparent danger.

Between the 17th and 20th there occurred numerous encounters along the Bull Run Mountains between the cavalries of Stuart and Pleasonton, but it was not until the later date that Pleasonton with infantry support managed to drive Stuart back to the Blue Ridge at

Ashby's Gap, and by that night the whole of Lee's troops were in the Valley. Two days later Lee made his first serious mistake in the campaign. He wanted to delay Hooker's crossing of the Potomac so as to be sure of anticipating him in Maryland and have time to collect there the supplies he needed. Stuart suggested to him that by moving through the Bull Run Mountains he could get behind Hooker, and cause him such damage as would hinder his passage of the river. He then proposed to pass between Hooker and Washington, cross into Maryland, and rejoin the army in Pennsylvania. Lee agreed and gave him an order which had such momentous consequences that I give it *in extenso:*

Maj. Gen. J. E. B. STUART,
  Commanding Cavalry.

June 23rd, 1863. 5 P.M.

1. General: Your notes of 9 and 10.30 A.M. to-day have just been received. As regards the purchase of tobacco for your men, supposing that Confederate money will not be taken, I am willing for your commissaries or quartermasters to purchase this tobacco and let the men get it from them, but I can have nothing seized by the men.

2. If General Hooker's army remains inactive, you can leave two brigades to watch him, and withdraw with the three others, but should he not appear to be moving northward, I think you had better withdraw this side of the mountain to-morrow night, cross at Shepherdstown next, and move over to Fredericktown.[1]

---

[1] That is, cover the flank of the army in its march into the Cumberland Valley.

3. You will, however, be able to judge whether you can pass around their army without hindrance, doing them all the damage you can, and cross the river east of the mountains. In either case, after crossing the river, you must move on and feel the right of Ewell's troops, collecting information, provisions, etc.

4. Give instructions to the commander of the brigades left behind, to watch the flank and rear of the army, and (in the event of the enemy leaving their front) retire from the mountains west of the Shenandoah Valley, leaving sufficient pickets to guard the passes and bringing everything clean along the Valley, closing up the rear of the army.

5. As regards the movements of the two brigades of the enemy moving toward Warrenton, the commander of the brigades left in the mountains must do what he can to counteract them, but I think the sooner you cross into Maryland after to-morrow the better.

6. The movements of Ewell's corps are as stated in my former letter, Hill's first division will reach the Potomac to-day and Longstreet will follow to-morrow.

Be watchful and circumspect in all your movements.

R. E. LEE, *General* [1]

Now Hooker did not remain inactive. He moved toward the Potomac at once with his army well concentrated. The second paragraph of this order, therefore, was inapplicable. The third paragraph directed Stuart to 'cross the river east of the mountains,' and east of the mountains might be anywhere between the mountains and the sea. It told him to feel the right of Ewell's troops, but did not tell him how soon he was required to do this. It is evident that Lee meant *just*

[1] O.R., vol. XXVII, part III. p. 923. The paragraphs are not numbered in the original.

east, and to have Stuart close on his flank as soon as possible. But it was dangerous to give so vague and general a direction to a commander of Stuart's well-known enterprise and penchant for sweeping raids. It apparently did not occur to Lee that Hooker's army might move promptly, get between his infantry columns and his cavalry, and make it impossible for Stuart to rejoin him in time to be of service. That is what actually happened.

On June 23d, Ewell moved toward Chambersburg and the remainder of the army began to follow him over the Potomac. On the 25th, Stuart started on his expedition round Hooker's rear with three brigades, the remaining two being left to close the gaps of the Ridge and protect Lee's communications and rear. On that day a considerable part of Hooker's army crossed the river, and Stuart had to make a wide détour. Thus the Army of Northern Virginia was almost without cavalry during the march through hostile territory, and while Hooker was well supplied with information as to Lee's movements, Lee knew very little about Hooker's. Four corps of the Army of the Potomac entered Maryland on the 25th, but it was not until the 28th, when Hooker had his whole army concentrated about Frederick, that Lee learned that he was over the Potomac. Upon that day, Hooker, who had had a quarrel with Halleck about the garrison of Harper's Ferry, was replaced in command by Meade.

RELIEF MAP OF THE CUMBERLAND VALLEY
From a photograph of the cast made by A. E. Lehman for the
Cumberland Valley Railroad Company

Lee was now in a dangerous position; believing Hooker's main body to be still in Virginia, he had ordered Ewell toward Harrisburg on the Susquehanna, and his main body was considerably scattered to make it easier to obtain supplies. Upon entering Pennsylvania, Lee had practically abandoned his communications and was living on the rich Cumberland Valley. For this he had made all preparations before crossing the Potomac, and those preparations illustrate the difference between his character and the fierce Puritanism of Jackson, who would have made war as terrible as it could be made. He directed that all supplies should be paid for, ordered his men to have scrupulous respect for the persons of the inhabitants, and for private property, and warned them that offenders would be summarily punished. He wrote to Davis on June 25th that these measures were necessary for military discipline, they were in accordance with the dictates of humanity, and in agreement with his policy, which was to promote a pacific feeling in the North.[1] But these methods, wise as they were, entailed a considerable dispersion of his army, and if dispersion had been devoid of danger during Lee's advance from the Rappahannock to the Valley, it was so only because he was able to watch his enemy, and now he had sent away his eyes. He did not know where Stuart was, Stuart did not know where he was.

[1] O.R., vol. XXVII, part III, p. 930.

On getting the news that Hooker was over the Potomac, Lee early on the 29th decided to concentrate his army. He therefore called back Ewell and sent Hill through and to the east of the South Mountain to act as a flank guard and cover the concentration. On the 29th, too, a division of Federal cavalry under General Buford was approaching Gettysburg which it occupied the next morning. Hill in his rôle of flank guard commander quite rightly endeavoured to investigate the strength of the force in Gettysburg. But Hill was without cavalry, and the small force of dismounted Federal troopers, skilfully handled, gave the impression of being a large body. Hill hesitated, and so the battle of Gettysburg began as it ended, with the Gettysburg Ridge in Federal hands. Had Stuart been present on June 30th, either Gettysburg would have fallen to Hill and the Federal corps would have been defeated in detail, or more probably the battle would have been fought on the South Mountain with Meade forced to attack in order to save Washington and Baltimore. Longstreet would have realised his dream of forcing by offensive strategy offensive tactics on the Federals, and the course of the war would probably have been vastly changed. The Confederate chaplain might have added to his prayer that not only Jackson's death, but Stuart's absence at a critical time, was a necessary prelude to the downfall of the Confederacy. For on June

30th, alarm in the North at the invasion of Pennsylvania was at its height, and it has, I think, been truly said that the Confederacy was never nearer to the peace it wished for than it was at the end of June, 1863. A fatal mistake had robbed Lee of the chance of bringing to fruition the opportunity for which he had been waiting since he recrossed the Potomac in September, 1862.

On July 1st, both armies were concentrating toward Gettysburg as rapidly as might be, for Hill and Buford were drawing their armies after them like magnets, and early that morning Hill began a cautious advance, cautious because he did not know what was in front of him. Buford, again handling his troopers skilfully, kept him off until Reynolds arrived with the First Corps of the Army of the Potomac. Some stiff fighting followed in which the gallant Reynolds was killed, but the arrival of Howard with the eleventh Federal Corps kept the Confederates at bay until Ewell began to come down on Gettysburg from the north, when the Federals were driven from the greater part of the town. Things were going badly with them, for the Confederates were in superior numbers, when Hancock, sent forward by Meade to take command, put new life into the defence. Meade had given him discretion to stand at Gettysburg or fall back on Pipe's Creek, and Hancock, knowing that reënforcements were coming up fast, and realising the natural strength and importance of the ridge south of Gettysburg, elected to hold it.

So far the two commanders-in-chief had done little more than direct their troops toward a place of strategical importance.[1] Neither had yet definitely decided on battle, and the course of events had been directed by their subordinates.

Lee reached the battlefield about 3 P.M., and soon learned that his men were engaged with two Federal corps, and that others were coming up. His troops had gained some preliminary success, but in view of his uncertainty as to the position of Meade's troops he decided not to press on immediately. He had now to consider what he would do next. He had four alternatives open to him. He could fall back on the South Mountains and there await attack, he could await attack where he was, he could move round the Federal left and interpose between it and Washington, and lastly he could make a direct attack on the Federal army where it stood. The first two of these Lee has disposed of in his report: 'It had not been intended,' he says, 'to deliver a general battle so far from our base unless attacked, but coming unexpectedly upon the whole Federal army, to withdraw through the mountains with our excessive trains would have been difficult, and

[1] Gettysburg is the point of junction of roads leading from Washington and Baltimore to the Cumberland Valley and across the Susquehanna to Philadelphia.

dangerous. At the same time we were unable to await an attack, as the country was unfavourable for collecting supplies in the presence of the enemy, who could restrain our foraging parties by holding the mountain passes with local and other troops. A battle had therefore become in a measure unavoidable, and the success already gained gave hope of a favourable issue.' [1] Lee had skinned the Cumberland Valley to feed his 73,000 men, and the greater part of its produce was either in his men's stomachs or in his wagons. When these were empty, he had no immediate means of refilling them. He could not, therefore, allow his adversary to take his own time in offering battle. The harassed Confederate Quartermaster General had said airily: 'If Lee wants supplies, let him seek them in Pennsylvania,' but quartermasters do not always realise how much their proposals affect the strategy of their generals. The poverty in resources of the Confederacy imposed strict limits upon Lee's choice of action.

During the night of the 1st–2d of July, Longstreet, as averse as ever to offensive tactics, urged a movement round the Federal left. But Lee rejected it, and rightly. It was from the direction of Washington that Meade was advancing, and Lee did not know where were the Federal troops, who were marching up to Gettysburg Ridge. Jackson's turning movement at Chancellors-

[1] O.R., vol. XXVII, part II, p. 318.

ville had been justified by exact knowledge of Hooker's position, but to have made a turning movement on July 2d, in the absence of Stuart's cavalry and of all detailed information, would have been wildly rash. It remained then to attack the Federals where they stood. During the night Lee received information that only a part of Meade's army was opposite him. He knew that the two Federal corps which had opposed him had suffered severely, and he decided to attack next morning as early as practicable. Obviously his greatest chance of victory lay in attacking before all Meade's troops were up. Lee's plan was to make his main attack against the Federal left with Longstreet's corps, while Ewell kept their right occupied. This was tactically the soundest plan, but it was a singular misfortune for Lee that the disposition of his troops forced him to entrust it to a lieutenant who was notoriously averse to initiating attack.

I do not propose to repeat in any detail the story so often told of the glorious struggle of the second and third days of Gettysburg. I will confine myself to Lee's leadership in the battle. The evidence that Longstreet received Lee's order to attack as soon as possible on July 2d seems to me to be overwhelming. Lee had been accustomed to deal with Jackson, who needed no more than an indication of his chief's purpose to carry that purpose through with all loyalty, and with the utmost expenditure of effort. But it is remarkable that, knowing Longstreet's character and opinions, he did not himself, or through his staff, work out the time when Longstreet's attack could have been made, and give him an explicit order in writing specifying that time. As it was, Longstreet found numerous reasons for delaying an enterprise he did not like. He says himself that, early on July 2d, 'I went to General Lee's headquarters at daylight and renewed my views against making an attack. He seemed resolved, however, and we discussed results.' Despite his instructions, Longstreet allowed the morning to pass in arranging his troops with little zeal to throw them into battle. Lee watched first impatiently, then anxiously, the opportunity slipping by. He said in Hood's hearing, 'The enemy is here, and if we don't whip him, he will whip us.' Even Longstreet observed that his chief's usual calm was ruffled, and said to Hood, 'The General is a little nervous this morning. He wishes me to attack. I do not want to do so without Pickett. I never like to go into battle with one boot off.' [1] Pickett did not come up till afternoon, but it was for Lee, not for Longstreet, to decide whether it was right to wait for him or not. In the event Longstreet's attack was not made till 4 P.M. Not long after that hour Sedgwick's Sixth Corps began to arrive, and its arrival saved the situation for Meade.

[1] Fitzhugh Lee: *General Lee*, p. 279.

Speculation as to what might have happened in battle if this body of troops or that had acted differently is not of much value, but it seems at least likely that if Longstreet's attack had been made, in accordance with Lee's intention, before noon on July 2d, it would have succeeded. Delivered as and when it was, it had no chance of carrying the ridge. No general has ever given way less to reproaches and recriminations after a defeat than Lee. His one public comment on Longstreet's dilatoriness was, 'General Longstreet's dispositions were not completed as early as was expected.'[1] But to a friend after the war he said: 'Had I had Stonewall Jackson at Gettysburg I should have won that battle';[2] and that is most probably the truth. But if the greater responsibility for failure must rest with Longstreet, a heavy share must devolve on Lee. Longstreet's strong and obstinate character seems to have exercised a curious power over Lee, who a second time failed to control his subordinate as a commander in battle should have done. As his nephew Fitzhugh Lee says of him: 'Lee to the strong courage of the man united the loving heart of the woman. . . . He had a reluctance to oppose the wishes of others, and to order them to do anything that would be disagreeable, and to which they would not consent.'[3] This unwillingness to enforce his will upon

[1] O.R., vol. XXVII, part II, p. 320.
[2] J. W. Jones: *Life and Letters of Lee*, p. 237.
[3] Fitzhugh Lee: *General Lee*, p. 280.

others was a serious defect in Lee's generalship. He failed in the very quality in which Grant so greatly excelled.

Of the further events of the battle it need only be said that Lee, on July 1st, at last succeeded in getting into touch with Stuart, who arrived on July 2d on Ewell's flank with weary men and still wearier horses, and there he was neutralised by a weaker body of Federal cavalry. His enterprise had, indeed, proved costly. Longstreet's attack gained some measure of success, but failed in driving the Federals from the ridge. On the evening of July 2d, Lee was, however, deeply committed; even the possibility of successful retreat depended on fighting the Federal Army to a standstill. He had again and again defeated Federal armies in the field, and it was not to be expected that he would abandon hope of victory while hope remained. As Lee says in his report: 'The result of the day's operations induced the belief that with proper concert of action, and with the increased support that the positions gained on the right would enable the artillery to render the assaulting columns, we should ultimately succeed, and it was accordingly determined to continue the attack. The general plan was unchanged. Longstreet, reënforced by Pickett's three brigades, which arrived near the battlefield during the afternoon of the 2d, was ordered to attack the next morning, and General Ewell was directed to assault the enemy's right at the same time.' [1] 'With proper concert of action' — concert of action had been lamentably absent on July 2d, and it was no more evident on July 3d. The unwilling Longstreet was still entrusted with the supreme effort, and again he refused to put his whole soul into support of his chief, who again failed to give him explicit instructions in writing. The result was the charge of Pickett's men, a charge as futile as that of the Light Brigade at Balaclava, and even more gallant, for to drive home a charge of infantry, 'stormed at with shot and shell,' requires a higher degree of courage than is needed to gallop into hostile ranks. The splendid gallantry of Pickett's 15,000 could never have availed to do more than show the world what glorious failures men will undertake. Whether the 25,000 Lee had meant to assault the ridge would have succeeded may well be doubted, but it is at least certain that the attack was not made as Lee had designed and Longstreet's disbelief in his chief's plan led him to make failure certain. Lee's bitter 'Oh! too bad! too bad!' [2] was, I believe, forced from him by his realisation that it was misunderstandings and blunderings which had sent Pickett's men to their death.

Keenly as he must have felt that if his orders had

[1] O.R., vol. XXVII, part III, p. 320.
[2] Spoken to General Imboden on the night of July 3d.

been carried out the issue would have been different, he showed in that moment of supreme trial a rare nobleness of character. An English officer, Lieutenant-Colonel Fremantle, who was present on the field, says: 'His face did not show signs of the slightest disappointment, care, or annoyance, and he was addressing to every soldier he met a few words of encouragement, such as: "All will come right in the end, we'll talk it over afterwards, but in the meantime all good men must rally. We want all good and true men just now." He spoke to all the wounded men that passed him, and the slightly wounded he exhorted to bind up their hurts and take up a musket in this emergency. Very few failed to answer his appeal, and I saw many badly wounded men take off their hats and cheer him. He said to me: "This has been a sad day, Colonel, a sad day, but we can't expect always to win victories."' [1] A flustered and angry officer came up to report the state of his brigade. General Lee immediately shook hands with him and said cheerfully, 'Never mind, General, all this has been my fault, it is I who have lost this fight, and you must help me out of it the best way you can.' [2] Small wonder that the Confederate army soon rallied after its disaster and that its men were willing to follow their chief to death.

July 4, 1863, is a memorable day in the history of the

---

[1] Fremantle: *Three Months in the Southern States*, p. 266.
[2] *Ibid.*, p. 268.

Union. Upon that day Lee began his retreat from Gettysburg; upon that day Grant received the surrender of Vicksburg. As Lincoln picturesquely put it, 'The father of waters again goes unvexed to the sea.' It was, as Sherman wrote to Grant, for the Union 'the best 4th of July since 1776.' The Union was saved, though few at the time realised the consequences of these two great victories. If Lee had not lost heart, he recognised that his policy of winning peace on Northern soil had failed, and that, with the diminishing resources of the South, the opportunity for trying that policy would never come again. Thenceforth the only prospect for the South was to weary the North into conceding the best possible terms. His retreat from the stricken field was skilfully conducted. Having lost the battle, nothing remained for him but to recover his line of communications with the Shenandoah Valley as speedily as possible. He reached Hagerstown on the 6th, and that day his trains were on the Potomac at Williamsport. But the river had risen in flood and his pontoon bridge had been destroyed, and for some days he had to accept the possibility of another battle with the swollen river in his rear. Meade, however, followed cautiously, and remembering the Antietam was in no hurry to proceed to extremes. He might have attacked with advantage on July 11th, and finally made up his mind to do so on the 14th. During the 13th the river fell, and that night Lee recrossed into Virginia. In his distress he turned as ever to his God, and on the 12th he wrote to his wife: 'The waters have subsided to about four feet, and if they continue by to-morrow I hope our communications will be open. I trust that a merciful God, our only hope and refuge, will not desert us in this hour of need, and will deliver us by His Almighty hand, that the whole world may recognise His power and all hearts be lifted up in adoration and praise of His unbounded loving kindness. We must, however, submit to His Almighty will whatever that may be. May God guide and protect us all, is my constant prayer.' [1] In disaster he blamed no one but himself, and in disaster his faith was unshaken.

[1] Fitzhugh Lee: *General Lee*, p. 306.

CHAPTER IX

DELAY AS A WEAPON OF WAR

FROM the time when Lee sadly recrossed the Potomac after his failure at Gettysburg, a complete change took place in his methods. As I have already said, he never considered the conquest of the North to be an object even worth attempting. Up to July, 1863, he had believed the defeat of the Army of the Potomac on Northern soil to be not only possible, but to be the one sure way of winning for the South the peace it sought; when the sun of July 2d crossed the meridian and its rays shone in the faces of the Federals still sheltering behind the boulders of the Gettysburg Ridge, the chance of a Southern victory north of the Potomac had gone forever, and Lee's strategy sought a new aim. No longer do we find him eagerly creating opportunities to force battle on his opponent, no longer do we see him chafing at the delays which lack of means or inclement weather have imposed upon him. Delay has become a friend and ally to be cultivated and used as skilfully as his first love, offensive manœuvre. The axes and spades of his men are now employed as, when his hopes were higher, were their blistered and bleeding feet. He sees that it is beyond his power to subdue the spirit of the people of the North by the dramatic overthrow of their chief army, but he may, he thinks, wear out their patience. So, though in the summer of 1864 Lee began as aggressive as ever, his attack was a weapon of the defence which was his object, and if his campaigns of 1862 are models of what may be accomplished by bold manœuvre against superior numbers, the campaigns of 1864 are not less remarkable examples of how to hold a strong, active, and skilful enemy in check.

The failure of the second invasion of Maryland was naturally a grievous disappointment to the South, and some of the newspapers of Richmond were free in criticism, not of the commander himself — his reputation was too firmly established — but of his subordinates. Lee on learning of this wrote to Davis on July 31st explicitly taking upon himself the whole responsibility: 'No blame can be attached to the army for its failure to accomplish what was projected by me, nor should it be censured for the unreasonable expectations of the public. I am alone to blame, in perhaps expecting too much of its prowess and valour. It, however, in my opinion achieved under the guidance of the Most High a general success, though it did not win to victory. I thought at the time the latter was practicable. I still think that if all things could have worked out together, it would have been accomplished. But with the knowledge I then had, and in the circumstances I was then placed, I do not know what better course I could have pursued. With my present knowledge and could I have foreseen that the attack on the last day would have failed to drive the enemy from his position, I should certainly have tried some other course.' [1] So after nearly a month's reflection, in the light of fuller information Lee came to the conclusion that the prime cause of his failure was that he had acted on insufficient knowledge of the enemy; he did not see how, with the knowledge he possessed on the battlefield, he could have acted differently, but he did see that he might have had fuller knowledge. [2] Though the blunders and mistakes of some of his subordinates were both grave and numerous, and have given rise to much controversy, his judgment on himself must, I think, be accepted as true. Certainly there have been few men who, with such opportunities for placing blame upon others, have so quickly reached and acted upon a just appreciation of the facts.

Feeling, as he did, Lee resented deeply the continuance of criticism of his army in the Press, and on August 8th he declared to the President: 'I know how prone we are to censure and how ready to blame others for non-fulfilment of our expectations. This is unbecoming in a generous people and I grieve to see its expression. The general remedy for the want of success in a military

[1] *Lee's Confidential Despatches to Davis*, p. 110.
[2] 'The absence of the cavalry rendered it impossible to obtain accurate information. . . . The march towards Gettysburg was conducted more slowly than it would have been had the movements of the Federal army been known.' Lee, July 31, 1863. O.R., vol. XXVII, part II, p. 307.

commander is his removal. This is natural and in many
instances proper. For, no matter what may be the
ability of the officer, if he loses the confidence of his
troops, disaster must sooner or later ensue. I have been
prompted by these reflections now more than ever since
my return from Pennsylvania to propose to Your Excellency the propriety of selecting another commander
for this army. I have seen and heard expressions of discontent in the public journals as the result of the
expedition. I do not know how far this feeling extends
in the army. My brother officers have been too kind to
report it, and so far the troops have been too generous to
exhibit it. It is fair, however, to suppose that it does
exist, and success is so necessary to us that nothing
should be risked to secure it. I, therefore, in all sincerity,
request Your Excellency to take measures to supply my
place. I do this with the more earnestness because no
one is more aware than myself of my inability for the
duties of my position. I cannot even accomplish what I
myself desire. How can I fulfil the expectations of
others?' [1] Lee felt, as every commander-in-chief in the
field who has any sensibility must feel, that he could not
bear his heavy burden of responsibility, that he would
not order men to their deaths, unless he had the confidence not only of his army, but of his Government and
of his people. The *moral* of an army is as delicate a thing

[1] O.R., vol. LI, part II, p. 752 *et seq.*

as the reputation of a woman; it is easily destroyed and without it victory is impossible. Those who lightly set out to loosen the bonds of confidence which must unite a general and his troops do a work more deadly than is accomplished by all the shells and poison gas from an enemy's lines. From Davis promptly came the answer that the confidence of Government and people was unabated, and with this assurance of support Lee began to prepare to apply his new methods of war.

As after the first invasion of Maryland, so now after the second his first care was to use the respite, which the weariness of both armies afforded, to improve the discipline and the meagre equipment of his troops. Desertion was still the cause of gravest anxiety to him and that anxiety he again expressed to Davis on August 17th: 'The number of desertions from the army is so great and still continues to such an extent that unless some cessation of them can be caused I fear success in the field will be seriously endangered. Great dissatisfaction is reported among good men in the army at the apparent impunity of deserters. In order to remove all palliation from the offence of desertion and as a reward to merit I have instituted in the army a system of furloughs, which are to be granted to the most meritorious and urgent cases at the rate of one for every hundred men present for duty.[1] I would now respectfully submit to Your

[1] A similar system was adopted in the Allied armies in France and Bel-

Excellency the opinion that all has been done which
forbearance and mercy call for and that nothing will
remedy this great evil which so much endangers our
cause except the rigid enforcement of the death penalty
in future in cases of conviction.' [1] When we remember
Lee's nature and his well-known aversion to enforcing
the death penalty, this letter is an adequate answer to
those who would make him to be lacking in appreciation
of the importance of discipline.

Of the autumn of 1863 and the winter of 1864 little
need be told. At first both armies needed rest after the
Gettysburg Campaign. Then Lee had to send away
Longstreet and two of his divisions to help restore the
waning fortunes of the Confederacy in the West. Meade
was weakened by the despatch of a considerable detachment from his army to deal with the serious rioting
which had broken out in New York as the consequence
of the enforcement of the Conscription Act of March,
1863. Meade was, therefore, in no hurry to force a battle upon Lee, who did not then desire one, and, when he
was called upon to send off Hooker with two corps to the
West, the Federal commander naturally thought it
prudent to wait. So the two armies watched each other
from either bank of the Rapidan.

gium in the Great War. An extension of the system of furloughs was one
of Pétain's methods of restoring the *moral* of the French army after the
failure of Nivelle's campaign of 1917.

[1] *Lee's Confidential Despatches to Davis*, p. 124.

In October, Lee finding that Meade showed no sign of attacking, started to manœuvre round the Federal right through the familiar ground of the eastern slopes of the Blue Ridge; but when Meade fell back to an entrenched position beyond Bull Run, with the Washington lines close in his rear, Lee, having no desire to assault defences, and no means to cross the Potomac again, fell back behind the Rappahannock. On October 19th, he wrote to his wife: 'Our advance went as far as Bull Run, where the enemy was entrenched, extending his right as far as Chantilly, in the yard of which he was building a redoubt. I could have thrown him back further, but I saw no chance of bringing him to battle, and it would only have served to fatigue our troops by advancing further. If they had been properly provided with clothes, I would certainly have endeavoured to have thrown them north of the Potomac, but thousands were barefooted, thousands with fragments of shoes, and all without overcoats, blankets, or warm clothing. I could not bear to expose them to certain suffering on an uncertain issue.'[1] The picture of his army which Lee here gives must be before our eyes as we approach the story of the continuous and desperate fighting of the Wilderness and of Spottsylvania; we shall then understand what a leader capable of inspiring his men may cause them to endure. The devotion of the Tenth

[1] Fitzhugh Lee: *General Lee*, p. 317.

Legion to Cæsar did not surpass that of the Army of Northern Virginia to Lee.

On November 7th, Meade in his turn started to manœuvre against Lee's right, and forced him back into his lines behind the Rapidan which were too strong to make attack inviting. A fortnight later, Meade made a well-planned attempt to turn those lines, but Lee read his mind and manœuvred his breastworks as rapidly and skilfully as he had his infantry in the days of Jackson's 'foot cavalry,' and Meade found his way barred by defences through which peeped so many Confederate rifles as to put the possibility of a direct assault from his mind. Thereafter Marshal Winter took command, to be succeeded, when Spring came, by the no less masterful Marshal Mud. So, broken by occasional excursions and alarms, Lee's chief labours were the strengthening of his position and the equipment of his ragged men.

On March 9, 1864, Lincoln took a decisive step. He appointed Grant Lieutenant-General in the Army of the United States, and, a measure of greater importance, placed the entire technical control of the war in his hands, with the solemn assurance that he would support him politically and with the whole military resources of the North. Thenceforward the conduct of the war by the North is, as I have already said, in my judgment, the best example in existence of the coördination of political and military effort in a democracy. In acting as he did Lincoln had established unity of command, but he abdicated neither his authority nor his responsibility. He watched Grant as carefully as he had watched any of the commanders of the Army of the Potomac, but he did not interfere with his military conduct of the war. Having found a man, he trusted him, and when the soaring hopes which the public in a crisis always forms of a newly discovered hero were disappointed, he refused to 'swop horses.' Grant spent the months of March and April in great preparation. He planned a coördinated effort for the subjugation of the South, and for the first time in the history of the war there was a common purpose behind the Federal armies in the West and in Virginia. He decided, while leaving Meade in command of the Army of the Potomac, to direct personally its movements against the chief enemy. At the end of April that army was rather less than 130,000 strong and to oppose it Lee had rather more than 60,000 in the Army of Northern Virginia.

Had Lee fallen on the field of Gettysburg, it might perhaps have been difficult to answer the criticism that his successes had been more due to the incompetence of his opponents and to the qualities of his troops than to his own genius. But in 1864 he faced a great soldier in command of an army twice as strong as his, an army, moreover, composed of experienced troops, whose high courage was raised by seeing at their head the conquerer of Vicksburg. As Sherman wrote some years after the war: 'It was not till after both Gettysburg and Vicksburg that the war professionally began. Then our men had learnt in the dearest school on earth the simple lesson of war. Then we had divisions, brigades, and corps which could be handled professionally, and it was then that we as professional soldiers could rightfully be held to a just responsibility.' Grant to innate ability added experience and the prestige of victory, and he handled a well-tempered weapon. Further, the circumstances which I have described gave him the initiative; he could choose how, when, and where to strike. No soldier with any experience of war can fail to understand how priceless an advantage that was. Lee on the defensive had to be forever ready at a moment's notice to anticipate that move even before its purpose was declared. The strain upon a commander in such circumstances is intense; the fortunes of his army and his country depend upon his prescience to a far greater degree than they do when he can choose his course, frame his plan, and march out to attack his foe. The alternatives open to Grant were many. He might repeat McClellan's campaign and land an army in the Yorktown Peninsula; he might strengthen the considerable Federal force at Suffolk and advance on Richmond, south of the James; he might move the campaign to the Valley of the Mississippi; he might elect to direct the operations in Tennessee, or he might, as he did, choose Lee's army as his chief objective. In some of these theatres of war there were many alternative lines of action open to him: in Virginia, he might, for instance, elect to make a direct attack upon the Confederate position on the Rapidan; he might, while holding them in that position by a threat of attack, move past their left down the Valley, or he might endeavour to manœuvre Lee out of his lines by marching on Richmond past his right. The task of reading his opponent's mind was, therefore, no light one for the commander of the Army of Northern Virginia. It was under such conditions that Lee met and checked Grant, and it was because the conditions were such that his generalship in the campaigns of the Wilderness and of Spottsylvania has special distinction.

At first Lee was disposed to think that the publicity given to Grant's appointment and the announcement that he had opened an office in Washington were blinds and that the new commander-in-chief would make Tennessee the theatre of this chief campaign, and on March 25th he so informed the Confederate President.[1] Five days later he began to change his mind, and on the 30th he told Davis: 'Their plans are not sufficiently developed to discover them, but I think we can assume that if General Grant is to direct operations on this frontier he will concentrate a large force on one or more

---

[1] *Lee's Confidential Despatches to Davis*, p. 140.

lines, and prudence dictates that we should make such preparations as are in our power.'[1] He continued to watch Grant as a cat does a mouse, and on April 30th he had come to the conclusion that 'everything indicates a concentrated attack on this front.'[2]

Grant came and looked at Lee's positions on the Rapidan, which in the winter and spring had grown greatly both in extent and in strength. He wished to manœuvre Lee out of them and force him to fight on open ground. Therefore, he determined to cross the Rapidan, below Lee's right, and to march across the Wilderness on Richmond, a manœuvre which he believed would compel Lee either to interpose between him and the Confederate Capital, or to attack him. Lee did attack him, but not as and when he was expected to do so. Grant began to cross the Rapidan at midnight May 3d–4th — a difficult operation, for to get round Lee's right he had to abandon his communications by the Alexandria railway, which ran past the Confederate left, and to carry with him ten days' supplies for his army in some five thousand wagons. To his relief he got over the river without interference, and on May 5th he started confidently on his march southward through the Wilderness.

As he had done before Chancellorsville, so now Lee had been carefully examining the various movements by

[1] O.R., vol. XXXIII, p. 1245.   [2] Ibid., p. 1332.

which his opponent might execute the attack he had foreseen, and had come to the conclusion that the most
probable was that on which Grant had started. At a
conference with his generals he had indicated the fords
of the Rapidan which Grant used as those by which the
Federals would be likely to cross, and was ready to move
quickly when the time to move came. To attack an army
twice as strong as his own seems an extraordinarily risky
proceeding on his part. But as is usual with Lee's plans
the risks are seen to disappear when they are carefully
examined. He decided not to attack while Grant was
crossing the river, because he knew that Grant would
expect to be attacked then and would be ready for him.
He wanted to choose his own battle-ground, and to
strike unexpectedly. He was familiar with the Wilderness, and so were his men. In that tangled forest the
Federal artillery, superior to his not only in number of
guns but also in supply of ammunition, would count for
little, and, if he would not be able to make much use of
his cavalry in such country, Brandy Station had taught
him that Stuart's troopers no longer held the preëmi-
nence which was theirs in '62. But he was influenced
chiefly by his recollection of Hooker's difficulties in
meeting Jackson's flank attack. In striking Grant's
flank, he could choose his avenues of approach and make
it comparatively easy for his men to deploy. Grant, on
the other hand, would have to change front quickly on

ground which he had not chosen, and would find it hard to bring the whole of his army into battle; Lee therefore reckoned that in the actual number of men who would be able to use their weapons he would not be inferior, and might even be superior to his enemy. So early on May 4th he left his entrenched lines and marched with Ewell and Hill in two columns for the Wilderness, to strike Grant's line of march at right angles, while Longstreet was ordered up from Gordonsville to form a third column on Lee's right. On May 5th, Grant, delayed by his long train of wagons, was still in the Wilderness, and there Ewell first struck his flank and so began two days' fierce fighting.

Though Grant and his men had been surprised, and in that forest some confusion was inevitable, there was no such disturbance of the Federal ranks as had followed Jackson's blow in the same country. The men of the Army of the Potomac were now experienced soldiers, and the influence of a leader who knew his mind and kept his head was all that was needed to give them confidence. So when night fell neither side could claim any pronounced advantage. The fights of May 5th showed the change which had taken place in the character of the war. The Southerners had during its progress shown themselves averse to 'niggers' work' and it had been hard to get them to entrench. But by 1864, Lee's teaching and Federal bullets had had effect. In the Battle of the

Wilderness as soon as a position was gained the axes were at work and breastworks sprang up like magic. From these either side, as reënforcements arrived or opportunities occurred, sprang forward to assault the opposite lines, and, if the enterprise failed, the baffled assailants returned to the shelter of their logs. So the front of battle changed but slowly. During the night of the 5th–6th, both the commanders decided to attack the next day, Grant determining to hit his enemy's front everywhere and as hard as possible, Lee to feign attack on the Federal right and drive in Longstreet against his left. But Longstreet was late in his march to the battle-field, and ere he arrived Hancock had made a fierce attack on Hill's lines and captured the greater part of them. Lee, who was with Hill, was quietly riding amongst his men and restoring order when Longstreet's Texans came. He was preparing to lead them in the right direction when a cry broke from the ranks, 'Go back, General Lee! Go back!' and a sergeant seized his horse's head and turned it to the rear. As Fitzhugh Lee says, 'The Texan soldiers were, like Scipio's, ready to die for him if he would only spare himself.'[1]

Longstreet, if tardy in movement, was a fierce fighter and skilful tactician. His attack, well directed, flung back Hancock with heavy loss, and like Jackson he fell wounded by his own men. Again it may be doubted if

[1] Fitzhugh Lee: *General Lee*, p. 331.

the fall of the leader of the successful attack affected greatly the issue of the battle. In such country the general has little control after he has sent his men into action, but it is at least probable that if Longstreet had been ready to assail the Federals at dawn on May 6th, as he might have been, Lee's success would have been more conspicuous. As it was, the issue of the battle was indecisive. That it did not end in a Federal defeat was due to Grant's courage and determination; a lesser man, finding his plan foiled, and unable to shake off a resolute enemy from his flank, would have retreated across the river as on like occasions commanders of the Army of the Potomac had done. Grant decided to advance. During the day of the 7th, the two armies remained behind their breastworks, Grant seeing that it would be useless to assault again Lee's lines. Instead he proposed to continue his march against Richmond, thus forcing Lee to leave his defences and come to meet him. The roads southward from the Wilderness converge on Spottsylvania Court-House, and that was Grant's immediate goal. To conceal his intention from Lee, he did not mean to move his troops till after dark, but he had to get his cumbrous wagon train started in the right direction during the afternoon. The watchful Stuart saw the wagons moving toward Chancellorsville, and at once told Lee, who guessed Grant's intention and ordered Anderson, now in command of Longstreet's

corps, to Spottsylvania. A stroke of good fortune rewarded Lee's prescience. The horrors of the Battle of
the Wilderness had been increased by a forest fire, many
wounded perishing in the flames. The fire spread, and
to avoid it Anderson marched off early and had just
reached a position covering Spottsylvania Court-House,
and supporting the cavalry, which, preceding him, had
skilfully delayed the leading Federal troops, when the
first of Grant's corps arrived. Again breastworks
quickly sprang up, and when Grant reached the front he
found his way barred. Lee had acted as surely and certainly as if he had been provided with a copy of Grant's
orders.

On May 9th, there began the Battle of Spottsylvania,
a nine days' struggle of trench warfare. Many a blunder
made in the Great War might have been avoided if the
lessons of Spottsylvania had been learned, but men are
slow to learn from the experience of others, and soldiers
are amongst the slowest. After spending three days in
tapping at Lee's front and investigating his flanks, Grant
discovered what he thought was a weak spot in the salient, popularly known as the 'Bloody Angle.' This he
assaulted with three divisions on May 12th. If com-
muniqués had been the fashion in 1864, that of May
13th would have read like a hundred of such pronouncements during the Great War. The attack was at first
completely successful; the Confederate lines were

carried, the greater part of Edward Johnson's division was overwhelmed, and the General himself was taken prisoner with several thousand of his men; twenty pieces of artillery were captured. But the preparations for attack had warned the defenders, as preparations for the attack of entrenched positions usually do, and Lee had his reserves ready. They came up led by General J. B. Gordon, and, as in the Wilderness, Lee in his eagerness to restore the battle was preparing to lead them himself. But again his men would not have him expose himself.[1] The counter-charge was made, the Federals were hurled back, and the Confederate line was restored, a portion only of the salient remaining in the hands of the attackers.

Again and again we read in the story of these assaults that the attacking troops were thrown by their very success into confusion, and so fell easy victims to reserves who had escaped the rough and tumble of capturing trenches; again and again we read that the turmoil of the battlefield prevented the arrival of supports in time to enable the assaulting troops to make good their success, or, as the jargon of the Great War had it, 'to consolidate their position.' Grant was learning the lessons which had to be learnt again by many a general between 1914 and 1918, that the problem before him was not how to carry the first lines of his enemy, but how to

[1] Fitzhugh Lee: *General Lee*, p. 336.

beat the reserves behind those lines. The solution he found was much the same as that found by the Allied Generals on the Western Front. By May 11th, the day before the assault on the 'Bloody Angle,' he had written to Halleck: 'I propose to fight it out on this line if it takes all summer.' His assaults were sometimes wasteful of human life, but the principle of wearing down the enemy was sound once that enemy had adopted delay and entrenchment as his means of defence.

Meantime the Confederacy had suffered a grievous loss, and Lee a brilliant lieutenant and true friend. On May 9th, Sheridan started with a large force of cavalry to ride round Lee's flank and rear to Richmond. Stuart on the 11th with two brigades threw himself across Sheridan's path, while a third brigade worried the rear of the Federal cavalry. By this means Sheridan was delayed long enough to allow Bragg to collect troops to man the defences of Richmond and save the Confederate Capital, but in the fighting Stuart was killed. Lee, who felt the loss of Stuart only less deeply than he had that of Jackson, himself penned and issued to his army as fine a tribute as one soldier may pay to another: 'Among the gallant soldiers who have fallen in this war, General Stuart was second to none in valour, in zeal, and in unflinching devotion to his country. His achievements form a conspicuous part of the history of this army, with which his name and services will be forever associated. To military capacity of a high order and to the nobler virtues of a soldier he added the brighter graces of a pure life, guided and sustained by the Christian's faith and hope. The mysterious hand of an All-Wise God has removed him from the scene of his usefulness and fame. His grateful countrymen will mourn his loss and cherish his memory. To his comrades in arms he has left the proud recollections of his deeds and the inspiring influence of his example."[1] At Chancellorsville Lee had lost one who had served as his right arm, and at Yellow Tavern he lost him who had been his ever-observant eyes. More and more as the grim struggle drew to a close had the burden of sustaining the Confederacy to be borne by him alone. I cannot but think that this mental strain was, as much as constant physical effort, the cause of the illness which, keeping him in his tent at a critical moment, was to deprive him of a chance of doing something more than delay his doughty opponent.

After again failing to catch Lee napping on May 18th, Grant decided to abandon his attempts to force the line of Spottsylvania, and to try once more to manœuvre Lee into a position in which he could be compelled to attack to save Richmond or be attacked with more prospect of success. Again he prepared his plans with the utmost secrecy, again he started his movement under

[1] Fitzhugh Lee: *General Lee*, p. 338.

the cloak of darkness, during the night of the 20th–21st, again he reached his destination only to find the Army of Northern Virginia in front of him. But it was not so easy to read Grant's mind as it had been to divine Pope's movements. On May 22d, Lee told Davis: 'The enemy left in his trenches the usual amount of force generally visible and the reports of his movement were so vague and conflicting that it required some time to sift the truth. It appeared, however, he was endeavouring to place the Mattapony River between him and our army, which secured his flank, and by rapid movements to join his cavalry under Sheridan to attack Richmond. As soon, therefore, as his forces on my front could be disposed of, I withdrew the army from its position and with two corps arrived here [1] this morning. . . . The Third Corps [Hill's] is moving on my right, and I hope by noon to have the whole army behind the Annas.' [2] Again Grant was free to choose one of several courses and again Lee had to be prepared to meet each of them. The only definite indication of his opponent's movements which the Confederate commander had was that the Federal base had been shifted to Fredericksburg and this indicated that Grant would continue to manœuvre by his left. Lee, therefore, watching carefully for the signs of a movement round his right, had his plans ready

---

[1] Hanover Junction.
[2] *Lee's Confidential Despatches to Davis*, p. 192.

when his cavalry reported those signs to him. He slipped quickly and quietly away from his entrenchments, keeping his corps so disposed that they could be moved readily in alternative directions, and, moving by the chord while Grant was marching round the arc, was on the 23d in position behind the North Anna as soon as it appeared that the main bodies of the Federal corps were marching toward the crossings over the river. That day Lee wrote to Mrs. Lee: 'General Grant, having apparently become tired of forcing his passage through, began on the 20th to move round our right toward Bowling Green, placing the Mattapony River between us. Fearing he might unite with Sheridan and make a sudden and rapid move upon Richmond, I determined to march to this point [1] so as to be within striking distance of Richmond, and be able to intercept him. The Army is now south of the North Anna. We have the advantage of being nearer our supplies and less liable to have our communications, trains, etc., cut by his cavalry, and he is getting further from his base.' [2] This was true; but if Lee was delaying his enemy and making him pay for the ground he gained, the enemy was steadily drawing nearer to the Confederate Capital.

There were five crossings over the North Anna by which Grant could approach Lee; opposite the Confederate right was the bridge of the Fredericksburg-

---

[1] Hanover Junction.   [2] Fitzhugh Lee: *General Lee*, p. 338.

Richmond railway, and a little to the west of that the Telegraph Road bridge; Lee's centre could be approached by a ford and his left by two other fords. To take advantage of these crossings the army of the Potomac had to advance in several columns. On the 23d, Warren with one of these columns crossed by Jericho Ford, on Lee's extreme left, before A. P. Hill arrived to oppose him. Hill then attacked with a part only of his corps and was repulsed, and Warren at once entrenched the ground he had won. Grant's centre and left, finding the Confederates strongly posted, made no serious attempt to cross. Lee was angry with Hill for letting Warren over the river, and there is little doubt that, if Hill had been more active or Lee himself on the spot, Warren's isolated corps could have been roughly handled. But Lee was beginning to feel the effects of an illness that soon after confined him to his tent, and a chance was missed, for Lee had been reënforced by nearly 9000 troops, including Pickett's division, while, though Grant had also received reënforcements, these hardly made up for the discharges of time-expired regiments.[1]

On the 24th, Lee executed a manœuvre which displays his remarkable capacity for using the accidents of ground. The North Anna makes a pronounced bend

[1] Between May 2d and July 4th no fewer than thirty-six regiments were discharged on the expiration of their terms of service.

NORTH ANNA - MAY 23ᴿᴰ

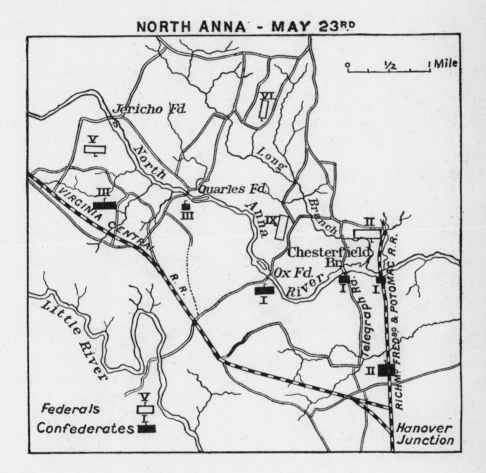

0   ½   1 Mile

Jericho Fd.

VI

V

North

VIRGINIA CENTRAL

III

III

Quarles Fd.

Anna

IX

Long

Branch

II

Chesterfield
Br.

Ox Fd.

River

I

I

I

Telegraph Rd.

RICHMᴰ FREDᴮᴳ & POTOMAC R.R.

R. R.

Little River

II

Federals   V

Confederates

Hanover
Junction

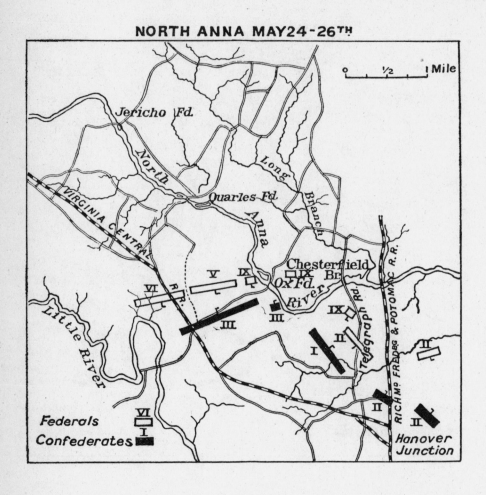

NORTH ANNA MAY 24-26TH

Jericho Fd.

North

Long

Branch

Quarles Fd.

Anna

VIRGINIA CENTRAL

Chesterfield

V

IX

Ox Fd.

Br.

VI

R.R.

River

IX

Little River

III

III

Telegraph Rd.

II

I

RICHMD. FREDBG. & POTOMAC R.R.

II

II

II

Federals

VI
I

Confederates

Hanover
Junction

½   1 Mile

southward near the central ford. The ground on the south bank of this ford and round the bend Lee strongly entrenched and held. He then drew back his flanks, resting them on the Little River which flowed behind him, and these, too, were protected by a series of defences admirably sited. As soon as he found the crossings on the flanks open to him, Grant passed his army over the river in two parts, leaving only one division on the north bank opposite the central ford. He at once found himself in a most uncomfortable position. His wings were widely separated by the bend of the river, and he could not get at the Confederate flanks; he was in fact completely checked. It has been suggested that Lee's illness alone saved Grant from disaster, but, if Lee was entrenched, so was Grant; if Grant could only make a frontal attack, Lee had no other choice; and in spite of his central position Lee was not strong enough to risk frontal attacks on entrenchments. He had baffled Grant, but for the present he could not hope to do more. The opportunity for the Confederates came before Grant had thrown up his works; once they were established, Grant was in no great danger, though he could achieve nothing.

During the night of the 26th, Grant withdrew across the river. Again it has been suggested that, if Lee had not been on his sick bed, Grant would not have escaped, but the experience of the Great War has taught us how difficult it is to detect withdrawals by night from behind entrenchments. There were on both sides between 1914 and 1918 a score of instances of withdrawals made unobserved from positions more perilous than that of the Army of the Potomac on the North Anna.

Having successfully withdrawn, Grant repeated his previous manœuvre. He again used the invaluable command of the sea, which gave the North access to all the estuaries of the Virginian coast, to change his base and shorten his line of communication, and again he marched round Lee's right. As before, Lee followed him on the inside of the circle. On May 31st, Sheridan drove Fitzhugh Lee's cavalry out of Cold Harbour. Now Cold Harbour was of importance because it lay barely five miles east of one of the railways to Richmond, by which Lee drew his supplies, and it was a place from which roads branched out to the bridges over the Chickahominy. Lee, therefore, when he heard that the Federals were there, sensed danger to his right flank and to his communications with Richmond, and determined to drive them out. Sheridan, however, had no difficulty on June 1st in holding off the first Confederate troops which came up, until he was relieved by infantry columns which drove in the troops opposed to him. This preliminary success seems to have had a fatal effect on Grant, for he determined to continue his attacks. Perhaps he was weary of finding Lee always in front of him whenever he attempted to get around the

Confederate right, and lost patience. He meant to renew the battle as early as possible on the 2d, but some of his troops had run out of ammunition, some of them were exhausted by marches in the June heat, and others were not yet in position, so the assault was postponed till the afternoon of June 3d. When it came it failed disastrously, for the delay had given Lee time not only to get his whole army into position, but to erect strong lines of defence. Grant's attack had no more chance of success than Burnside's at Fredericksburg, for he had not the superiority of numbers to enable him to overwhelm the Confederates in a plain frontal attack.[1] Cold Harbour was for him a bloody failure, as he himself recognized. The two armies remained facing each other till the night of June 12th, when Grant marched off for the James River, and so began a new phase in the war.

It had taken Grant rather more than a month to advance from the Rapidan to the Chickahominy, a distance of some seventy miles; he had been made to fight almost the whole way and his casualties amounted to 54,929 men, nearly one half of his effective force at any one period of the campaign. Including the reënforcements he had received from time to time, he had under his orders about 180,000 men,[2] and Lee during the same

[1] The approximate Union strength at Cold Harbour was 108,000; that of the Confederates, 59,000.

[2] Against this figure must be set Grant's losses from discharges which amounted to nearly 20,000 men.

period had commanded 80,000. Therefore the Confederate claim that every soldier in Lee's army had put
out of action a man in the Army of the Potomac is a very
mild exaggeration. If we consider Grant's performance
in the light of recent experience, we will, I think, view it
with more kindly eyes than have some of the critics who
wrote before the Great War. Cold Harbour was a costly
blunder, but it was a blunder in execution as well as in
conception, and for the execution Meade, the actual
commander of the attacking troops, must take a great
share of the responsibility. Despite that blunder, Grant's
campaign had brought the war appreciably nearer its
end, and that justifies his policy of fighting hard and
often. The suggestion that he could have reached
Petersburg without losing a man comes from that wisdom after the event, which it is often easy but rarely
useful to apply to war. If he had followed McClellan's
example and gone round by sea, he would have found
before him a very different army from that which in the
event held the defences of Petersburg and Richmond.
The situation in the middle of June, 1864, was curiously
like that on the Western front in November, 1916, at
the end of the Battle of the Somme. I have not been
able to find any reliable evidence that there was after
Cold Harbour more than such a temporary depression
in the Army of the Potomac as would naturally follow a
reverse. Certainly Grant had not lost confidence either

in himself or in his men. But the heavy tale of casualties had shaken public opinion in the North, and had alarmed many of the politicians in Washington; just as the casualties of the Somme had made the people of Great Britain realise, as they had not realised before, the terrible nature of modern war, and had convinced certain of the statesmen in Downing Street that that battle had been a ghastly and costly failure. Fortunately for the North, they had at Washington a man who had the courage to look beyond lists of casualties, and the imagination to picture the effect of Grant's methods of exhaustion on the South. Lincoln refused to withdraw his support from Grant, and so made victory possible in 1865. Had the Allies possessed the Lincoln of 1864 in 1916, it is well within the bounds of possibility that they could have ended the war victoriously in the following year.

Once the vastly superior resources of the North were applied systematically and resolutely to the prosecution of the war, the end was certain. The fact that, though opposed by system and resolution, Lee accomplished what he did in the summer of 1864 is an index of the quality of his generalship. He began the campaign by forcing upon his opponent battle on ground of his own choice, ground which by its nature neutralised the superior numbers of the Army of the Potomac, and was peculiarly favourable to the Army of Northern Virginia.

He continued the campaign foreseeing every movement which his enemy made, opposing every manœuvre by timely counter-manœuvre. He showed that as a tactician he was, in his employment of entrenchments, years ahead of his time, and as a strategist he never allowed himself to be surprised by an able enemy who throughout held and used the initiative.

If the campaign of 1862, from Richmond to the Potomac, is a model of what an army inferior in numbers may achieve in offence, the campaign from the Wilderness to Cold Harbour is equally a model of defensive strategy and tactics. Some commanders have excelled in the one method, some in the other; few in both, and amongst those few must be remembered Robert E. Lee.

CHAPTER X

THE CATASTROPHE

A STUDY of the actions and reactions of popular opinion under the strain of war, of how far it has been held together by national character, and how far it has been influenced by faith in causes and by dominating personalities, would be both interesting and valuable. For since war on the grand scale has tended more and more to involve the whole resources of the nations concerned, and to be no longer a matter for soldiers and sailors to deal with apart from the rest of the nation, the ultimate object of war has come less and less to be the destruction of the enemy's armies and navies in the field, and more and more the destruction of the will of the opposing people to continue the struggle. There may be circumstances in which it is possible to reach this end without defeating the opposing armies. For example, it is not inconceivable that the people of Great Britain might be forced by continuous air attacks upon the home-land, or by the cutting-off of their supplies of food, to accept the terms of an enemy while their armies were actually victorious in some foreign theatre of war. It is notorious that in Germany it is still a matter of acrimonious dispute whether the German armies were defeated in the field in the Great War, or whether her surrender was caused by the collapse of the will of the people behind the armies.

If I have made myself clear so far, Lee's prime purpose in 1864 will be seen to have been the exhaustion of the patience of the people of the North, and it is highly probable that but for Lincoln and Grant he would have succeeded. It is true that, by his march to and across the James after Cold Harbour, Grant had very nearly out-manœuvred Lee; it is true that but for the lack of enter-prise of a subordinate he might have stormed the lines of Petersburg against Beauregard's gallant handful before Lee arrived. But these things were hidden from the public. They saw that Grant's assaults on those lines were being repulsed, that the tale of casualties was lengthening daily, that their sons were being sacrificed, their treasure exhausted, and that the end appeared to be no nearer than before. They were unable to look beyond their own troubles to the steady exhaustion of the South, which was increasing progressively as the combined plan of attack from north, east and west, devised and directed by Grant, became more and more effectual, and as the last avenues of communication between the South and the outer world were closed by the Federal fleet. They saw that Lee, so far from ap-pearing to be harassed by Grant's costly attacks, had actually detached troops from himself and sent them into the Valley.[1] They saw these troops under Early apparently achieve an even greater measure of success than had been gained by Stonewall Jackson in '62. For Early, after defeating the troops sent to meet him, appeared on July 11th at the gates of Washington. It is possible that with a little more resolution Early might have entered the Capital that evening. He could not have stayed there, for he knew that reënforcements sent by Grant were arriving, but had he entered the Capital, raided the Treasury, and withdrawn, the effect upon the elections then in preparation might have been disastrous. But in July, 1864, there were none of the panic measures that followed Jackson's appearance at Win-

[1] While the campaigns of the Wilderness and Spottsylvania were in progress, Sigel, in command of the Union forces in the Shenandoah Valley, had advanced. He was opposed only by a small force under General Imboden, and to meet this menace General Breckinridge was brought with reënforcements from Southern Virginia. Breckinridge defeated Sigel at Newmarket on May 15, 1864; that is, while the fighting at Spottsylvania was in progress. After this battle Sigel was removed, and General Hunter took command of the Union forces. Breckinridge, too, was withdrawn by Lee and joined him on the North Anna.

Hunter then began to advance triumphantly up the Valley, and on June 5th defeated the Confederate forces near Port Republic, the scene of Jackson's victory of 1862. Having repulsed Grant at Cold Harbour, Lee first sent Breckinridge back to the Valley, and on June 13th despatched Early with his whole corps in the same direction. As in 1862, Lee, while warding off the advance of the main Federal army on Richmond, was also watching the approaches to the Confederate capital from the west, and, as in the days of Stonewall Jackson, thought of defending Richmond by menacing Washington. Hunter had turned eastward from the southern end of the Valley toward Lynchburg, when Early came up and the Federals retreated westward leaving the Valley open. Early then boldly proceeded to spread alarm once more in Washington. He reached Winchester July 2d, crossed the Potomac on July 6th, on the 9th he entered Frederick City, and on the 11th was before the western defences of Washington.

chester two years before.[1] Lincoln trusted Grant, and Grant, though he delayed the despatch of troops to Washington until the very margin of safety was reached, and perhaps passed, refused to be alarmed. Lee's war upon the *moral* of the leaders of the North was no longer successful, but if he failed there his campaign against the *moral* of the people added greatly to the difficulties and perplexities of Lincoln.

I have already drawn more than one parallel between the events of the Civil War and of the Great War. I must here draw yet another. Just as in the late autumn of 1917, Germany's facile success in Roumania appeared to the anxious-minded to show that the desperate and gallant defence of Verdun and the costly assaults of the Somme had been in vain, that those tremendous battles had in fact resulted far more in exhaustion of the Allies than of Germany, so, in the summer of 1864, Early's enterprise seemed to prove to many in the North that Grant's campaign from the Rapidan to the James had been a failure, and, as in the one case so in the other, unofficial negotiators appeared on the scene to urge a peace by agreement. Two of such missionaries from the North appeared before Davis in the middle of July, 1864. To them Davis answered: 'We are not exactly shut up in Richmond. If your papers tell the truth, it is your

---

[1] 'Let us be vigilant, but keep cool. I hope neither Baltimore nor Washington will be taken.' — Lincoln. O.R., vol. xxxvii, part ii, p. 173.

capital that is in danger, not ours. Some weeks ago
Grant crossed the Rapidan to whip Lee and take Richmond. Lee drove him back in the first battle, and then
Grant executed what your people call "a brilliant flank
movement" and fought Lee again. Lee drove him a
second time, and then Grant made another flank movement, and so they kept on, Lee whipping and Grant
flanking until Grant got where he is now. And what is
the net result? Grant has lost 75,000 or 80,000[1] men —
more than Lee had at the outset — and is no nearer
taking Richmond than at first, and Lee, whose front
has never been broken, holds him completely in check
and has men enough to spare to invade Maryland and
threaten Washington; Sherman, to be sure, is before
Atlanta, but suppose he is, and suppose he takes it?
You know that the farther he goes from his base of
supplies the weaker he grows, and the more disastrous
defeat may be to him. And defeat may come. So, in a
military view I should certainly say our position was
better than yours.'[2] Making all allowances for the circumstances in which this statement was made, it repre-
sents very fairly the general opinion in the South at the
time, an opinion shared by quite a number of people in
the North. It is a remarkable tribute to the ascendancy
which Lee had obtained over the minds of his fellows

[1] If discharges and sick be added to the battle losses, this is a fairly
accurate estimate.
[2] Rhodes, vol. IV, p. 515.

of the Confederacy that such should have been their
confidence when war was pinching them more and more
cruelly, and when Grant, with an army increasing in
numbers as Lee's was dwindling, was hammering al-
ternately at the defences of Richmond and Petersburg.

But this very ascendancy proved, owing to faulty
organisation, to be rather a hindrance than an advantage to the cause of the Confederacy. Lincoln was able
to tide over the crisis of the summer and autumn of
1864 because in making emancipation a prime issue of
the war he had created for the North a reserve of enthusiasm upon which he could draw at need, because he
had established a real unity of command, because he
supported his chosen general, and because he left to that
general the technical conduct of the war. Grant had
tried his political chief very highly by his tardy arrangements to meet Early's raid. But in reply to an enquiry
from Grant as to whether the President thought he
should come to Washington, Lincoln answered: 'What I
think is that you should provide to retain your hold
where you are, certainly, and bring the rest with you
personally and make a vigorous effort to destroy the
enemy's force in this vicinity. I think there is really a
fair chance to do this if the movement is prompt. That
is what I think upon your suggestion and it is not an
order.'[1] It would be hard to find in history a finer

---

[1] July 10. O.R., vol. XXXV.I, part II, p. 155.

example of wise restraint. Grant did not go to Washington, but the President's words were not wasted on him. He appointed Sheridan to the command in the Valley, providing him with ample force, and Sheridan both defeated Early and destroyed one of Lee's few remaining granaries. Sheridan's victories in the Valley, Farragut's success in Mobile Bay, and Sherman's capture of Atlanta acted as a wholesome corrective to despondency in the North. Lincoln was triumphantly returned to power and Lee's campaign against the *moral* of the North was finally defeated.

Now let us look at the other side of the picture. To display that completely I must turn back to the events preceding the Battle of Cold Harbour. On May 17th, while Lee and Grant were still facing one another at Spottsylvania, Beauregard, after Butler's ill-planned attempt upon Richmond at Drewry's Bluff, advanced, and, to use an expression of Grant's, 'bottled up' Butler on the south bank of the James.[1] Grant, to whom the command of the sea gave freedom to use the estuaries and safe communications with Butler, ordered the latter to send to the Chickahominy all troops not required to

[1] Part of Grant's concerted plan for the attack upon Richmond was a movement against Petersburg by the south bank of the James. Butler entered the James on May 5th and landed at City Point, in the Bermuda Hundred, near the junction of the James and Appomattox Rivers. Conducting his operations with little skill and prudence, Butler was, on May 16th, defeated at Drewry's Bluff on the James, midway between Petersburg and Richmond, and was there skilfully bottled up by Beauregard in the Bermuda Hundred.

hold his lines against Beauregard defensively, and a corps
of some 16,000 men under Smith joined him before the
Battle of Cold Harbour was fought. Lee was anxious
that at least corresponding reënforcements should come
to him from Beauregard. Now Davis had appointed
Bragg as his chief of the staff, but Bragg had no authority to act in important matters without consulting
the President, and the President was often too occupied
to give his whole mind to military problems, even if he
were competent to solve them correctly. The result was
correspondence and delay, when speedy action was
needed. On May 30th, Beauregard telegraphed Lee in
reply to a request for further reënforcements: 'War
Department must determine when and what troops to
order from here. I send to General Bragg all information I obtain relative to movements of enemy's
troops in front.' Lee at once answered: 'If you cannot
determine what troops you can spare, the Department
cannot. The result of your delay will be disaster.
Butler's troops will be with Grant to-morrow.' And at
the same time he telegraphed to Davis: 'General
Beauregard says the Department must determine what
troops to send from him. He gives it all necessary
information. The result of this delay will be disaster.
Butler's troops (Smith's corps) will be with Grant to-
morrow.' [1] As it turned out, the delays in this instance

[1] O.R., vol. XXXVI, part III, p. 850.

October 7½ P.M. 30 May '64

Genl G T Beauregard
Hancock's House —

If you cannot determine what troops to you
Can spare the Dept Cannot — The result ~~will~~
~~be disaster~~ If you delay will be disaster —
Butler's troops will be with Grant tomorrow

R E Lee

2 7/3 40 Chg

did no harm and Grant was repulsed at Cold Harbour, but a fortnight later the Confederacy was only saved by good luck from having to pay a heavy penalty for a bad system. Lee's telegram to Beauregard was for him unusually petulant in tone, probably because Lee was ill when he sent it. The fault was not with Beauregard. No general likes to take the responsibility of weakening his own front, and Beauregard was not in a position to judge of Lee's needs. Such responsibility can only be taken by some one who is able to view the theatre of war as a whole, and who has authority to decide promptly.

When Grant moved to the James, Lee was for once uncertain as to what his opponent was about. He did not in fact discover the full import of Grant's movements until late on June 16th. On the 15th and 16th, Beauregard at Petersburg was in great danger, and it was Lee who withheld reënforcements from him because he was rather expecting that Grant would advance directly upon Richmond, and was not fully informed of the situation on Beauregard's front. The reputation which Lee had established in the South and the confidence which he inspired was such that Bragg never, and Davis only spasmodically, attempted to direct him when the situation required that the movements of his army should be coördinated with those of other forces. Davis at the very moment when he should have been exercising his functions as Commander-in-Chief to control the situation round Petersburg and Richmond, or have conferred them on some one with the means and authority to use them, was in fact using them disastrously elsewhere. For on June 17th he removed from the command of the army opposing Sherman, J. E. Johnston, who was certainly, next to Lee, the ablest soldier the Confederacy then had, and replaced him by Hood. Lee showed his opinion of this measure when he eventually became Commander-in-Chief by again putting Johnston in charge of the troops fighting his old enemy Sherman, but by then the blunders of Hood had caused injuries which were beyond repair. The story of the Civil War in the latter half of 1864 is, indeed, an example of both how greatly a commander-in-chief is reënforced by a sound system and by the coördination of political and military policy, and of how even the best general is crippled by bad organisation of what in the Great War we learned to call the Higher Command.

This does not mean, as many historians of the war have hitherto assumed, that Grant by his movement to and across the James completely hoodwinked Lee; for the publication of Lee's 'Confidential Despatches to Davis,' which I have freely quoted, proves the contrary. Grant had made up his mind that the best way into Richmond was from the south, and during the night of June 12th he began to move his army south from Cold

Harbour across the Chickahominy toward the James. He took advantage of the Federal command of the sea, as he had done throughout his campaign in Eastern Virginia, to change his base once more, and he embarked a part of his army on the York River and shipped it round to the James. These manœuvres, skilfully screened by Federal troops, were difficult for Lee to discover. A force in ships might be landed at one of a number of places; the direction of trails through the forests and the position of the fords over the rivers could not help Lee, as they had done before, to guess the destination of an enemy moving by sea.

On the night of June 14th, General Smith, with the Eighteenth Corps, had disembarked in the James and joined Butler in the Bermuda Hundred. But that day the rest of Grant's army was so disposed that it might either be going to cross the James or to advance on Richmond by the north bank of the river. At 12.30 P.M. on June 14th, Lee wrote to Davis: 'I have just received your note of 11½ P.M. yesterday. I regret very much that I did not see you yesterday afternoon, and especially after your having taken so long a ride. If the movement of Early meets with your approval, I am sure it is the best that can be made, though I know how difficult it is with my limited knowledge to perceive what is best.[1] I think the enemy must be preparing to move

[1] A very clear hint to the President that effective central direction was needed.

south of the James River, for scouts and pickets yesterday stated that General Grant's whole army was in motion for the fords of the Chickahominy from Long Bridge down, from which I inferred that he was making his way to the James River as his new base. I cannot, however, learn positively that more than a small part of his army had crossed the Chickahominy, and our contest last evening, as far as I am able to judge, was with a heavy force of cavalry and the Fifth Corps of his army.[1] They were driven back until dark, as I informed you, by a part of Hill's corps. Presuming that this force was either the advance of his army, or the cover behind which it would move to James River, I prepared to attack it again this morning, but it disappeared from before us during the night, and as far as we can judge from the statements of prisoners it has gone to Harrison's Landing.[2] The force of cavalry here was pressed forward early this morning, but as yet no satisfactory information has been obtained. It may be General Grant's intention to place his army within the fortifications around Harrison's Landing, which I believe still stand, and where by the aid of his gunboats he could offer a strong defence. . . . It is reported by some of our scouts that a portion of his troops marched to the White

[1] This was correct. Grant's cavalry, supported by his Fifth Corps, covered the movement to the James and threatened to advance on Richmond by the north bank of the river.

[2] The scene of McClellan's last stand on the Peninsula.

House, and from information derived from citizens were there embarked.[1] I thought it probable that these might have been discharged men, especially as a scout reported under date of the 9th instant that transports loaded with troops have been going up the Potomac for three days and nights passing above Alexandria. On the night of the 8th, upwards of thirty steamers went up, supposed to be filled with troops; no doubt many of them were wounded and sick men. Still I apprehend that he may be sending troops up James River with a view of getting possession of Petersburg before we can reënforce it. We ought, therefore, to be extremely watchful and guarded.'[2]

It is not often that history allows us so fascinating a peep into the mind of a general trying to divine the intentions of a skilful opponent who has both the initiative and alternative lines of attack open to him. With the care of his own army upon his shoulders, Lee could not do more than place the central authority in possession not only of remarkably accurate information, but also of a very shrewd guess at the enemy's plans. The one important movement of Grant's army of which he was unaware was the shipment of the Eighteenth Corps to the Bermuda Hundred; such is the advantage which command of the sea confers. He foresaw the

[1] Grant's Eighteenth Corps.
[2] *Lee's Confidential Despatches to Davis*, p. 226.

possibilities of such a manœuvre, but he did not know that it was actually taking place when he wrote. Therefore, while he was fearful, and quite rightly fearful, for the safety of Richmond, he was unaware of the danger to which the gallant Beauregard in front of Petersburg was exposed.

Smith, with the Eighteenth Corps and Butler's troops, advanced cautiously against Petersburg on June 15th, but, being ignorant of Beauregard's weakness, he attempted no attack until late in the evening and was then content with driving the Confederates from their front lines. A great opportunity was missed, but it must be remembered that the experiences of Spottsylvania and Cold Harbour had naturally made the Federal generals careful in attacking trenches.

Three hours after the despatch to Davis of the letter of June 14th which I have quoted, Lee, with more definite information of the enemy's movement, wrote to him: 'As far as I can judge from the information I have received, General Grant has moved his army to James River in the vicinity of Westover. A portion of it I am told moved to Wilcox's Landing, a short distance below. I see no indications of his attacking me on this side of the river,[1] though, of course, I cannot know positively. As his facilities for crossing the river and taking possession of Petersburg are great, and as I think it will more

---

[1] The north bank of the James.

probably be his plan I have sent General Hoke with his command to a point above Drewry's Bluff ... He will execute any orders you may send him there.' [1] Hoke's division reached Beauregard on the evening of the 15th, but Smith had by then received larger reënforcements and again if he had acted with energy Petersburg must have fallen. As late as 10.30 A.M. on the 16th, Lee wrote to Beauregard: 'I do not know the position of Grant's army and cannot strip north bank of James River.' And at 4 P.M. on that day he was still asking: 'Has Grant been seen crossing James River?' [2] At 7.30 P.M. that evening, Lee wrote Davis: 'I have not learned from General Beauregard what force is opposed to him in Petersburg, or received any definite account of operations there, nor have I been able to learn whether any portion of Grant's army is opposed to him.' [3] Nonetheless on the 16th, Lee had further reënforced Beauregard whose splendid defence just kept Grant at bay until the main body of Lee's army came up and the siege of Petersburg began. Grant had very skilfully kept Lee in doubt; he had refused to be alarmed by Early's demonstration, and his generalship together with the defective organisation of the Confederate Higher Com-

---

[1] Another clear hint that central control was needed. *Lee's Confidential Despatches to Davis*, p. 232.

[2] O.R., vol. XL, part II, p. 1659.

[3] *Lee's Confidential Despatches to Davis*, p. 245. Certain of Beauregard's reports to Lee seem to have gone astray, but it is strange that Davis and Bragg should not have kept Lee informed.

mand very nearly brought him a success, which might
have been decisive.

Until the middle of June, 1864, the methods of Lee
and Grant had been in marked and interesting contrast.
On the one side there was the skilled fencer whose
fascinating blade work was marked by perfect timing,
the result of confident interplay of brain and hand; on
the other side one, who, disdaining the niceties of fence,
took the bludgeon as his weapon and, relying on his
physical strength, careless of pricks, disregarding loss of
blood, at length forced his opponent into a corner in
which he had no room to use his skill of fence. No one
saw this quicker than Lee. Hardly was he established in
the lines of Petersburg than he wrote to the President:
'I hope Your Excellency will put no reliance in what I
can do individually, for I feel that it will be little. The
enemy has a strong position, and is able to deal us more
injury than from any other point he has ever taken.
Still we must try and defeat him. I fear he will not
attack us, but advance by regular approaches. He is so
situated that I cannot attack him.' [1]

The siege of Petersburg dragged on through the
summer and autumn into the winter; knowing as much
as we do now about trench warfare, it is easy to see that,
without a far greater preponderance of artillery than he
possessed, Grant had at no time much chance of carrying

[1] June 21st. *Lee's Confidential Despatches to Davis*, p. 253.

the Confederate lines. The rifles of 1864 were precise enough and could be fired sufficiently rapidly to make assault a dangerous expedient unless the defences had been flattened out and the defenders driven from them by accurate bombardment, or unless the attack could be made in overwhelming numbers and regardless of loss. Throughout the siege Grant's superiority in numbers was rarely more and often less than two to one, while Lee's watchfulness was such, and his handling of his reserves so masterly, that, though Grant was always free to choose his point of attack on a very lengthy front of defence, he was never able to accumulate sufficient strength to crash through the defences. The Battle of the 'Crater' ended in a similar failure to that of the 'Bloody Angle' of Spottsylvania and for much the same reasons.[1] Grant would, indeed, have been better advised to have avoided a direct attack and have relied earlier upon the policy into which he was forced by events of continually extending his left and so gradually cutting off Lee's lines of supply. But his plan of keeping Lee tied to the defences of Richmond and Petersburg, while elsewhere the Federal forces steadily reduced the area from which the troops in those defences could draw men, food, and munitions, was the best possible. Lee's great weapon was manœuvre, and Grant had taken it from

[1] The attack by Grant of July 27, 1864, was begun by the explosion of a mine under the Confederate trenches.

him; events proved that no plan was better calculated to undermine the *moral* of the people of the South. While Lee was free to out-manœuvre his opponents, the Confederacy as a whole was quick to appreciate his generalship and refused to be frightened by continuous loss of territory. But the strain of a prolonged siege, accentuated by privations due to ever-dwindling resources, could not be relieved by the mere repulse of attacks, and, when unkindly nature brought in winter to make the strain heavier and the privations less endurable, the confidence of the South steadily waned. Desertion increased in the Confederate ranks. Until the winter '64–'65 numbers of the Confederate soldiers had gone off during pauses in the campaign to see their wives and families, or to have a look at their farms, but when fighting was resumed numbers of them had come back. Now they left and did not return. The stories of burnt farms and wasted lands, of wives and children pinched by the difficulties of getting food as prices soared and currency became of less and less value, were too much for them. A new symptom of exhaustion of the Confederacy appeared, deserters in increasing numbers, as the avenues of escape from Petersburg to the States of the Confederacy grew fewer, came over with their arms to the Union lines. Lee's anxiety to keep up the confidence of his army, therefore, became as urgent as that to parry Grant's efforts to cut off his communications. 'The struggle,' he wrote, 'now is to keep the army fed and clothed. Only fifteen in one regiment had shoes and bacon is only issued once in a few days'; and again a little later he told Seddon that 'the troops were exposed in the line of battle two days, had been without meat for three days, and in scant clothing took the cold hail and sleet. The physical strength of the men if their courage survives must fail under this treatment.' On November 2d, he said plainly to the President, 'I fear a great calamity will befall us.' [1]

Nor was despondency in the ranks, due to prolonged undernourishment and bad news from home, the sole reflection of the desperate state of the Confederacy. Discontent became more and more pronounced in political circles. One of the most striking tributes that Lee received was the open display of confidence in himself made during these days of stress. In such crises men are not prone to be judicial in criticism, or to be careful in their aim when they fling the stones of abuse, and in the crises of a war the general is an obvious and natural target. But it did not occur, even to the most bitter of the critics, to assail Lee. The grumbling and murmurs were directed against Davis, and important influences were at work to make Lee a dictator. Lee would have nothing to do with such proposals, and when in February, 1865, under pressure from the Virginian

---

[1] *Lee's Confidential Despatches to Davis*, p. 305.

Legislature and from the Confederate Congress, he was made Commander-in-Chief of all the forces of the South, he accepted the office only as the subordinate of the President. His first act in his new position was symptomatic. Few generals have been less inclined than he to resort to such Napoleonic pronouncements as McClellan loved. He relied upon personal influence and example rather than upon words. It is then an indication of his view of the situation that he issued to his men a stirring and finely worded appeal to endure, ending with the words: 'Let us oppose constancy to adversity, fortitude to suffering, and courage to danger, in the firm assurance that He who gave freedom to our fathers will bless the efforts of their children to preserve it.' [1]

Lee has been accused of a certain timidity, a reluctance to accept responsibility, because he refused offers to extend his powers of command, and in particular because he rejected the unofficially proffered dictatorship. I have already indicated that I think he, as a soldier, was well advised to turn his back upon any suggestion that he should be vested with political power. His reluctance to have the scope of his command extended was, I think, due to the form in which the proposals were made him, and are an indication that he understood fully the principles which should govern the organization of

[1] General Orders, no. 2, February 11, 1865. O.R., vol. XLVI, part II, p. 1230.

command. More than once during the war it was suggested to him that, while still commanding the Army of
Northern Virginia in the field, he should simultaneously
control forces in other theatres. He saw that this was
faulty organisation. When he began his advance from
the Rappahannock to Gettysburg, in June, 1863, D. H.
Hill had been, after Longstreet's departure from Suffolk
to join the main army in Virginia, left in command in
the neighbourhood of Richmond. To Hill Lee sent some
general instructions for the guidance of his actions.
Hill replied asking for precise orders, and Lee at once
telegraphed to the President: 'I gave General Hill
discretionary orders from Richmond to apportion his
force to the strength of enemy and send what could be
spared. He declined to act and requested positive orders.
I gave such orders as I could at this distance. Now he
objects. I cannot operate in this manner. I request you
to cause such orders to be given him as your judgment
dictates.' [1] This was to tell the President plainly that
if he was commander-in-chief of the Confederacy he
should increase the functions of that office.

In January, 1865, Davis was subjected to considerable
political pressure to induce him to confer on Lee greater
power, and the President proposed to Lee that he should
take command of all the armies of the Confederacy
while still directing the defence of Richmond and

---

[1] May 29, 1863. *Lee's Confidential Despatches to Davis*, p. 99.

Petersburg. The answer came: 'I received to-night your letter of the 18th instant stating that it had been reported to you that I had changed my opinion in regard to the extension of my duties, while retaining command of the Army of Northern Virginia. I do not know how such a report originated, nor am I aware of having said anything to have authorised it. I do not think that while charged with my present command, embracing Virginia and North Carolina and the immediate control of this army, I could direct the operations of the armies in the S. Atlantic States. If I had the ability, I would not have the time. The arrangement of the details of this army, extended as it is, providing for its necessities and directing its operations engrosses all my time and still I am unable to accomplish what I desire and see to be necessary. I could not, therefore, propose to undertake to do more.' [1]

The reasons Lee here gives why he, when in command of one army, could not command another are of universal application. Yet in the Great War the Germans, during the first march of their right wing through Belgium and Northern France, placed their First Army, commanded by von Kluck, under the command of von Bülow, who at the same time commanded their Second Army, and this was one of the causes of the failure of their initial campaign in the west. Again, in 1917, the

---

[1] *Lee's Confidential Despatches to Davis*, p. 322.

British Army in France and Flanders was placed under the command of General Nivelle, who retained executive command of the French army, and this defective organisation was one of the reasons for the failure of Nivelle's campaign. Such measures lead to disorganisation, not to unity of command. Lee finally accepted the command-in-chief of the Confederate armies because he was assured that such a measure was necessary to restore the waning confidence of the South, but he accepted it with reluctance knowing the arrangement to be a bad one and knowing also that at that stage he could not give up the command of the defenders of Petersburg and Richmond in order to devote his whole attention to the coördination of the military effort of the Confederacy.

It has been said by many competent critics that Lee hung on too long at Petersburg, and that his one chance of continuing the war was to have abandoned Richmond earlier, and joined hands with Johnston against Sherman. It has been suggested by some that Davis's influence kept him tied to Richmond. I can find little evidence of that. That Lee had contemplated leaving the Capital to its fate during the winter is clear. Why, then, did he not do it? The answer is, I think, to be found in his letter to Breckinridge of February 21st: 'You may expect Sheridan to move up the Valley and Stoneman from Knoxville. What then will become of those sections of the country? Bragg will be forced back by Schofield, I fear, and until I abandon James River nothing can be sent from the army. Grant is preparing to draw out his left with the intent of enveloping me; he may be preparing to anticipate my withdrawal. Everything of value should be removed from Richmond. The cavalry and artillery are still scattered for want of provisions, and our supply and ammunition trains, which ought to be with the army in case of a sudden movement, are absent collecting provisions and forage in West Virginia and North Carolina. You will see to what straits we are reduced.'[1] Lee foresaw his opponent's plans as clearly as ever he did, but to counter them he needed an army which could manœuvre with the swiftness and precision of the Army of the Wilderness. He knew in February, 1865, that he had no such army. His men were as ready as ever to die for him, but hunger and exposure had sapped their vitality, their old spring and snap had gone, and Grant's steady pressure on all parts of the Confederacy had made it impossible for him to re-create such a system of supply for a moving army as is the first essential condition of successful manœuvre. On February 24, 1864, Lee wrote to the Governor of North Carolina: 'The state of despondency that now prevails among our people is producing a bad effect upon the

[1] Fitzhugh Lee: *General Lee*, p. 370. General Breckinridge had, when the Confederate Higher Command was reorganized, become Secretary of War.

troops. Desertions are becoming very frequent, and there is good reason to believe that they are occasioned to a considerable extent by letters written to the soldiers by their friends at home. In the last two weeks several hundred have deserted from Hill's corps. . . . The deserters generally take their arms with them. . . . So far as the despondency of the people occasions this sad condition of affairs, I know no other means of removing it — than by the counsel and exhortation of prominent citizens.' [1]

Lee knew that the combined effect of Grant's pertinacious siege, of Sherman's continuous advance through Georgia, of Sheridan's destructive sweep through the Shenandoah Valley, and of the relentless pressure on the coast was breaking the spirit of resistance in the Southern people. Stalwarts there were, who asked nothing better than to continue the struggle as long as life remained, but the will to fight of the people as a whole was ebbing fast. Lee, however, decided to make a last effort to break the chain which bound him. At the beginning of the siege he had told Davis that Grant was so situated that he could not be attacked. But by the middle of March, I believe, he had come to the conclusion that the abandonment of Petersburg and Richmond meant the end, and before resigning himself to that he determined to try one assault upon

[1] J. W. Jones: *Life and Letters of General Robert E. Lee*, p. 359.

the works of the besiegers. The attack was made upon March 25th against Fort Stedman, a strong defence near the south bank of the Appomattox.[1] The attackers entered the fort, but were driven out by a counter-attack and the attempt to stop Grant's envelopment of the Confederate lines failed. On March 26th, Lee wrote the President: 'I have been unwilling to hazard any portion of the troops in an assault upon fortified positions, preferring to reserve their strength for the struggle which must soon commence, but I was induced to assume the offensive from the belief that the point assailed could be carried without much loss, and the hope that by the seizure of the redoubts in the rear of the enemy's main line, I could sweep along his entrenchments to the south, so that, if I could not cause their abandonment, General Grant would at least be obliged so to curtail his lines, that upon the approach of General Sherman, I might be able to hold our position with a portion of the troops, and with a select body unite with General Johnston and give him battle. If successful, I would then be able to return to my position, and if unsuccessful I should be in no worse condition, as I should be compelled to withdraw from James River, if I quietly awaited his approach. But, although the assault upon the fortified works . . . was bravely accomplished, the redoubts commanding the line of entrenchments were

---

[1] The approximate total strength of the Confederate forces in Petersburg and Richmond at this time was 50,000; that of Grant's army 110,000.

found enclosed and strongly manned, so that an attempt to carry them must have been attended with great hazard, and even if accomplished, would have caused a great sacrifice of life in the presence of the large reserves which the enemy was hurrying into position. I therefore determined to withdraw the troops, and it was in retiring that they suffered the greatest loss the extent of which has not yet been reported. I fear now it will be impossible to prevent a junction between Grant and Sherman, nor do I deem it prudent that this army should maintain its position until the latter shall approach too near.... General Johnston estimates General Sherman's army, since its union with Schofield and the troops that were previously in North Carolina, at sixty thousand. I have no correct data upon which to form an estimate of the strength of General Grant's army. Taking their own account it would exceed one hundred thousand, and I fear it is not under eighty thousand. Their two armies united would therefore exceed ours by nearly a hundred thousand. If General Grant wishes to unite Sherman with him without a battle, the latter, after crossing the Roanoke, has only to take an easterly direction toward Sussex, while the former moving two days' march toward Weldon, provided I moved out to intercept Sherman, would render it impossible for me to strike him without fighting both armies.' [1]

[1] *Lee's Confidential Despatches to Davis,* p. 342 *et seq.*

Thus the President was clearly told that withdrawal from Petersburg and that soon was inevitable and that it was a desperate expedient.

I believe that Lee did not leave Petersburg earlier because he knew that to do so would be a measure of despair, and that he left it knowing that the end was near. The retreat from Petersburg began on April 2d. Grant's conduct of the pursuit to Appomattox Court-House was masterly, and Lee's avenues of escape were promptly closed, but it was a pursuit of a force crippled before it began to move.[1] Lee had ridden out from Petersburg with calm face, but despair in his heart. 'How easily I could get rid of this and be at rest. I have only to ride along the lines and all will be over. But it is our duty to live, for what will become of the women and children of the South if we are not here to support and protect them?' On April 9th, when he learnt that his attempt to drive back Sheridan had failed, he said: 'Then there is nothing left me but to go and see General Grant, and I would rather die a thousand

[1] The story given with much corroborative detail by R. H. McKim in "A Soldier's Recollections," p. 265 et seq., that the efficacy of Grant's pursuit is accounted for by the fact that a plan of Lee's proposed retreat, prepared by him, fell into Grant's hands is hard to credit. It seems very unlike Lee either to have prepared such a plan or to have put it, if it was prepared, in the hands of others. It is not in this case a question of an order for the first day's march or for the marches of the first few days but of a plan for the entire retreat. The movements of the Confederate army would necessarily depend on the action of the Federal forces and no one would have been better aware of this than Lee, who never attempted to plan for more than he could forecast with reasonable certainty.

deaths.' So in surrender and defeat ends Lee's career as a soldier. In surrender and defeat, as in victory, he asked himself only — what is right? To the counsellors who would have him take to the mountains and prolong a useless struggle by guerilla warfare, he refused to listen, and to one who said to him, with agony in his heart, 'Oh! General, what will history say of the surrender of the army in the field?' he answered: 'Yes, I know they will say hard things of us: they will not understand how we were overwhelmed by numbers. But that is not the question, Colonel; the question is — Is it right to surrender this army? If it is right, then I will take all the responsibility.' [1]

[1] A. L. Long: *Memoirs of Robert E. Lee*, p. 422.

CHAPTER XI

LEE'S PLACE IN HISTORY

JOMINI, the exponent of Napoleon's strategy, makes, with a happy touch of imagination, his master defend his conduct in war before a tribunal composed of Alexander, Hannibal, and Cæsar. Of these three one fought for a losing cause and his career ended in disaster, but it has occurred to no one to question on that account Hannibal's right to a place between the Conquerors of the old East and of the new West; nor has any historical critic suggested that because Wellington was victorious at Waterloo his generalship should be estimated as highly as that of the man whom he defeated. We must not then allow the final scene of Appomattox to prejudice our judgment of Lee's generalship, nor must our estimate of the worth of the cause for which he fought be permitted to affect one way or the other our opinion of Lee the soldier, though we may fairly make it an important item in summing up the character of Lee the man.

For some time after the close of the Civil War the majority of those who attempted to review Lee's career found it difficult to keep the man apart from the soldier, and were, consciously or unconsciously, moved to enthusiasm for or condemnation of his generalship, by sympathy with or dislike of his political opinions. Thus his qualities were very variously estimated. We have on the one side the warm-hearted hyperbole of old comrades such as General Gordon, who declaimed: 'Even the greatest of captains in his Italian campaigns, flashing his fame, in lightning splendour, over the world, even Bonaparte met and crushed in battle but three or four (I think) Austrian armies, while our Lee, with one army badly equipped and in time incredibly short, met and hurled back, in broken and shattered fragments, five admirably prepared and most magnificently appointed invasions. . . . Lee was never really beaten. Lee could not be beaten! Overpowered, foiled in his efforts, he might be, but never defeated until the props which supported him gave away.' [1] Indeed, the number of Southern writers who have declared Lee to be the equal or even the superior of Napoleon is not small. One, however, of his comrades has been severely critical. 'On the defensive,' says Longstreet, 'Lee was absolutely perfect . . . but of the art of war, more particularly of that of giving battle, I do not think General Lee was a master. In science and military learning he was greatly the superior of General Grant, or any other commander on either side. But in the art of war I have no doubt that Grant and several others were his equals, and on the field his characteristic fault was headlong combativeness.' [2]

[1] J. W. Jones: *Reminiscences*, p. 50.
[2] H. D. Longstreet: *Lee and Longstreet at High Tide*, p. 83.

I would rather suggest that Lee's greatest defect as a general was his unwillingness to control Longstreet, but the latter's testimony is so clouded and influenced by bitter controversy that we may dismiss it as, for our purpose, unreliable.

Of contemporary opinion on the other side, by far the most important is that of Grant. During his voyage round the world he is reported to have said to his friend, J. R. Young: 'I never ranked Lee so high as some others in the army; that is to say I never had so much anxiety when he was in my front as when Joe Johnston was in front. Lee was a good man, a fair commander, who had everything in his favour. He was a man who needed sunshine . . . Lee was of a slow, cautious nature, without imagination, or humour, always the same, with grave dignity. I never could see in his achievements what justified his reputation. The illusion that heavy odds beat him will not stand the ultimate light of history. I know it is not true. Lee was a good deal of a head-quarters general, from what I can hear and from what his officers say. He was almost too old for active service — the best service in the field.' [1] Any opinion coming from such a source must be treated with respect, but in weighing it, we must remember that Grant never met Lee until after the Confederate failure at Gettysburg, when Lee was confined strategically to the defensive, and was

[1] J. R. Young: *Around the World with General Grant*, vol. II. p. 459.

therefore fighting with one arm tied behind his back. Grant would hardly, had he when he spoke known more of the facts, have described the man who designed the campaigns which drove McClellan from the Peninsula, routed Pope, and defeated Hooker, as lacking in imagination, and we may legitimately be surprised that he should have discovered the lack of that quality in the general who foresaw, and met in time, his advance through the Wilderness, his movement to Spottsylvania, his attempt to cross the North Anna, and his subsequent flank march on Richmond. I will return to Grant's criticism when I have considered some of the more recent commentators of Lee's campaigns.

As time has passed, so have the bitter feelings which all war, and in an especial degree civil war, arouses, and we have had from both sides a number of admirable and judicial studies of Lee's campaigns. Allan and Alexander on the one side, Swinton and Palfrey on the other, have succeeded remarkably in freeing themselves from prejudice, while in more recent days Ropes, W. R. Livermore, and Rhodes have patently endeavoured to be temperate and fair in judgment. But these latter historians, from the very fact that they have told their story from the Northern point of view, have not always been able to devote the space needed for an exposition of the qualities of Lee's generalship. With Ropes's chief criticism of Lee, a criticism which Livermore accepts, I

have already endeavoured to deal. Ropes, who pays
many a handsome tribute to Lee's soldierly qualities, in
particular ascribes to him an unjustifiable rashness, a
contempt of the quality of the generalship of his opponents, and of the fighting powers of their men, which
inevitably brought him to disaster. 'It is certainly a
mistake,' he writes, 'for a general to overestimate his
adversary's strength and powers; and it is no less a mistake, however, to underrate them. But this was, as we
know, the habit of General Lee's mind, and his subsequent successes confirmed him in it. It was not until the
disastrous assault on the heights of Gettysburg that he
found out his mistake.'[1] In respect of this criticism it is,
I think, fair to ask which of Lee's manœuvres was bolder
in conception than his first attack upon Grant in the
Wilderness, remembering, as we put the question, that,
when Lee made that attack, the sun of victory had for
the first time warmed the hearts of the soldiers of the
Army of the Potomac, the clouds of defeat for the first
time chilled the enthusiasm of veterans of the Army of
Northern Virginia. If the view of Gettysburg, which I
have presented, be correct, then it was not rashness or
contempt of his enemy which led him to hurl his men
against the ridge of Gettysburg. He was, through an
initial oversight, dragged into battle against his will,
and being involved in battle had no alternative but to

[1] Ropes: *The Story of the Civil War*, vol. II, p. 352.

attack, though it is true the methods of attack might well have been different. I have condemned Lee's decision to fight behind the Antietam, because no general should fight a battle which is not forced upon him unless the chances of obtaining decisive results are preponderatingly in his favour, and, as I have tried to show, Lee had on the Antietam no chance of routing McClellan's army. But I do not think Lee's decision, in this case, can be condemned on the ground of rashness. His training and skill as an engineer, his quick and accurate eye for the tactical possibilities of ground, showed him at once the defensive strength of the position on either side of Sharpsburg and enabled him to estimate that McClellan would require a greater superiority of force than the Federal commander was likely to possess, if the Confederates were to be driven into the Potomac. At Malvern Hill, Lee attacked rashly, but again it is the method rather than the fact of attack which should be criticised. The Army of the Potomac was retreating, it had been retreating for five days, when it stood to meet attack on Malvern Hill. All the experience of war teaches that the utmost vigour and boldness is not only justifiable but required in a pursuit. I suggest that Lee would and should have been even more criticised than he has been if he had allowed McClellan, after the battle of June 30th, to retreat unmolested to Harrison's Landing.

Of the contemporary foreign critics, the most voluminous, the Comte de Paris, followed the war with the Northern armies and drew most of his information from Northern sources. Of British critics Colonels Fremantle and Chesny were both pronouncedly Southern in their sympathies, while Lord Wolseley, whose opinion of Lee's soldiers I have already quoted, undoubtedly, during his short visit to the Confederate army in 1862, fell under the spell of Lee's personal charm. 'He was the ablest general, and to me seemed the greatest man I had ever conversed with, and yet I have had the privilege of meeting von Moltke and Prince Bismarck. . . . General Lee was one of the few men who ever seriously impressed and awed me with their natural and inherent greatness.' [1] Henderson is the first of British military historians who can be said to have entered upon the study of the Civil War free from any possibility of bias and of any direct association with the participants in the struggle, and, while in his chief work on the war he has skilfully turned the limelight on the picturesque figure of Stonewall Jackson, he has left us in no doubt as to his opinion of Jackson's Chief: 'Lee, with his extraordinary insight into character, had played on Pope as he had played on McClellan, and his strategy was justified by success. In the space of three weeks he had carried the war from the James to the Potomac. With an army that at no time exceeded 55,000 men, he had driven 80,000

[1] Wolseley: *Story of a Soldier's Life*, vol. i, p. 135.

into the fortifications of Washington. . . . So much had
he done for the South; for his own reputation he had
done more. If as Moltke avers, the junction of two
armies on the field of battle is the highest achievement
of military genius, the campaign against Pope has sel-
dom been surpassed; and the great counter-stroke at
Manassas is sufficient in itself to make Lee's reputation
as a tactician. Tried by this test alone, Lee stands out as
one of the greatest soldiers of all times. Not only against
Pope, but against McClellan at Gaines's Mill, against
Burnside at Fredericksburg, and against Hooker at
Chancellorsville, he succeeded in carrying out the operations of which Moltke speaks; and in each case with the
same result of surprising his adversary. None knew better how to apply the great principle of strategy, "to
march divided, but to fight concentrated." . . . It was
not due to the skill of Lee that Pope weakened his left at
the crisis of the battle [of Manassas]. But in the rapidity
with which the opportunity was seized, in the combination of the three arms, and in the vigour of the blow,
Manassas is in no way inferior to Austerlitz or Salamanca.' [1] The result of these reasoned and temperate if
highly laudatory appreciations of Lee's generalship has
been a steady increase, in the Northern States of the
Union, in recognition of Lee's claim to a place among
the great Americans. I have already quoted Charles

[1] Henderson: *Stonewall Jackson*, vol. II, p. 231 *et seq.*

Francis Adams's generous tribute. I will end my survey
of Lee's critics by bringing forward another greater
Northerner. 'As a mere military man,' said Roosevelt,
'Washington himself cannot rank with the wonderful
war-chief who for four years led the Army of Northern
Virginia'; [1] and in another place he declared Lee 'will
undoubtedly rank as without any exception the greatest
of all the great Captains that the English-speaking people have brought forth — and this, although the last and
chief of his antagonists may claim to stand as the full
equal of Marlborough and Wellington.' [2] So in passing
the critics in review, I close much as I began: there is not
much difference between the eulogy of Gordon and the
praise of Roosevelt; as time has passed, the enthusiasm
of the partisan is no greater than that of those in whom
no grain of political sympathy with Lee or with his ·
cause, can be found.

It is curious how many of the comments on Lee
balance one another. Ropes found that Lee 'showed a
singular lack of caution'; Grant found him to be 'of a
slow and cautious nature.' To another critic, who used
almost the same words of Lee as did Grant, Jackson,
the designer with Lee of those very enterprises which
have been most criticised as lacking in prudence, said:
'I have known General Lee for twenty-five years; he is

[1] Roosevelt: *Gouverneur Morris*, p. 52.
[2] Roosevelt: *Thomas H. Benton*, p. 38.

cautious; he ought to be. But he is not slow.' Longstreet maintained that Lee's prime defect was 'headlong combativeness.' Grant thought him to be 'a good
deal of a headquarters general'; his own staff and his
troops were in constant anxiety because of his habit of
exposing himself in battle. 'I wish,' Lee once said,
'some one would tell me my proper place in battle. I am
always told I should not be where I am.' [1] I have already told stories of the feeling of Lee's men, during the
fighting in the Wilderness and at Spottsylvania, as to
their commander's habit of risking his life. During the
'Seven Days' the Confederate President felt called upon
to check that same habit. 'When I remonstrated,' says
Davis,[2] 'with General Lee, whom I met returning from
his reconnaissance, on account of the exposure to which
he had subjected himself, he said he could not get the
required information and therefore had gone himself.'
I have given proof of Lee's frugal life in the field and of
his insistence in refusing the offers of hospitality show-
ered upon him. General Grant's impression of him as an
'office general' seems, indeed, to have been wide of the
truth. So critic answers critic.

And when we have heard the critics, when we have
studied the campaigns, where are we to place Lee among
the commanders of history? I have not attempted to

---

[1] J. W. Jones: *Life and Letters of General Robert E. Lee*, p. 242.
[2] Davis: *Rise and Fall of the Confederate Government*, vol. II, p. 144.

slur over what I believe to have been his mistakes, Stuart should not have been sent off on a wild-goose chase at the beginning of the campaign of the 'Seven Days'; the attack on Malvern Hill should not have been made as it was made; the Antietam was, I believe, an unnecessary battle; the orders to Stuart before the advance to Gettysburg were loosely framed with dire consequences; on two critical occasions Lee failed to control and direct Longstreet as a commander should control and direct a subordinate. Of how many generals who have commanded for three years in the field is it possible to sum up the mistakes committed in so few words?

It may be said that I have omitted Lee's gravest error. He not only espoused, but was the main prop of a cause history has proved to have been wrong. That is the tragedy of his life, and his conduct after the war makes it clear that he realised that it was tragedy. Though, as I have shown, he remained convinced after the war that Virginia had constitutionally the right to secede if she desired to do so, the whole tenor of his life from the surrender of Appomattox to his death is evidence that he believed in his heart of hearts that his State was wrong in exercising that privilege, that the Union was too precious a possession to be sacrificed to the wishes and aspirations of single States. Undoubtedly he believed also that the North was wrong in seeking to keep the Southern States in the Union by force of arms; he hoped up to the moment of the final breach that some means of peaceful adjustment of the quarrel might be found and that the seceding States would, if discreetly handled, return voluntarily to the Union. If he did not doubt that it was his duty to defend his State when she was attacked, after she was beaten he set himself resolutely to make the Union a reality. A few months after the war ended he justified this apparent contradiction to his friend General Beauregard: 'I need not tell you that true patriotism sometimes requires of men to act exactly contrary, at one period, to that which it does at another and the motive which impels them — the desire to do right — is precisely the same. The circumstances which govern their activities change and their conduct must conform to the new order of things. History is full of illustrations of this. Washington himself is an example. At one time he fought against the French under Braddock in the service of the King of Great Britain, at another he fought with the French at York Town, under the orders of the Continental Congress of America, against him. He has not been branded by the world with reproach for this, but his course has been applauded.'[1] Distinguished as was Lee's conduct while an officer of the Army of the United States, splendid as was his career as a general in the field, nothing in his life

[1] Oct. 3, 1865. J. W. Jones, *Life of Lee*, p. 390.

became him more than its end. His resolute refusal, in circumstances of great difficulty and temptation, to take part in any of the controversies which the war evoked, his devotion to the success of his work, as President of Washington University, in training young men of the South to forget the quarrels of the past and to be good Americans, all displayed even more surely than did the tests of the battlefield, high courage, sincerity of purpose, devotion to principle, and nobility of mind. No man took upon himself more earnestly Lincoln's charge, and with real abnegation of self set himself, 'with malice toward none,' 'to bind up the Nation's wounds.' But all this has to do with Lee the man, not with Lee the General.

Generals cannot be ticketed and classified like specimens in a museum, for the problems which each has faced, the conditions under which each has worked, vary so greatly that the prudent historian will not attempt to do more than to place each, judged by his achievements, in a certain group, and the best way of finding the right group for a new candidate for a position amongst the great commanders is to compare him with some other commander for whom history has already found a niche. But before proceeding to that investigation, we must take account of certain circumstances of Lee's campaigns for which no parallel can be found in those of other great commanders. In the first place, Lee

fought almost entirely and gained all his greatest
successes, not only in his own country, but in that part
of his own country with which he was best acquainted.
'If,' said Frederick the Great, 'we had exact information
of our enemy's dispositions, we should beat him every
time'; and he told his generals: 'If I were mindful only
of my own glory, I would choose always to make war in
my own country, for there every man is a spy and the
enemy can make no movement of which I am not informed.' The information which Lee obtained was remarkable for its abundance and its accuracy. Every
Virginian was a spy in his service, and so were many of
the slaves. The Southerners, indeed, from their long
practice in dealing with the negroes, were much better
able to get news from them than were the Northerners,
who found them so unreliable as to be almost useless.
The usual negro answer to a Northern query as to the
strength of a body of Southern troops was 'Guess about
a million.' Again, the fact that the combatants spoke
one language made it far more easy to acquire information than is usually the case in war. A conversation
between two Northern officers, overheard by a Virginian, was instantly understood and often quickly
transmitted to the opposite camp. As I have told, Lee
was saved, during his first invasion of Maryland from
the full effect of the discovery of his plans and orders by
McClellan, by the fact that a sympathiser with the

South was present when the momentous news came to the Northern General. But let us make every allowance for these advantages which Lee possessed; let us even suppose that in the middle of May, 1862, he knew the exact position and strength of each of the Federal forces in Virginia, which is far from being the case; let us take it that he could, as we can now, set out correctly on the map of Eastern Virginia the daily position of each of those several bodies; even then the conception of the manœuvres by which the problems of the defence of Richmond were solved is startling in its brilliance.

There is a further consideration which we must take into account. Lee, as I have shown, was intimately acquainted with many of the commanders by whom he was opposed. But if Lee knew McClellan, McClellan knew Lee; the one could use his knowledge, the other could not. It happened that Lee was at least as successful in foreseeing the movements of Grant as he was in guessing the plans of McClellan, Pope, and Burnside, but he had very little acquaintance with Grant before the war. One of the few recorded meetings of Lee and Grant before they opposed each other in war took place in Mexico during the advance from Vera Cruz. Scott had issued an order that officers coming to Headquarters should present themselves in full-dress uniform. One day Lieutenant Grant came in to Headquarters with a report; he was never at any time very particular about his appearance, and on this occasion he was in field kit, plentifully bespattered with Mexican mud. He was received by Captain Lee, who was as usual faultlessly appointed, and the staff officer sent the infantry lieutenant back to his quarters with orders that he was to return properly dressed. As Grant left the army a few years after the close of the Mexican War, Lee had no further opportunities of getting to know his characteristics.[1]

Having taken account of these two special features of the war in Eastern Virginia, let me proceed with my task. I choose Wellington for my comparison with Lee. In that I make no claim to originality either of method or in the selection of the commander who is to serve as the measure of Lee's generalship. Henderson has, in his 'Stonewall Jackson,' adopted the same method and has chosen the same man. Like Lee, Wellington had to endure the test and strain of long years of war, to create his opportunities for striking, and to use every artifice of offensive and defensive strategy. Both of them were masters in the art of keeping their own counsel and in mystifying and misleading the enemy. Both of them had the faculty of what Wellington called 'Guessing what was going on on the other side of the hill,'[2] though, it

[1] Grant resigned his commission in July, 1854.

[2] If Wellington did not fight in his own country like Lee, the majority of the inhabitants during the campaigns of the Spanish Peninsula and of Waterloo were friendly.

seems to me that Lee perhaps possessed that particular quality of generalship in a higher degree than did Wellington, for Lee was never out-manœuvred, save when his army was almost incapable of manœuvre, as Marmont out-manœuvred Wellington on the Douro and between the Douro and the Tormes in the marches which preceded the Battle of Salamanca, nor as Napoleon out-manœuvred Wellington and Blücher in the opening phase of the campaign of Waterloo. Taking all the circumstances into consideration, and after making every allowance for the special advantages which Lee possessed, I can find in Wellington's campaign no such brilliant example of imaginative strategy, no such bold acceptance of risks, after mature and careful calculation, as brought Jackson to the Peninsula to fight McClellan and kept McDowell defending Washington. Henderson, in a passage which I have quoted, has compared the counter-stroke of the Second Battle of Manassas with that of Salamanca, but it will, I think, be agreed that the counter-stroke of Chancellorsville was more remarkable than either. At Salamanca, Wellington opposed 44,000 men to Marmont's 47,000; at Chancellorsville, Lee overthrew Hooker's 130,000 men with less than half that number.

Nor can there be found in Wellington's campaigns more noteworthy examples of what may be accomplished by defensive strategy and tactics than are to be found

in Lee's campaign of 1864 against Grant. Lee's handling
of entrenchments in that campaign should, if it had been
studied and appreciated at its true value, have marked
an epoch in the history of tactics, but it was fifty years
before the use which trenches might play in manœuvre
was understood as Lee understood it.

As an organiser Wellington was probably superior to
Lee, but the conditions which confronted the two men
were so utterly different that here any just comparison is
difficult. Both men had to create the armies with which
they fought, and, if Wellington was far more abundantly
supplied with the necessary means than was Lee, he had
to meet at once skilled generals and soldiers accustomed
to victory. On the other hand, as the war in Spain continued, and while Wellington's army improved in quality and in experience, the efficiency of the French troops
diminished; for the strain of a prolonged struggle told
upon France and Napoleon's needs in other theatres of
war grew greater and greater. In the Civil War, Lee's
resources like Napoleon's grew steadily smaller and the
efficiency of the troops opposed to him as steadily increased. If the endurance of the Southern troops amidst
privation must stir any heart capable of being moved by
human valour, the stark courage of the Army of the
Potomac, which survived defeat after defeat and carried
its colours to final triumph, is a notable example of that
Anglo-Saxon spirit which never knows when it is beaten.

In one quality of generalship Wellington was incontestably Lee's superior. Both men were supremely self-possessed and self-controlled in the crises of battles. There is little to choose between Wellington's conduct during the long anxious hours of waiting for Blücher on the field of Waterloo and Lee's superb calm when his plans had collapsed at Gettysburg; but Wellington would never have permitted a Longstreet twice to thwart his plans, and as the director of an army in battle he displayed a firmness in which Lee was lacking. In yet another quality Lee was, as incontestably, the Superior of Wellington. Wellington was never loved by his troops as the soldiers of the South loved Lee. The reception of the Confederate Commander-in-Chief by his men, when he returned after his interview with Grant to tell them of the surrender, is, I think, more remarkable than is the story of any ovation accorded by his troops to a conqueror. I cannot improve upon the story of that scene as told by Lee's old comrade General Long:

'When, after his interview with Grant, General Lee again appeared, a shout of welcome instinctively ran through the army. But instantly recollecting the sad occasion that brought him before them, their shouts sank into silence, every hat was raised, and the bronzed faces of thousands of grim warriors were bathed with tears.

'As he rode along the lines, hundreds of his devoted veterans pressed around the noble chief, trying to take his hand, touch his person, or even lay a hand upon his horse, thus exhibiting for him their great affection. The General then, with head bare and tears flowing freely down his manly cheeks, bade adieu to his army. In a few words he told the brave men who had been so true in arms to return to their homes and become worthy citizens.' [1]

Such was the farewell of the army. The farewells of the people of the South, their testimony of devotion, were as extraordinary. Many a victorious general has been welcomed home to the capital of his country by the plaudits of his grateful countrymen, but I know of only one instance in history, of the people flocking to cheer a defeated general. When Lee rode into Richmond, a parolled prisoner of war, he was welcomed vociferously by a crowd of men and women waving hats and fluttering handkerchiefs. The character of the man had placed him, in the hearts of his comrades and his people, above the rebuffs of fortune.

For these reasons then I place Lee as a general above Wellington. 'Read and re-read,' said Napoleon, 'the eighty-eight campaigns of Alexander, Hannibal, Cæsar, Gustavus, Turenne, Eugène, and Frederick. Take them as your models, for it is the only means of becoming a

[1] Long: *Memoirs of Robert E. Lee*, p. 423 *et seq.*

great leader, and of mastering the secrets of the art of war.' To that select band of great commanders the name of Robert E. Lee must be added. His exact precedence amongst them I will not attempt to determine, but that they have received him as a soldier worthy of their fellowship, I do not doubt.

THE END

CHRONOLOGICAL TABLE

CHRONOLOGICAL TABLE

THE CIVIL WAR, 1861–65

EVENTS AND OPERATIONS WITH WHICH GENERAL R. E. LEE WAS CONCERNED

OTHER EVENTS AND OPERATIONS

1861

April 12.
Bombardment of Fort Sumter.

April 20.
Lee resigns his commission in United States Army.
April 23.
Assumes command of naval and military forces of Virginia.
June 14.
Appointed General, Confederate States Army.

July 11.
McClellan's victory at Rich Mountain, Western Virginia.
July 28.
Lee commands Confederate forces in Western Virginia.
July 21.
First Battle of Manassas or Bull Run.
September 12.
Failure of Lee's campaign against Reynolds.

November 5.
Lee commands in South Carolina, Georgia, and Florida (Atlantic Coast).
November 1.
McClellan appointed Commander-in-Chief of Federal armies in the field.

1862

February 6.
Grant captures Fort Henry.
February 16.
Fall of Fort Donelson.
March 13.
Lee ordered to Richmond as chief military adviser of the Confederacy.
March 17.
McClellan's army begins embarkation for Yorktown Peninsula.
March 23.
Jackson's attack at Kernstown.

| EVENTS AND OPERATIONS WITH WHICH GENERAL R. E. LEE WAS CONCERNED | OTHER EVENTS AND OPERATIONS |

1862

April 6–7.
   Battle of Shiloh. General A. S. Johnston killed.

May 3.
   J. E. Johnston retreats from Yorktown lines.

May 1.
   Federals occupy New Orleans.

May 5.
   Battle of Williamsburg.

May 8.
   Jackson wins Battle of McDowell.

May 25.
   Jackson defeats Banks at Winchester.

May 31.
   J. E. Johnston attacks McClellan at Seven Pines and is wounded.

June 1.
   Lee assumes command of Army of Northern Virginia.

June 8.
   Battle of Cross Keys.

June 9.
   Battle of Port Republic.

June 26.
   Pope assumes command of troops in Virginia.

June 26.
   Jackson joins Army of Northern Virginia.

June 26–July 1.
   The Seven Days.

July 2.
   McClellan's retreat ends at Harrison's landing.

August 29–30.
   Second Battle of Bull Run or Manassas.

July 11.
   Halleck appointed military adviser to Lincoln.
   Grant takes command in Tennessee and Mississippi.

September 4.
   Lee invades Maryland.

September 2.
   McClellan placed in command of troops in Washington.

September 15.
   Jackson captures Harper's Ferry.

September 17.
   Battle of the Antietam or Sharpsburg.

September 5.
   Resumes command of Army of Potomac.

September 19.
   Lee recrosses the Potomac.

October 3.
   Battle of Corinth.

EVENTS AND OPERATIONS WITH
WHICH GENERAL R. E. LEE
WAS CONCERNED

OTHER EVENTS AND OPERATIONS

1862

October 8.
Battle of Perryville.

November 7.
Burnside replaces McClellan.

November 24.
Grant begins advance on Vicksburg.

December 13.
Battle of Fredericksburg.

December 31.
Battle of Murfreesborough.

1863

January 26.
Hooker replaces Burnside.

April 30.
Grant crosses the Mississippi.

May 1–6.
Battle of Chancellorsville and
Second Battle of Fredericksburg.

May 12.
Battle of Raymond.

May 10.
Death of Jackson.

May 16.
Battle of Champion's Hill.

May 17.
Confederates retreat into Vicksburg.

June 15.
Lee invades Maryland.

June 28.
Meade replaces Hooker.

June 30–July 3.
Battle of Gettysburg.

July 4.
Surrender of Vicksburg.

July 9.
Surrender of Port Hudson.

July 14.
Lee retreats into Virginia.

September 19–20.
Battle of Chickamauga.

October 9–18.
Lee advances against Meade and
falls back.

October 19.
Meade advances to Rappahannock.

November 24–25.
Battle of Chattanooga.

November 26–December 2.
Meade crosses Rapidan and retreats.

EVENTS AND OPERATIONS WITH
WHICH GENERAL R. E. LEE
WAS CONCERNED

OTHER EVENTS AND OPERATIONS

1864

March 9.
Grant appointed Lieutenant-General of United States Armies.
Sherman takes command in the West.

May 4.
Grant crosses the Rapidan.

May 4.
Sherman begins advance on Atlanta.

May 6.
Butler lands at Bermuda Hundred, James River.

May 5–7.
Battle of the Wilderness.

May 9–19.
Battles of Spottsylvania.

May 16.
Beauregard "bottles up" Butler.

May 24.
Lee checks Grant on North Anna.

June 1–3.
Battle of Cold Harbour.

June 27.
Battle of Kenesaw Mountain.

June 12.
Grant moves to the James.

July 11.
Early appears before Washington.

June 13.
Early moves to Shenandoah Valley.

July 14.
Early recrosses Potomac.

June 15–18.
First attacks on Petersburg.
Siege of Petersburg begins.

July 22.
Battle of Atlanta.

August 5.
Battle of Mobile Bay.

August 7.
Sheridan takes command in Shenandoah Valley.

July 30.
Battle of the Crater.

September 2.
Confederates retreat from Atlanta.

September 19.
Second Battle of Winchester.

September 22.
Battle of Fisher's Hill.

October 19.
Battle of Cedar Creek.

November 15.
Sherman begins march through Georgia.

December 15–16.
Battle of Nashville.

December 21.
Sherman enters Savannah.

EVENTS AND OPERATIONS WITH WHICH GENERAL R. E. LEE WAS CONCERNED

OTHER EVENTS AND OPERATIONS

1865

February 1.
Sherman begins advance through Carolinas.

February 9.
Lee becomes Commander-in-Chief Confederate Armies.

February 18.
Fall of Charleston.
February 22.
Fall of Wilmington.

March 25.
Failure of Lee's sortie from Petersburg.
April 2.
Lee begins retreat from Petersburg.
April 9.
Lee surrenders at Appomattox Court-House.

March 19.
Battle of Burtonsville.
March 23.
Sherman occupies Goldsboro'.
April 26.
J. E. Johnston surrenders at Greenboro'.

AUTHORITIES CONSULTED

Official Records of the Union and Confederate Armies. 52 vols.

Lee's Confidential Despatches to Davis.

Military Historical Society of Massachusetts Papers.

Southern Historical Society Papers.

Battles and Leaders of the Civil War. 2 vols.

Davis, Jefferson: Rise and Fall of the Confederate Government. 2 vols.

Lee, R. E.: Recollections and Letters of General Robert E. Lee.

Long, A. L.: Memoirs of Robert E. Lee.

Lee, Fitzhugh: General Lee.

Jones, J. W.: Personal Reminiscences, Anecdotes, and Letters of General R. E. Lee.

Jones, J. W.: Life and Letters of General Robert E. Lee.

McCabe, J. D.: Life and Campaigns of General Robert E. Lee.

Ropes, J. C.: Story of the Civil War, 1861-62. 2 vols.

Ropes and Livermore: Story of the Civil War, 1863. 2 vols.

Livermore, Colonel T. L.: Numbers and Losses in the Civil War.

Rhodes, J. F.: A History of the United States from the Compromise of 1850. 5 vols.

Henderson, Colonel G. F. R.: Stonewall Jackson and the American Civil War. 2 vols.

Wood, W. B., and Edmonds, Colonel J. E.: History of the Civil War in the United States.

Allan, W.: Jackson's Valley Campaign.

Longstreet, James: From Manassas to Appomattox.

Johnston, J. E.: Narrative of the Operations in the late War between the States.

Gordon, J. B.: Reminiscences of the Civil War.

Palfrey, F. W.: The Antietam and Fredericksburg.

Alexander, E. P.: Military Memoirs of a Confederate.

Doubleday, H.: Chancellorsville and Gettysburg.

Humphreys, A. H.: The Campaigns of Grant in Virginia.

INDEX